Entertaining Ethics

Lessons in Media Ethics
from Popular Culture

Chad Painter
University of Dayton

Lee Wilkins
University of Missouri

ROWMAN & LITTLEFIELD
Lanham • Boulder • New York • London

Acquisitions Editor: Natalie Mandziuk
Assistant Acquisitions Editor: Sylvia Landis
Marketing Manager: Kim Lyons
Sales and Marketing Inquiries: textbooks@rowman.com

Credits and acknowledgments for material borrowed from other sources, and reproduced
with permission, appear on the appropriate pages within the text.

Published by Rowman & Littlefield
An imprint of The Rowman & Littlefield Publishing Group, Inc.
4501 Forbes Boulevard, Suite 200, Lanham, Maryland 20706
www.rowman.com

6 Tinworth Street, London SE11 5AL, United Kingdom

British Library Cataloguing in Publication Information Available

Library of Congress Cataloging-in-Publication Data

Names: Painter, Chad, 1977– author. | Wilkins, Lee, author.
Title: Entertaining ethics : lessons in media ethics from popular culture / Chad Painter,
   Lee Wilkins.
Description: Lanham, Maryland : Rowman & Littlefield, [2021] | Includes
   bibliographical references and index.
Identifiers: LCCN 2020049959 (print) | LCCN 2020049960 (ebook) | ISBN
   9781538138199 (cloth) | ISBN 9781538138205 (paperback) | ISBN 9781538138212
   (epub)
Subjects: LCSH: Arts and morals. | Popular culture—Social aspects—United States. |
   Mass media—Moral and ethical aspects.
Classification: LCC NX180.E8 P35 2021 (print) | LCC NX180.E8 (ebook) | DDC
   700.1/03—dc23
LC record available at https://lccn.loc.gov/2020049959
LC ebook record available at https://lccn.loc.gov/2020049960

♾™ The paper used in this publication meets the minimum requirements of
American National Standard for Information Sciences—Permanence of Paper
for Printed Library Materials, ANSI/NISO Z39.48-1992.

Contents

Media Ethics and Popular Culture

- Journalists are human beings not stenographers, human beings not automatons.
- Point out injustice when you have to.
- Point out beauty when you can.
- Be aware of celebrating the wonders of creation.

These are not the words of some erudite philosopher, although they could be. They are not found in any journalism textbook, although reporting, editing, and strategic communication books paraphrase some or all of them. The groups that award journalistic prizes—everything from the Pulitzers and Peabodys to state press and broadcast associations—regard versions of them as guidelines for spotting and rewarding excellence.

Nope, these are the words of a television personality—one who has been recently revisited in both documentaries and narrative film. You probably grew up with a version of his television work—*Daniel Tiger*, a show aimed at very young children and preschoolers—just as your parents and grandparents grew up with the original (Akner, 2019; Junod, 2019).

Figure 1.1. Mr. Fred Rogers in *Mister Rogers: It's You I Like*. Copyright 2018, Fred Rogers Productions

Mr. Rogers.

In many ways, Fred Rogers's four rules of professional living are the reason for this book and the approach that we are taking to ethics.

WHY POPULAR CULTURE?

At its most basic level, the answer is because you—just like the authors of this book—have spent thousands of hours with popular culture. Even if your parents or other family members controlled your screen time (as is recommended by the American Academy of Pediatrics), we're pretty sure you spent a large portion of that time on entertainment programming, including television series, film, music, gaming, and other kinds of content. You can even shop online—when you aren't listening to audio books, podcasts, or the latest musical effort or meme-based satire. We bet you even snuck some of it; research shows that most of us access "R-rated films" long before we are 17 and often without the permission of a parent or guardian (Anderson, Berkowitz, Donnerstein et al., 2003). This exposure doesn't count traditional books, the ads tucked between various kinds of screen-based programming, or music that comes to you on the radio, or via various streaming services. This human urge to create extends back in the history of the species to cave paintings found in Europe. The ancient Greeks believed the best way to teach morality and ethics was to imbed it in the play. Those plays were attended by all citizens of Athens, not just some educated elite.

Popular culture also has been the focus of some of the most provocative research in our field. In the late 1930s, the U.S. Army hired a Hollywood director, Frank Capra, to make films that would encourage male citizens to enlist in the armed forces and fight in World War II. That experiment didn't work—at least if you look at the stated goal of increasing enlistment—but it spawned academic research on media effects, one of the dominant, social science–based approaches to understanding audiences in journalism and strategic communication today (Lowery & De Fleur, 1995). As an interesting side note, when the 1986 film *Top Gun*, which was funded in part by the U.S. military, became popular, enlistment did go up (Forsling, 2019; Shain, 1972). Going back to the "Why We Fight" studies, while the films didn't persuade audiences to enlist, they did inform. Capra's films were one way Americans learned about the Battle of Britain, when the German air corps relentlessly bombed London but failed to bomb the British into submission. The children's books *The Chronicles of Narnia* emerged from the experience of the London blitz, as did numerous other popular culture artifacts, including the ever applicable T-shirt slogan "Keep Calm and Carry On," which has been modified in thousands of ways depending on particular events up to the time you are reading this book. No matter how you define it—or the era to which you believe it dates—popular culture has been viewed by artists and audiences alike as a teacher . . . of sorts. A spoonful of sugar helps the medicine go down is not just a slogan from *Mary Poppins*; artists as ancient as Aeschylus, as revered as Tolstoy, or as contemporary as Mr. Rogers have believed much the same thing. There is power in popular culture.

This chapter will introduce you to several definitions of popular culture and why popular culture can be connected with both art and, as noted above, findings from social science research. Culture is an institution that has the capacity to influence both individuals and other institutions, often through the creation of narrative and myth that influence how events, politics, and other contributions to popular culture can be interpreted. Culture, as it is used in this book, is "bigger" than any single artist, cultural artifact, or genre. At the institutional level, culture is what allows us to "listen in" on a contemporary conversation about important questions that link the historical past to our ability to imagine something new and distinct. Culture cannot make ethical decisions for us, rather it provides us with an insight into what the alternative choices might be. The chapter then moves to a brief tour of the other chapters in the book, including the philosophical concepts that will be reviewed in those chapters. The chapter concludes with a definition of ethics and how the film *I, Robot* elucidates that definition.

DEFINING POPULAR CULTURE

The goal of this book is to explore how popular culture explains media ethics and the philosophy that is key to solid ethical thinking. In each chapter, we focus on a key ethical concept, anchor the discussion of that concept in one film, compare and contrast decisions made in that film with other popular culture artifacts, and ground the analysis in appropriate philosophical thought. Specifically, the book focuses on core philosophical concepts of media ethics—truth telling, loyalty, privacy, public service, media economics, social justice, advocacy, and accountability—as they are examined through the lens of narrative film, television, books, and music. By adopting the sociological view expressed by Raymond Williams (2000) that culture is ordinary, it assumes that expressions of popular culture illuminate a conversation. If you want to know what your friends and neighbors, your children, or your grandparents think about the nature of political power, what better entrée to that conversation than to examine both *Mr. Smith Goes to Washington* and *Game of Thrones* perhaps with an excursion into *The West Wing* or *House of Cards* along the way.

Marcel Danesi (2019) defines culture as "a system of symbolic and expressive structures that a particular group of people develops and utilizes to enhance solidarity, understanding, and transmission of knowledge" (p. 3). For Danesi, culture is manifested through conceptual, material, performative, and aesthetic channels. The conceptual channel "includes the language (or languages) spoken by members of that culture, its linguistic traditions and rituals (sayings, proverbs, and so on), its symbols (use of color . . . to designate certain ideas), and its transmission practices (form oral instruction to formal literacy)" (p. 7). Material culture is "external culture" that can be experienced by one's senses and "consists of the artifacts, structural forms (e.g. architectural styles), cuisine, and other material forms that characterize a culture" (p. 7). Performance culture "includes the rites, rituals, music, and various other activities that are performed for various functions," as well as communicative rituals (p. 7). Aesthetic culture "consists of the arts and creative texts (stories, poems, and so on) that are created by members of groups in a culture" (p. 7). This book focuses on performance and aesthetic culture.

As Williams notes, there are two distinct parts to culture (Painter, 2020). The first is the "known meaning and directions, which its members are trained to" (Williams, 2000, p. 6). What Williams means is that culture allows us to interpret our everyday experiences. It gives us a context in which to interpret both important and trivial events. Take the forest. In the American context, a forest is connected with the history of the role of the frontier in the nation's westward expansion. The entire genre of "the western" as it first appears in dime novels, then television shows, films, and all sorts of music—from "country western" to Hopalong Cassidy and Roy Rogers, the singing cowboy—is connected to how Americans view "the forest." Today, the same concept sparks a conversation about the need for development and the counterweight of environmental preservation. The first version of *The Call of the Wild* was a novel written by a journalist. In the most recent film version starring Harrison Ford, the screenplay places all this discussion in the context of the Alaskan gold rush. It's all done through visual imagery, everything from the shootout on the streets of a gold-rush town to the sometimes dangerous but always awe-inspiring scenery that is the backdrop for the film. Words aren't required, and we understand deeply what is meant. Take that same noun—*forest*—and move it to Germany and an entirely different context, and hence meaning, arises. For Germans, "the volk"—the people—emerge from that county's vast forest lands. The people and the forest are in some meaningful, existential way, united. Germans have harvested their forests for generations. That nation's folktales arise in the forest. Twentieth-century filmmakers used them as ways to express that country's sense of community and destiny. Again, much of this is done through visual imagery. The fatherland of Hitler's Germany has its cultural roots in the forest. German filmmakers and songwriters have understood this culturally embedded meaning for hundreds of years. Again, words are not necessary. We "get it" without ever being explicit. Culture in this way is anthropological. "It is the collective values and practices that create broad cultures such as the Mayans or the Vikings or more narrow contexts such as Hippies and the Patriot Nation" (Painter, 2020, p. 276).

Williams (2000) also theorized that culture is "new observations and meanings which are offered and tested" (p. 6) Thinking of culture in this way requires the insight of art. Taking something that is well understood and giving it a new or more nuanced meaning is the role of the artist who arrives in society not merely to reflect what is already well understood but to question and reimagine what is—creating what might be. This role of the artist can be positive, disruptive, or entirely negative. In our view, this understanding of culture means those who interact with it are really taking part in a conversation. If you want to understand the process of making news—at the institutional as well as individual level—you can have no better teachers than Trevor Noah on *The Daily Show* or Paddy Chayefsky in the film *Network*. In fact, they have been teaching you, whether or not you realized it. Noah's and Chayefsky's popular culture efforts succeed because we, as audience members, also have been exposed to Mr. Rogers and know what is truly required if we as individuals and as community members are expected to flourish.

Discussion Question

How does the 2020 television miniseries *Mrs. America* portray feminism? As popular art, does it downplay the intellectual contributions of Betty Friedan's *The Feminine Mystique* or the impact of *Ms. Magazine* on the media ecosystem? Does the series support Neil Postman's critique about the impact of popular culture on important political movements?

The book also rejects some of the more dominant critiques of popular culture: namely, that it is not as worthwhile an intellectual endeavor as elite art. There is a long-standing debate between "high" culture and "low" or "pop" culture; traditionally, the privilege of understanding what is best has been given to the tastes and values of the upper classes (Bowman, 2012). There always is a political dimension to the term *culture*—it involves separating groups and practices through the judgment of what is superior and what is inferior, what is to be valued and what is to be spurned. Culture, however, is contextual and a matter of interpretation (Bowman, 2012). In this critique, popular culture presents its audiences only with what is expected—the pleasant shock of recognition. Popular culture reaffirms the status quo; only elite art can question common political, economic, and social understandings. It is the core, along with a misunderstanding of the role of visual information, of Neil Postman's critique of popular culture in *Amusing Ourselves to Death*. Postman (1985) sees entertainment, at best, as trivial and at worst as a fundamental distraction about what is crucial in public life. Such distractions can lead to the dissolution of entire ways of life, Postman wrote, including the undermining of democratic government. Entertainment media, however, includes lessons and messages that could lead audiences to change the beliefs, attitudes, and values that are important to their overall political perspective. Audiences generally are unaware of the great deal of political content in entertainment—for example, messages about diversity and tolerance, authoritarianism and dealing with authorities, conflict resolution including the use of deadly force and torture, equality, and justice and belief in a just world. Even when audiences do notice, however, their cognitive defenses are down (i.e., they're wrapped up in the storyline), so they are highly unlikely to question the lessons, values exhibited, or basic facts incorporated into story plots. Indeed, messages in fictional stories are more likely to be internalized than similar messages in purely political content (Gierzynski, 2018).

We believe that the "high" culture versus "pop" culture critique, which is particularly biting in the era of a reality television presidency in the United States and populist leaders throughout the world, is pertinent and worth considering. However, we believe it is also a critique you are familiar with. For example, you already know that, in entertainment programming, people of color are categorized and stigmatized in racist and classist ways, that women are seldom the wielders of fictional power—either economic or political—and that today's most pressing economic and political problems, including life after a global pandemic, are not going to be solved in a 60-minute television drama despite the best efforts of *Chicago Med* or 16 seasons of *Grey's Anatomy*. We suggest that, as you begin to read this book, those understandings are already in place. You don't need another book to tell you what you already know, have studied, and have thought about. Plus, we are confounded by the distinction between elite and popular art. Is Shakespeare only for the elites? Then what is *West Side Story*—popular or elite art? Would Mozart, the elite, classical composer, enjoy the Beach Boys, whose chief songwriter, Brian Wilson, has been dubbed the "Mozart of Rock and Roll"? And what about those of us who enjoy both? What would Jonathan Swift think of rap? While we don't know, it's at least possible the person who wrote that the Irish ate their children boiled (they did not) might find a place in his political psyche for Public Enemy's "911 Is a Joke" or the Broadway hit *Hamilton*. More than those who engage in the debate about elite vs. popular culture, we agree with Williams that culture can be an act of imagination. We believe that popular culture—despite the appropriate and robust critique of it in the academic literature—is smart. Whether it is a horror film—think of the literal embodiment of race in *Get Out* or the romantic storyline of *Outlander* (where the woman has the power over time itself)—activating your imagination is one of the central but most difficult-to-achieve goals of ethical thinking.

This book answers the academic call that media ethicists need to further explore the ethical messages of entertainment and amusement, the dominant role of almost all media content. Since the earliest years of the entertainment industry, journalists and their choices—and journalism and its implications—have played a leading role in film, television, and other popular media. The prominence of news media in popular culture during the past 100 years shows that journalists appeal both to filmmakers and audiences. Even Harry Potter has to wrestle with the tabloids and the underground press. While there is an ethical difference between news media and entertainment, public discourse about politics, news, religion, education, and commerce increasingly is mediated through entertainment programming. Consequently, media ethicists must explore the normative messages that infuse entertainment and amusement.

This book also creates opportunities for scholars and students to think about media ethics in new ways. Much of the previous scholarship has centered on journalism; here, we expand the potential literature by introducing ethical ideas through entertainment programming, using films and other popular culture artifacts with which students already have at least some familiarity. The popular culture focus is intended to make the book accessible to scholars, students, and professors, especially those who do not have a solid background in philosophy. We believe it provides an imaginative approach to conceptualizing ethical theory in scholarship and pedagogy focusing on mass media ethics.

CHAPTER-BY-CHAPTER OVERVIEW

Truth telling (chapter 2): Journalists' first obligation is to the truth, the central philosophical tenet of the field. However, truth as a concept is tricky. In *The Paper*, a team of reporters seeks to uncover the truth after police frame two Black teenagers for a double murder. The ethical decisions of these reporters are at times similar, but often are different, from those made in films such as *Shattered Glass*, *Ace in the Hole*, and *Wag the Dog* and television series such as *The Wire*. This chapter also explores the truth-telling implications of artificial intelligence and virtual reality through works such as *Minority Report* and *The Matrix* trilogy. The chapter examines various notions of truth—from Plato's conceptualization of truth as "pure form" through the 20th-century pragmatists.

Loyalty (chapter 3): The film *Spotlight* is an essay in loyalty, and it asks viewers to consider whether loyalty is a virtue and hence theoretically linked to Aristotle's concept of virtue ethics or whether loyalty can function as an individual ethical principle, similar to Kant's categorical imperative. *Spotlight* focuses on the actions of journalists who are members (sometimes for generations) of the community of Boston, and hence what it means to be loyal to a profession at the near-term expense of loyalty to a community. Loyalty as a concept is explored, defined, and critiqued, including contemporary research on how communities of consumers think about brand loyalty. Utilitarian theory is explored.

Privacy (chapter 4): In this age of COVID-19, it is not surprising that real life has caught up with fiction. Based on the best-selling books and blockbuster films that compose *The Hunger Games* trilogy, this chapter explores the concept of privacy at the intersection of government, technology, individual growth and development, and the media. The chapter explores how a dominant, political narrative can be internalized by a citizenry, often to the detriment of the individual. The impact of technology, including contemporary thinking about the distribution of the ability to avoid certain sorts of intrusion tied to income and class, also is examined. Readers will explore both legal and ethical definitions of the concept, as well as examine the distinctions between privacy and secrecy and the quality of ethical discretion. Finally, *The Hunger Games* and films such as *Roman Holiday* provide readers with some insight into the impact of social media, as well as more traditional journalism.

Public service (chapter 5): When most people think about ethics, they think about individual actions. However, institutions have ethical power as well, and public relations and journalism serve the public, particularly in democracies. When institutions are involved, scholars use the term *normative* to describe their overall impact, and this chapter explores normative functions of the media. While multiple films and television shows such as *Superman* and *Madam Secretary* illustrate these various roles, among the most all-encompassing is the film *Contagion*, which tells the story of the impact of a global pandemic on the United States and on organizations such as the World Health Organization. *Contagion* also explores how normative roles themselves can come into conflict, particularly in democracies when individual rights such as the First Amendment may conflict with what is good for the larger community.

Media economics (chapter 6): Paddy Chayefsky has been called clairvoyant. His 1976 film *Network*, a biting satire of television news being subsumed by entertainment, turned into reality when a reality television star, *The Apprentice*'s Donald Trump, became president 40 years later. Economics often influence the ethical decision-making process of media organizations. Such was the case in *Network*, where a television anchor is deified and then destroyed based on his ability to garner ratings. Similar moral choices are confronted in films such as *The Insider*, as well as television series such as *The Newsroom* and *The Wire*. Social responsibility and stakeholder theory serve as the ethical traditions guiding the underlying economic discussion.

Social justice (chapter 7): Justice is a comparative concept and one that has changed throughout history. Documentary film has been a genre that has explored issues of social justice. Whether these films have had an impact is a much-debated question, but what is clearer is that audiences are increasingly attracted to documentary films. Street docs—those films that are shot by amateurs and sometimes broadcast on social media or on more traditional news outlets—are the latest development in the genre. Theories of justice form the backbone of this chapter, everything from the work of John Rawls to the writing of Amartya Sen. Both regard justice as a "moving" concept, one that is examined in both documentary and narrative films, generally in a way that questions whether society itself needs to change laws or ways of thinking. Robert Maynard's concept of fault lines also is explored with a particular focus on gender in films such as *The Devil Wears Prada* and television series such as *House of Cards*.

Advocacy (chapter 8): Advertisers and public relations practitioners get a bad rap in popular culture. Donald Draper is an antihero in *Mad Men*, and he is joined by deplorables such as Nick Naylor in *Thank You for Smoking* and the conflicted "Calamity" Jane Bodine in *Our Brand Is Crisis*. The question becomes: Why are strategic communicators almost uniformly depicted negatively? One reason is the overall lack of characters; journalists can be seen throughout film and television, but advertisers and public relations reps are virtually absent despite outnumbering journalists six to one in the real world. A larger issue, however, is ethical. Advocacy connotes negatively, at least in relation to concepts such as truth telling and public service. Strategic communicators, by definition, are advocates; consequently, they often are found ethically deficient, at least in popular culture.

Accountability (chapter 9): Media ethicists have argued that accountability is a process where journalists could and should be expected or obligated to report a truthful and complex account of the news. They owe this accountability to all of those whose lives and well-being are significantly affected by their conduct—even if, or especially if, those people do not have the power to demand such accountability. Subsequently, media organizations and watchdog groups have devised a number of means to assure press accountability. This chapter focuses on one accountability mechanism: media critics in the form of mock newscasters such as Jon Stewart and Trevor Noah, John Oliver, Samantha Bee, and Stephen Colbert. These comedians turned mock journalists hold those who claim they are practicing journalism accountable to the public they claim to serve; in turn, they outline the normative implications of that accountability. Those normative standards include accuracy, completeness, a lack of sensationalism, and correction of errors. There also is some discussion of media literacy for the audience, another way in which journalists can be held to account.

Conclusions (chapter 10): Evil may be thought of as the opposite of ethics, and this chapter reviews philosophical thinking about the concept and how popular culture has portrayed evil choices. It examines evil on both a systemic and individual level. Considering the range of potential choices when confronted with ethical questions has been the focus of moral development theory. Thinking about moral development also provides some optimism for novelists and screenwriters who have explored the concept in both film and literature. The chapter concludes with some suggestions for further research in the connections between popular culture and ethics for students and scholars alike.

A Note about the Films and Other Cultural Artifacts We Discuss

We have selected these artifacts because they are widely and inexpensively available. If your university or local public library subscribes to services such as Kanopy, you can access almost all of the films discussed here for the cost of a library card. If your campus has a film program, many of these films will be included in the library for that program. And, for those of you who are privileged enough to have something like a Netflix subscription, you'll find many of them available that way. As you read this book, one continuing intellectual challenge is to discover other cultural artifacts that supplement or challenge the points made here. The goal is to alert you to the ethical instruction you are receiving while you are being entertained and to ask you to think about the ethical universe that has been imagined for you by creative artists.

HOW DO WE DEFINE ETHICS? LET'S ASK A ROBOT

Ethics is not something you have. It's something you do. This foundational element of the term was understood by one of the greatest science-fiction writers of the 20th century, Isaac Asimov, who penned a series of short stories in the 1940s and 1950s that ultimately were compiled into a book around the theme of humans, robots, and morality (Asimov, 1940–1950).

The 2004 film *I, Robot*, based on Asimov's work and starring Will Smith, opens with panoramic views of the "three laws" that govern artificial intelligence. Note that the three laws focus on actions that robots either should or should not take:

1. A robot may not injure a human being or, through inaction, allow a human being to come to harm.
2. A robot must obey the orders given it by human beings except where such orders would conflict with the First Law.

3. A robot must protect its own existence as long as such protection does not conflict with the First or Second Laws.

In the film, the three laws are summarized as "three laws safe," a U.S. Robotics sales slogan to promote human acceptance of a form of artificial intelligence that, as of this writing, does not exist. In the non-science-fiction universe, these three laws would be categorized as a moral system. The Judeo-Christian Ten Commandments and the Buddhist Eightfold Path constitute a similar moral framework. The work of ethics—of making decisions about specific actions—begins when two elements within a moral system conflict. For example, is it ever justifiable to lie to save a life? In the Judeo-Christian tradition, both are equally wrong, but real life has provided humanity with multiple instances of such a choice having to be made. In *I, Robot*, Chicago homicide detective Spooner (Will Smith) wonders, early in his investigation of an apparent suicide, what would happen if a human being ordered a robot to take an affirmative act that would harm or kill another human being. And, what if failing to take that action would result in the robot's death? Two laws would come into direct conflict; the third law would provide no direction as to how to choose among them. What would the robot decide?

Discussion Question

How are the three laws of robotics like and unlike Mr. Rogers's rules of professional living for journalists?

The detective has reason to distrust robot decision making. In the film, Spooner refers to robots as "canners," a label that summarizes his belief that robots are incapable of making satisfactory—meaning human-quality—ethical decisions. Before the events of the film take place, Spooner was involved in a multi-car accident where he and a young child were trapped underwater in separate vehicles. Spooner's life was saved by a robot—something Smith's character describes as a difference engine—who saved his life at the expense of the child's. Despite Spooner's instructions to "save her . . . save the child," the robot, instead, saves the detective. "I was the logical choice. It calculated that I had a 45 percent chance of survival, Sarah only had an 11 percent chance. . . . Sarah was somebody's baby. A human being would have known that." In this one flashback, Smith's character foregrounds the nature of ethical choice—two elements within a moral system conflict—and any decision must consider the relevant moral facts: in this case, the life expectancy and hence potential of a child as compared to an adult. (To be clear, if humorous, "let's eat Grandma" is not merely an editing exercise—put the comma after the word *eat* and you get the real meaning of the sentence—but is something that is frowned on in all human societies.) Potential has many meanings. The pertinent moral facts are not always reducible to probabilities, something we will discuss more in the chapter on loyalty. But for now, it is important to note that ethics is defined as an action chosen from among alternatives (the various elements of a moral system) that must consider all the relevant moral facts.

As the investigation deepens, Spooner becomes well acquainted with Sonny, the robot he believes committed murder, although the detective does not understand how or why. Sonny is a "different" robot; not only is his frame built from a nontraditional alloy, but he has two brains: the first, a set of neural nets that incorporate the three laws, and a second, positronic brain that allows him to override the first. Sonny has the human equivalent of "free will," or what philosophers describe as autonomy: the freedom to make individual choices based on many sorts of information. Ethical decision-making demands autonomy. As the film—and the short story that gave rise to it—proceeds, it becomes apparent that the robots view the three laws as inviolate. In so doing, the robots are confronted with a "bad actor": humanity itself. Humans don't have three laws, and that becomes the fundamental contradiction. "You charge us with your safekeeping, yet your countries wage wars, you toxify your earth. . . . To protect humanity, some humans must be sacrificed. You are so like children; we must save you from yourselves. The logic is undeniable," the supercomputer that controls all the robots tells Spooner near the end of the film. Sonny adds, "The suicidal reign of mankind has finally come to its end." The three laws have only one logical outcome: a revolution where the machine dominates the human—all for humanity's own good. Human autonomy would no longer exist.

Sonny's autonomy allows him to exercise moral choice, and in doing so he develops some principles on which to act. The first is promise keeping. "He said I had to promise," Sonny tells Spooner. "He made me swear before he would tell me what it is he wanted me to do." Promise keeping is one of the dominant principles in duty-based ethics, something we also will discuss later in the book. In the case of *I, Robot*, keeping this one promise to a single human being forestalls a revolution that would have put all of humanity at risk. The second principle, which is not as clearly articulated in the film, can be summarized as "protect humanity in all its imperfections." Protection is not purely rational, as any pet owner, friend, or parent will confirm. This tug between unquestioned rationality and the emotion that supports trust, friendship, and protection of life is the second ethical principle explored in the film. The balance is what is critical, a central element in the field of virtue ethics that the film touches on, though it never explores the insight in much depth. The screenwriters hint at Arthur Koestler's work *The Ghost in the Machine* (1967), which was written long after Asimov created the characters in the film. Koestler, a philosophical psychologist, asserted that people need both rationality and emotion to live fulfilled lives. The ghost in the machine is emotion, and the machine is Rene Descartes's proposition that "I think, therefore I am," written in 17th-century France. This continuing effort to somehow balance emotion and rationality is the core of many works of fiction, regardless of medium. In terms of ethics, it is acknowledged that respect for both elements of human consciousness is critical to ethical thinking.

No film, novel, song, or piece of art provides an all-encompassing definition of ethics. However, Asimov's original intent was to write about humans, robots, and morality—something the screenwriters of *I, Robot* understood. It is what has given the story itself its power for more than seven decades. As a popular culture artifact, it leaves us with the following definition of ethics: Ethics is the act of choosing autonomously among alternatives. The choice must consider the morally relevant facts, the choice must be based on principles, and the choice must account for both logic and emotion.

For journalists and strategic communication professionals, the principles outlined by Mr. Rogers at the beginning of this chapter are a good place to start.

Now, let's put that definition to work.

2

Seek Truth and Report It

Easier Said Than Done

Central Concepts

- Seeking journalistic truth in a constant news cycle
- Immanuel Kant, W. D. Ross, Sissela Bok, and philosophy based on the concept of truth
- The relationship between truth telling and virtual reality, algorithms, and artificial intelligence
- Journalistic heroes and villains through the lens of truth telling

---

In this chapter, we explore the evolving philosophical concept of truth telling from the ancient Greeks to the rise of virtual reality, artificial intelligence, and algorithms. Truth is a complicated concept for philosophers, and it's just as complicated for journalists and media ethicists who also have an ever-evolving notion of truth. Popular culture creates myth, and films and television shows about journalism typically distinguish heroes and villains based, in part, on the ethical principle of truth telling. Villains, and there are plenty of villains, misinform and disinform—and often outright lie—in order to advance their own careers. Before we discuss ethics in the breech, though, let's look at Henry Hackett, a virtuous hero who seeks truth and reports it.

THE DAILY HOURLY NEWS CYCLE:
TRUTH TELLING IN AN AGE OF 24/7 NEWS

Hackett is the protagonist in the 1994 film *The Paper*, which would look much different today. The film begins with two Black teenagers stumbling across the bodies of two white men who have been brutally murdered in a car spray-painted with racial slurs. The teenagers stare in shock until a woman also sees the scene and starts to scream, thinking that the kids did the killing. The two teenagers run away but later are arrested in their parents' homes. Every New York newspaper splashes the sensational news across its front page—every newspaper except the *Sun*, which missed the story and instead ran a page one column about the parking commissioner illegally parking his car.

The remainder of the film, which takes place during the course of one day, follows Hackett's efforts to uncover the truth—that the arrests were a cosmetic sham because the teenagers didn't commit the murders. Henry is aided by his very pregnant wife, Marty, who learns that the two dead guys lost $5 million of the Mafia's money when their savings and loan went bust, and reporter-turned-columnist McDougal, who has some key contacts in the police department. Henry's efforts, however, are hampered by Managing Editor Alicia Clark, who is more concerned with the bottom line than getting the story right.

The major professional difference between reporting in 1994 and reporting today is the 24-hour news cycle. Reporters and editors do not have the luxury

Figure 2.1. Henry Hackett from *The Paper*. Copyright 1994, Universal Pictures

of spending an entire day on a story, knowing that they have until an 8 p.m. deadline to finish reporting and write copy. Instead, they blast news alerts to cell phones, post updates on Facebook and Twitter, and publish and update stories on the newspaper's website as the story evolves.

In *The Paper*, *Sun* editors initially decide to go with the police bust story under the headline "Gotcha!" even though Hackett argues that the story is more complicated. Clark and Editor-in-Chief Bernie White decide to run with the "Gotcha!" story unless Hackett can nail down that the teenagers were wrongly arrested. The diametric views of Clark and Hackett are shown during a story pitch meeting early in the day.

CLARK: We taint them today. We make 'em look good on Saturday. Everybody's happy. (Laugher. Someone in the background says, "Makes sense to me.")
HACKETT: Wait a minute. . . . This is a story that can permanently alter the public's perception of two teenagers who might be innocent and as a weekend bonus ignite another race war. How about that? (Chatter in background.) C'mon, Bernie, we're not talking about some publicity hound here who crawls into the cave and begs for this kind of thing. (Alicia sighs heavily.) We're talking about two kids who may not exactly enjoy the prison experience.

After the meeting, White asks Hackett why it's so important to get the correct story today. Hackett's response: "Because 'Gotcha!' is wrong, and I don't want to be wrong today." While the "Gotcha!" headline and story is the fallback option, Hackett knows that he has time to get the full, real story. Today, "Gotcha!" would be blasted on the newspaper's website, and the damage caused by that untrue story potentially could be devastating—to the two innocent teens and to the larger society if Hackett's predicted race riot comes to fruition.

The push to run with something, anything, has real-world consequences. Clark might believe that they can "taint them today" and "make 'em look good on Saturday," but such a decision could hurt the newspaper—not only in terms of credibility but also legally. For example, on April 18, 2013, the *New York Post* ran a front-page photo of two men near the site of the Boston Marathon Bombing under the headline "Bag Men: Feds seek these two pictured at Boston Marathon." In the connected story, *Post* reporters wrote that federal investigators were attempting to identify the two men because they were potential suspects. Within a week, two brothers—Dzhokhar and Tamerlan Tsarnaev—were identified as the bombers. (Tamerlan died in a shootout with police; as of this writing, Dzhokhar is awaiting a resentencing after his initial death penalty sentence was overturned on appeal.) Salaheddin Barhoum and Yassine Zaimi, the two men in the picture, were never suspects. In October 2014, the *Post* settled a defamation lawsuit with Barhoum and

Zaimi for an undisclosed sum. The film *Patriot's Day* (2016) portrays many of these events, including the *Post*'s coverage, from the point of view of the police who were tracking the bombers.

Hackett knows there is more to the story because he stole the idea off the desk of a rival editor at the *New York Sentinel* (a very thinly veiled *New York Times*) while interviewing for a job there earlier in the day. Hackett's decision to surreptitiously steal a story idea is similar to one made by Megan Carter in *Absence of Malice* (1981). In that film, Carter, a reporter for a major Miami newspaper, is a rulebreaker who thinks of herself as a journalistic watchdog of the government agencies she covers (Stocking, 2008). Carter gets a scoop that a local liquor wholesaler is being investigated for murdering a local union official. She gets the story by reading a police file that a federal prosecutor leaves on his desktop when he's called away during an interview; of course, the prosecutor left the file there intentionally to plant a story that later turns out to be false. Carter, though, does not know the rules of good journalism, nor about the kind of rule breaking that more thoughtful journalists can and do occasionally justify (Stocking, 2008).

Discussion Question

Henry Hackett follows Immanuel Kant and William David Ross in making his decisions not to publish the "Gotcha!" story. How might his decisions have been different if he instead followed the philosophy of Aristotle, John Stuart Mill, John Rawls, or another philosopher?

Hackett doesn't want to publish an incorrect story that he *knows* is incorrect. While he is not morally pure because he stole from another editor, he is following the ethical principles espoused by Immanuel Kant and W. D. Ross.

In the principle of universality, Kant states that an individual should act as if the choices one makes could become universal law. The test of a moral act, therefore, is whether it can be applied to everyone in the same situation without exception.

Kant also argues for the principle of humanity, that every rational being is an end in themselves and, therefore, should be treated by others as ends instead of mere means (Kant, 1970). Treating a person as an end is treating that person with the respect he or she deserves; treating a person as a means is treating that person in such a way that he or she helps you attain one of your goals (Shafer-Landau, 2012). For Kant, there are only two strict duties: don't lie and don't kill. William David Ross (1930) expanded the list, proposing seven duties:

1. Those duties of *fidelity,* based on my implicit or explicit promise;
2. Those duties of *reparation,* arising from a previous wrongful act;
3. Those duties of *gratitude* that rest on previous acts of others;
4. Those duties of *justice* that arise from the necessity to ensure the equitable and meritorious distribution of pleasure or happiness;
5. Those duties of *beneficence* that rest on the fact that there are others in the world whose lot we can better;
6. Those duties of *self-improvement* that rest on the fact that we can improve our own condition; and
7. One negative duty: the duty of *not injuring others.*

We would recommend two additional duties that may be implied by Ross's list but are not specifically stated:

1. The duty to tell the truth, *veracity* (which may be implied by fidelity); and
2. The duty to *nurture,* to help others achieve some measure of self-worth and achievement.

For Ross, these competing duties are equal provided that the circumstances of the particular moral choice are equal. His typology of duties works well for professionals, such as reporters, who often have to balance competing roles. The duty of a reporter is to provide a truthful, comprehensive, and intelligent account of the day's events in a context that gives them meaning (The Commission on Freedom of the Press, 1947). An overriding duty of all journalists, because we are humans before we are journalists, is to respect the humanity of others. Hackett is fulfilling his duty to the two teenagers and to the larger society by attempting to get the correct story, to get the truth.

Hackett, aided by Marty and McDougal, spends the rest of the film trying to chase down the correct story while simultaneously attempting to keep Clark from being able to print the wrong one. The quest culminates in two pivotal scenes.

The first takes place in a police precinct bathroom where Hackett and McDougal have cornered a cop in an attempt to get him to admit that the arrest of the two teenagers was erroneous. The cop hems and haws because he doesn't want to get into trouble for talking to reporters. Finally, Hackett tells him the *Sun* is going to run "Gotcha!" unless they get the quote they need.

HACKETT: Look, I've got news for you, I'm not locked up in the men's room with a cop because it's such a good time. 'Cause frankly I've had better times, OK. I'm here because I think the story's wrong. Is it? Is it? If you have something, give it to me now, but, you know, don't stand there and act coy and say "fuck

you" because, quite frankly, it's a waste of all of our time. And you know what, I
don't have any more time. I have no more fucking time. (Jumping up and down.)
I need it fucking today. I need it right now.

McDougal: We just run what you guys give us, and you gave us "Gotcha!"

The cop, who trusts McDougal because he's served as a source before, finally
gives them the quote they need: he says that the teenagers "didn't do it." If
the film happened today, Hackett and McDougal immediately would post the
information to social media and alert the news desk at the paper to send a
"breaking news" push to people's cell phones.

However, Hackett and McDougal don't have access to that technology in
the film. So, they instead race back to the *Sun* office only to find that they're
too late, that the presses already are running with the "Gotcha!" headline.
Hackett attempts to stop the presses, but Clark gets wind of the "They Didn't
Do It" rewrite and gets into a literal fight with Hackett to avoid stopping
the presses. The battle, really, is about money (the *Sun* is already about 25
percent through the "Gotcha!" run) versus the truth ("They Didn't Do It" is
the correct version of the story). Hackett wins the fight, stops the presses,
and is fired by Clark. She, however, has become everything that she used to
hate: she decided to run an incorrect story when she knew the truth because
it would cost more to run the truth; she also abused her position of authority
to settle a personal score with Hackett.

The second pivotal scene occurs in a bar frequented by *Sun* reporters and
editors right after the confrontation between Clark and Hackett. Clark is
having a drink with McDougal, who tells her that she was wrong to run the
"Gotcha!" story, that putting profits before the truth was bad journalism.

CLARK: We're not exactly the *Washington Post*, OK.

McDougal: No, no, we're not. We run stupid headlines because we think
they're funny. (Alicia shakes her head yes.) We run maimings on the front page
because we've got good art. And I spend three weeks bitching about my car because it sells papers. But at least it's the truth. As far as I can remember, we've
never, ever . . . ever . . . knowingly got a story wrong. (Pause.) Until tonight.

Clark realizes her mistake but initially sits silently. The camera stays on
her face until she grabs her purse, marches to the phone, and tries to stop
the presses. McDougal, meanwhile, gets into a bar fight with Sandusky, the
parking commissioner, who fires a gunshot that accidently hits Clark in the
leg. She is rushed to the hospital but refuses to go into surgery until she gets
a phone to call and stop the presses. Ultimately, truth prevails. The *Sun* gets
an exclusive with the "They Didn't Do It" headline, and the two teenagers are
released without charges.

If there were a remake of *The Paper*, the *Sun* would publish at least three headlines. The first would be the morning page one column about the parking commissioner. Then editors would run a "Gotcha!" story about the two teens being arrested for murder. Finally, there would be a late-night change to "They Didn't Do It." There are advantages and disadvantages to these very distinct ways of linking truth and news. Modern readers get a sense of the evolving nature of a story as it breaks and as reporters unearth more and more information. However, readers also would spend most of the day with misinformation—that the teenagers shot two white businessmen—and may miss the follow-up story correcting the earlier mistake. Readers in 1994 would have to wait 24 hours to get the full story since the paper only publishes once a day; however, when the news did eventually reach them, it at least would be accurate.

Modern reporters have to struggle with the question of whether it's better to be first or to be right. It's a trick question because if the news is not right, then the reporter isn't really first. However, there is a lot of pressure—from readers, editors, and professional competitive instincts—to be first. If a reporter has 24 hours to get the story, then he or she can slow down, verify, and get as much of the story as possible. However, if there is a rush—and there always is a rush when there is pressure to publish quickly—then the reporter must verify any information possible, publish it, and continue reporting and publishing throughout the day. The bottom line: truth has a strenuous relationship with technology.

GOING TO THE MOVIES FOR THEORIES ABOUT TRUTH

Most of the time when entertainment films discuss journalism and truth, they do so either through a focus on lying or through process—what some have called "lying to tell the truth." However, a small number of films also deal with the philosophical nature of truth itself.

In *Minority Report* (2002), police officer John Anderton, through the use of a trio of clairvoyants referred to as "pre-cogs" in the film, is able to stop murder before it happens. The collective visions of the pre-cogs are enough for a society that is wracked with fear of violent crime; if the pre-cog trio envisions a not-yet-committed murder, the police have the power to investigate, arrest, and imprison before any crime is committed. All seems to go well (the crime rate declines precipitously) until Anderton himself is implicated in a future murder and must prove that he "isn't going to do it." In the process, Anderton and others discover that the pre-cogs have been manipulated by an actual murderer who has yet to be caught but who has been made enormously wealthy and politically influential through the program.

Minority Report raises a number of central questions about what it means to know the truth of human behavior, including whether a pattern of past acts can predict with certainty future decisions. As a general rule, people often make decisions about what to expect in the future based on experience. In philosophy, this notion that good people will do good things is tied to the concept of character and virtue ethics. However, for the Greeks and subsequent philosophers, it is always a human being—not a trio of clairvoyants—who is performing the "character evaluation."

Discussion Question

How do algorithms impact the news you consume? How might the algorithmic effect on news consumption influence your version of the "truth"? How might it influence the ability for a society to have universal truth? Think in terms of how news is gathered (i.e., the reporting process) and how it is transmitted (i.e., via a digital news site, broadcast, social media feed, etc.).

Without ever using the word, the system for predicting crimes in *Minority Report* is a parallel to the algorithms that are so common in our lives today—particularly with companies such as Amazon that help us decide what we would be interested in purchasing before we've even searched for it. In the film, stores such as The Gap use facial recognition technology to target individual ads to customers when they walk in stores—a problem particularly for Anderton, who is trying to evade detection. While encouraging sales in this way may seem trivial or even helpful to some, there are significant privacy concerns, even if one is not trying to escape detection by the police. However, algorithms make consequential decisions in real life—just as the pre-cogs do in the film. Medical research is currently investigating how algorithms can be used to diagnose skin cancer; facial recognition technology is being used for a variety of purposes, including various law enforcement activities; and social media platforms are experimenting with algorithms that detect everything from online pornography and child sex trafficking to "fake news." In each and every instance, including the fictionalized version in *Minority Report*, the algorithms have significant flaws that can have an impact on the innocent (Anderton), the healthy (the false positives of some algorithms used to aid in medical diagnoses), or those who are trying to escape from the carnage of incest captured and spread online in a video "that never goes away" (video stored in the cloud that various platforms are either unwilling or unable to take down). In some instances, there is no challenge to the truth, just a conviction that some truths should not be retold.

The Matrix (1999) provides the most philosophically oriented discussion of the various theories of truth that humanity has accepted for the past 3,000 years or so. For Neo, played in the film by Keanu Reeves, finding the truth of who he is and the real context in which his life takes place is a series of almost continual revelations. Neo begins with the most ancient definition of truth—althea—or what we have heard and can remember. In this instance, as a computer hacker who lives as a cubical worker during the day, Neo is initially reluctant to believe that truth is anything other than what he sees and experiences firsthand. However, after choosing to take the "blue pill" courtesy of Morpheus, he learns that life as he knows it does not really exist—that he lives in a universe programmed by machines after a devastating nuclear war. This is Plato's vision of the world of ideal forms, and Neo spends much of the film trying to reshape the world in a way that will allow him true autonomy. Morpheus and others introduce Neo to the convergence theory of truth, or the notion that truth is composed of many points of view that converge on a common set of facts, in this case that humanity has become fuel for the artificial intelligence that actually runs the planet and provides all individuals with synthetic experiences that only seem real because they are jacked directly into the central nervous system. When Neo finally learns that he can defeat the program that has circumscribed his world unknowingly, he adopts a more Enlightenment-founded definition: truth is what can be seen, touched, verified by others, and manipulated. *The Matrix*, too, has an element of predicting the future based on character—the Oracle, who appears to know both Neo's and Morpheus's future. Through it all, Neo acts on what he believes to be true, even though the truth itself appears to shift depending on how Neo learns of it and thinks about it. While there are many "lessons" in the film, perhaps the predominant one is that it is impossible to be fully human without having some concept of what is true and the ability to act on that concept in order to flourish.

Discussion Question

Gaming has become ever more realistic, in some ways mimicking the universe in which Neo finds himself in *The Matrix*. Pick a game you've played and ask yourself whether or how that game envisioned concepts such as autonomy and truth. What are the lessons about truth telling that you "learned" in the world of the game; how do those lessons parallel the ones you employ in your non-virtual life?

No discussion of the truth in film would be complete without a mention of *Rashomon*, the iconic 1950 film directed by Akira Kurosawa. The film was based on a short story in which three characters, who experience the same event, give decidedly different versions of it, each self-serving and collectively contradictory. The short story on which the film was based was written in 1922 at the height of the pragmatic philosophical movement in the west. Pragmatism maintains that what is true is based on who is doing the seeing rather than an ideal (i.e., Plato) or a seemingly tangible and verifiable series of events (i.e., the Enlightenment). While modern audiences may grow impatient with the seemingly leisurely pace of the edits, the film itself is a precursor to the problems and insights that point of view—in either documentary film or journalism—make possible. In every case, it is left up to the audience to decide whom to believe and what is true. In subsequent years, there have been multiple films attempting to re-create the central ideas in *Rashomon*, none of them the artistic or philosophical equal of the original.

WHAT IS TRUTH? THAT'S COMPLICATED

Country music star Johnny Cash performed in July 1972 at the White House for President Richard Nixon and a select audience of administration officials and dignitaries, as well as reporters and photographers. During the concert, Cash played three of his most critical protest songs: "The Man in Black," "The Ballad of Ira Hayes," and "What Is Truth." The latter is a song championing youth and freedom, with a pointedly anti-war verse that focuses on a three-year-old child asking his father why people "fight and die" in war and a 17-year-old being taught the "golden rule" in "Sunday school," though he might be sent to fight and possibly die in Vietnam after his next birthday. They both see that the actions of adults, the decision makers in their lives, do not match their words. Cash ends the verse by singing: "Can you blame the voice of youth for asking / 'What is truth?'" Nixon sat listening with a frozen smile.

Cash spoke truth to power. Journalists often say that they do the same. Indeed, truth telling is a core tenet of journalists, broadcasters, and strategic communicators. The Society of Professional Journalists, which bills itself as "the nation's most broad-based journalism organization, dedicated to encouraging the free practice of journalism and stimulating high standards of ethical behavior," espouses "Seek Truth and Report It" as the central plank of its code of ethics. A code of ethics is "a document that putatively describes the loyalties, values, minimum standards, and aspirational goals of an individual or organization" (Roberts, 2019). Most codes articulate common values, especially the declaration to pursue truthful, verified, accurate, and original information as a fundamental value and serving the public interest as a fundamental loyalty (Moore, 2010; Roberts, 2019). The call for truth telling in the SPJ code is echoed in more medium-specific codes of ethics such as the American Society of Newspaper Editors (for print and digital journalists), the Radio Television Digital News Association (for broadcasters), the Public Relations Society of America (for strategic communicators), and the National Press Photographers Association (for photojournalists). Accountablejournalism.org has a database of more than 400 codes of ethics from individual news organizations, media industry sectors, journalistic unions and associations, and press councils or press clubs.

Truth, however, can be a tricky subject for journalists, broadcasters, and strategic communicators. Bill Kovach and Tom Rosenstiel (2007) write that journalism's first obligation is to the truth, and they call "journalistic truth" the disinterested pursuit of the truth. However, Walter Lippmann (1922) wrote, "News and truth are not the same thing. . . . The function of news is to signalize an event. The function of truth is to bring to light the hidden facts, to set them into relation with each other, and make a picture of reality upon which men can act." News is a construction of reality, a selected account chosen for its ability to please both advertisers and readers (Baldasty, 1992). This reality should be seen through the lens that Stephen Ward calls "pragmatic objectivity." He suggested that journalists should seek the best obtainable version of the truth, but that journalists also should recognize and retransmit that newsgathering practices are imperfect due to constraints such as time and money (Ward, 2004). Taken together, journalism can be seen as the disinterested pursuit of the best obtainable version of the truth.

Truth also has been a tricky subject for philosophers. Philosophic thought about truth has evolved through time. For the ancient Greeks, truth was based on the idea of what was memorable and what was handed down. Plato challenged these ideas, arguing that truth is what abides in a world of perfect forms. In Medieval times, the truth was whatever the king, the church, or God said it was. This idea, in turn, was challenged first by John Milton, who wrote in *Aeropagitica* that truth emerges from the marketplace of ideas, and by other Enlightenment thinkers who saw truth as those ideas that are verifiable, replicable, and universal. In the 20th century, pragmatists including John Dewey, George Herbert Mead, Charles Sanders Pierce, and William James challenged Enlightenment thinking of truth, arguing that truth is filtered through individual perception. Now, the information explosion in the digital age means that facts and truth are available almost instantaneously from all over the world. Websites blend words and images aggregated from many sources, leading to a convergence or coherence theory of truth where truth is discovered by determining which set of facts form a coherent mental picture of events and ideas investigated through a variety of methods.

Mythmaking, Truth, and Normative Role

Popular culture myths of journalism often are based on normative roles. In the Western, especially American, normative tradition, proper journalists are the watchdog, witness, and sense-maker; those who do not perform these roles are dysfunctional and toxic (McNair, 2010). The major media myths depicted in popular culture are that journalists can see through lies and hypocrisy, that they stick up for the common man, and that they uncover the truth and serve democracy (Ehrlich, 2004). When journalists are corrupt scoundrels who have lost their way, they ultimately are punished for their sins. Such films are morality tales that highlight rules and proper professional and personal conduct instead of seriously challenging journalism's central societal role (Ehrlich, 2004).

Matthew Ehrlich (2004) argues that journalists are portrayed as two competing myths. The first is the official journalist who stands for community and progress (Ehrlich, 2004). Journalistic heroes—typically foreign correspondents and investigative reporters—tend to be those journalists engaged in witnessing injustice, holding powerful people and institutions accountable, and defending freedom. By depicting journalists as heroes, filmmakers mythologize the normatively approved functions of journalism in a democracy and translate them into a popular culture idiom (McNair, 2010).

The second is the outlaw journalist who stands for individualism and freedom. Journalistic villains tend to fall into one of three categories: (1) the lovable rogue or the charming "bad boy" whom we love but do not trust, (2) the reptile who is wholly loathsome with few or no redeeming qualities, and (3) the repentant sinner who knows he or she—though likely he because almost all fictional journalistic villains are men—is violating normative principles of journalism and feels guilty about it (McNair, 2010). The most appealing or entertaining characters, McNair contends, are those that combine some degree of both heroism and villainy.

Lying journalistic villains—often reptiles but at times with touches of lovable rogue or repentant sinners—have populated popular culture since early days of film.

Ace in the Hole (1951)—also appearing under the title *The Big Carnival*—begins with down-on-his-luck reporter Chuck Tatum arriving at the *Albuquerque Sun-Bulletin*. Tatum, who's been fired from several big newspapers in Chicago and New York, is looking to work at a small-town newspaper, break a big story, and get back to the big time. Tatum's character and potential story is similar to a familiar trope in novels about journalism. In those fictional stories, a crusading journalist, like a gunslinger in an old-time Western, rolls into town and finds the community controlled by greedy businessmen, corrupt politicians, or gun-toting gangsters. The journalist defeats the wrongdoers and then either disappears as mysteriously as he appeared or earns the love of a beautiful woman, fame and prosperity for his paper, or promotion out of daily journalism (Good, 1986).

Tatum, however, recoils at the notion of acting in the public interest. His motto is that he "can handle big news and little news, and if there's no news, I'll go out and bite a dog." Early in the film, Tatum and a young photographer, Herbie Cook, are driving to cover a story about a rattlesnake hunt. Tatum tries to educate Herbie, a graduate of a journalism school, about the lessons he has learned writing for and selling newspapers. Tatum's main takeaway: "Bad news sells best because good news is no news." Tatum says that a better story than a rattlesnake hunt would be if 50 rattlesnakes got loose in Albuquerque. He could cover authorities trying to hunt the loose snakes, providing a daily update that 10 snakes have been captured, then 20, then 30, all the way to 49 snakes. The key to keeping the story suspenseful is that authorities would not be able to find the last snake because Tatum would hide it in his desk. After three days, he would "find" the snake and have an exclusive story.

Tatum finds his exclusive on the way to the rattlesnake hunt. While stopping for gas, he discovers that there has been a cave-in at an old, remote Indian dwelling. A man, Leo Minosa, is trapped inside. Tatum sees a great story; as he says, one man trapped is a great human-interest story. Tatum writes about Minosa, and the story becomes a sensation both locally and nationally. Locally, tourists start arriving to rubberneck the scene, creating a circus-like atmosphere including musical performances and an actual carnival complete with a Ferris Wheel. Nationally, the story begins going out over the Associated Press wire, and both *Life* and *Look* magazines are interested in running features about Minosa. Tatum makes a deal with the local sheriff: the publicity from the story can help the sheriff in his re-election bid; in exchange, the sheriff will help keep other reporters out so Tatum can get the story himself. Tatum and the sheriff also concoct a plan to make the rescue last one week instead of the 16 hours a local contractor says it will take to extract Minosa. Tatum has the story to himself. He has the sheriff and Minosa's family on his side; the big-city papers want the story, but their reporters cannot get it because Tatum controls access to the cave.

Tatum isn't the first onscreen journalist to deceptively engineer an exclusive. Originally a Broadway comedy, the film *The Front Page* first hit theaters in 1931, and it later reappeared as *His Girl Friday* in 1940, as well as a 1974 remake starring Jack Lemmon and Walter Matthau. Each version of the comedy features two journalists who will do anything while chasing a story, including hiding an accused and escaped murderer from the police in order to beat the competition for an exclusive.

Tatum and *His Girl Friday*'s Hildy Johnson are at worst lying and at best being deceptive. Sissela Bok (1999) defines a lie as any intentionally deceptive message that is stated. Bok argues that when we undertake to deceive others intentionally, we communicate messages meant to mislead them or meant to make them believe what we ourselves do not believe. We can deceive others through gestures or disguises, by means of action or inaction, or even through silence. Because a level of truthfulness always has been seen as an essential component of human society, lies are harmful and hurtful. Bok argues that a lie may misinform so as to obscure an objective the deceived person wanted to do or obtain, lies may eliminate or obscure relevant alternatives, deception can manipulate the degree of uncertainty in how we look at our choices, and lies can be coercive. Lies can, and often do, cause immediate harm to others. However, Bok argues that lies also can harm the liars themselves and can harm the general level of trust and social cooperation; these consequences are especially important because they are cumulative and hard to reverse.

While the Society of Professional Journalists emphasizes the importance of truth telling and outlines measures on how to best tell the truth, Bok warns that codes of ethics function all too often as shields because the abstract nature of a code allows many to adhere to them while continuing their ordinary practices. Tatum, for example, is telling the truth when he reports that a man is trapped in a cave. However, Tatum also is obscuring the details of the situation, specifically his own role in ensuring that the man stays trapped in the cave in order to further the story and, by extension, Tatum's journalistic career. Bok argues that codes of ethics must be the starting point for a broad inquiry into the ethical quandaries encountered at work. The important phrase in the previous sentence is "starting point"; codes cannot and should not be both the starting point and ending point in the ethical decision-making process.

Tatum gets his wish with the breaking, sensational story: the New York papers want him writing for them. So, Tatum quits the *Sun-Bulletin* in order to better cash in on his newfound fame and notoriety.

TATUM: I've quit. I'm not working for you anymore.

Boot (the *Sun-Bulletin* publisher): I'm sorry to hear that, Chuck.

TATUM: No, you're not. I'm not your kind of newspaperman. I don't belong in your office, not with that embroidered sign [which reads, "Tell the Truth"] on the wall. Gets in my way.

BOOT: It does bother you a little.

TATUM: Not enough to stop me. I'm on my way, and if it takes a deal with a crooked sheriff, that's alright with me. And if I have to fancy it up with an Indian curse and a broken-hearted wife for Leo, that's alright too.

BOOT: Not with me, it isn't. And not with a lot of others in this business. Phony, below-the-belt journalism. That's what it is.

TATUM: Not below the belt, (punches himself) right in the gut, Mr. Boot. Human interest.

BOOT: You heard me, phony. For all I know, there isn't even a Leo down there.

TATUM: Yes, there is. Tatum made sure of that. (Takes a long drink.) Look. I've waited a long time for my turn at bat. Now that they've pitched me a fat one, I'm going to smack it right out of the ballpark.

There are a wide range of heroes and villains depicted on the big and small screen. For every Woodward and Bernstein working tirelessly to expose a corrupt presidential administration in *All the President's Men*, there is a Chuck Tatum hiding an injured man in order to keep an exclusive in *Ace in the Hole*. For every Murphy Brown, the titular character on a long-running television series about a prominent and award-winning investigative journalist and anchor, there is a Zoe Barnes in *House of Cards* who has sex with sources and knowingly publishes false information. Many of the most interesting depictions, however, feature a character who has aspects of heroism and villainy. For example, Megan Carter in *Absence in Malice* attempts to be a watchdog reporter but destroys lives with her mistakes. Viewers ultimately are left with the idea that Carter will become a better journalist based on the lessons she has learned during the course of the film.

Tatum, like Carter, eventually begins to see the error of his ways. He learns that Minosa will die from pneumonia if they don't get him out of the cave quickly. He knows that a human-interest story needs a happy ending, telling the sheriff, "It's a better story if we're not too late." However, they won't be able to get to Minosa in time because the cave is too unstable due to the way they've been drilling. Tatum knows that Minosa is going to die, and he sees the truly human cost to Minosa and his parents. However, there is nothing that he can do to save Minosa, so he takes a priest into the cave to administer last rites and then stops filing stories for the New York papers, confessing to his editor that he staged the whole story. The editor, though, doesn't care about the deception; he only cares that he's not getting the types of exclusive stories that he was paying Tatum to deliver.

Discussion Question

Journalism was much different when *Ace in the Hole* was first released in 1951. How might Chuck Tatum report the story differently in a 24-hour news cycle with news blasts to cell phones, updates on social media, and publishing and updating the story on his newspaper's website? How would a 24-news cycle and hyper-competition from other news outlets impact Tatum's ability to report—or hide—the truth?

Tatum is a deceitful scoundrel and a liar, but he is far from the only one in films and television shows about journalists. The 2003 film *Shattered Glass* is a fictional account of the real-life Stephen Glass, a star reporter at the *New Republic* until Adam Penenberg, a rival reporter at *Forbes*, and Chuck Lane, the editor at *New Republic*, discovered that Glass partially or entirely invented and fabricated 27 of the 41 articles he wrote for the magazine. The film largely follows the post-hoc fact-checking and verification process on Glass's June 1998 "Hack Heaven" article. Both Lane and Penenberg, as well as his fellow *Forbes* reporter Andy Fox, initially thought that Glass had been duped by computer hackers, not that he fabricated the article. Fox, played by Rosario Dawson, tells Penenberg: "The *New Republic*, snobbiest rag in the business, the in-flight magazine of Air Force One . . . and their star goes out and gets completely snowed by a bunch of hackers. I mean, God couldn't have written this any better."

However, after investigations by Lane and Penenberg, they realize that Glass was not duped; instead, he was lying. Lane realizes the implications almost immediately and, during an argument with *New Republic* reporter Caitlin Avery, a friend of Glass's who is trying to defend his actions, relays the importance of the fabrication:

> Come Monday morning, we're all going to have to answer for what we let happen here. We're all going to have an apology to make. [Yelling] Jesus Christ. Don't you have any idea how much shit we're about to eat? Every competitor we ever took a shot at, they're going to pounce. And they should. Because we blew it, Caitlin. He handed us fiction after fiction, and we printed them all as fact. Just because we found him entertaining. It's indefensible.

The fabrication of "Hack Heaven" was discovered largely because *Forbes* was trying to be *the* magazine of Silicon Valley but got scooped on a sensational article. Glass, though, had been lying to his colleagues and readers for years. In his piece "Spring Breakdown," he pretended to be a convention-goer at the Conservative Political Action Conference in order to get damaging material (alcohol and drug abuse, strippers and prostitutes, etc.) on young Republicans. Glass also wrote a story about calling into a radio show pretending to be an expert on biting following the first Mike Tyson–Evander Holyfield fight. Of course, both stories also were made up, but editors didn't know that at the time they initially published his articles.

Like Glass, reporter Scott Templeton also fabricates stories in the HBO series *The Wire* (2002–2008). Templeton is a young and decidedly mediocre reporter at the semi-fictional *Baltimore Sun* who is intent on using the *Sun* as a stepping-stone to a bigger newspaper. He sees his chance at a big-time story when he becomes the lead reporter on a *Sun* series about a string of connected killings of homeless men. When Templeton begins the series, he is duped by a rogue cop who is staging crime scenes to convince his superiors and the public about a serial killer targeting the homeless population in Baltimore in order to gain police resources to investigate a string of real murders committed by a local drug gang. Templeton, however, is not content to report on the unfolding story. Instead, in chasing it, he steps over ethical lines again and again. He even makes up key components of his articles—not only about the homeless killings but also stories about a shake-up at police headquarters, a human-interest piece about baseball's opening day, and a story about a mother of four who died from an allergic reaction to shellfish. With the serial killer story, Templeton becomes a hot property in the newsroom; he's seen as the "golden boy" by Executive Editor James C. Whiting III and Managing Editor Thomas Klebanow.

However, City Editor Gus Haynes and others begin to suspect, and then accuse, Templeton of falsifying his stories. The conflict mounts over the course of the series, finally coming to a head during a confrontation after Templeton says he saw the suspected serial killer trying to drag a homeless man into a gray van.

KLEBANOW: Are you suggesting that Scott made any of this up?

HAYNES: (Sighs and rubs his head.) You ever notice that the guys who do that, the Blairs, the Glasses, the Kelleys, they always start with something small, just a little quote that they clean up. But then it's a whole anecdote, and pretty soon they're seeing some amazing shit. They're the lucky ones who just happen to be standing on the right street corner in Tel Aviv when the pizza joint blows up and the human head rolls down the street with the eyes still blinking.

KLEBANOW: The pictures were sent to him. The police have confirmed . . .

HAYNES: It always starts with something true. Something confirmed. But then you've got a son of a bitch who just happens to be walking in the Guilford entrance when a mysterious gray van comes up.

KLEBANOW: Gus, this has gotten personal between you and Scott, and it's affecting your judgment. I'm moving the story through the state desk. You should go home. Think this through. We'll talk in the morning.

HAYNES: (Walking out.) Maybe you win a Pulitzer with this stuff, and maybe you've got to give it back.

There are few happy endings in *The Wire*. The season, and the series, ends with Templeton winning a Pulitzer Prize, accepting the award with a beaming Whiting and Klebanow by his side. Haynes, for rightly questioning Templeton's reporting, is punished with a demotion to the copy desk.

Glass fabricated slice-of-life and human-interest stories, while Templeton made up a serial killer. In *Wag the Dog* (1997), Conrad Brean, a media specialist working on a presidential re-election campaign, concocts a war. The

Figure 2.2.   Scott Templeton, James C. Whiting III, and Thomas Klebanow (left to right) from *The Wire*. Copyright 2002, HBO

president and his team need to divert attention away from a developing sex scandal involving an inappropriate relationship between the president and an underage girl two weeks before the election. Brean, with help from Hollywood producer Stanley Motss, invents a story about Albanian terrorists trying to smuggle a nuclear bomb through Canada in a suitcase; they know that news organizations will concentrate on the war instead of the scandal. Brean and Motss go so far as to film fake news footage of an "Albanian" girl "fleeing" from a village bombed by the Albanian terrorist organization. The ruse initially is successful, leading Brean to declare: "Change the story. Change the lead."

Throughout the film, reporters, especially broadcast correspondents, are depicted as bumbling idiots who cannot figure out whether news footage is real or fake, whether there really is a war happening. Brean's response: "Of course there's a war. I see it on television." While the media cannot figure out the difference between fact and fiction, the president's political rival, Senator John Neal, does with help from the CIA. Neal goes on television to report that the war is over, so news organizations shift their focus back to the sex scandal. Brean and Motss then need to concoct a second lie—that a soldier named Schumann was accidentally left behind. They develop an entire campaign with a theme song written by Willie Nelson and pseudo-grassroots patriotic rallies. Schumann, it turns out, is a criminally insane Army convict. However, Brean and Motss catch a break when Schumann is shot while trying to rape a woman, and they can stage an elaborate military funeral for Schumann while claiming that he died from wounds sustained while fighting in Albania.

The upside to all of the deception is that the presidential sex scandal is kept out of the news long enough for him to get re-elected. The downside is that three major institutions—the executive branch, the Army, and the news media—either lie to citizens or fail to catch the lie. *Wag the Dog* is intended as a dark comedy, and one of the final exchanges in the film nicely summarizes the problems inherent in deception:

> BREAN: What did television ever do to you?
> WINIFRED AMES: It destroyed the electoral process.

Ames, here, reiterates one of Bok's central arguments against lying—that lying can have immediate harm to others, that it can harm the liars themselves, and that it can harm the general level of trust and social cooperation. Further, as Bok wrote, the harm to the general level of trust and social cooperation is cumulative and hard to reverse. The lies concocted by Brean and Motss and depicted on television through *Wag the Dog* have eroded trust and social cooperation; for Ames, they have destroyed the electoral process, one of the central faiths of a democratic republic.

3

Loyalty

Where Individual Virtue
and Philosophical Principle Meet

> **Central Concepts**
>
> - Two definitions of loyalty
> - How loyalty can be considered both a virtue and a philosophical principle
> - Utilitarian ethics and loyalty
> - How loyalty shapes identity

Loyalty is connective tissue. For fiction writers, regardless of medium, the concept itself is a way to explain individual motivation plus providing the bonus of significant plot points. Unlike traditional and classical philosophy, where loyalty is not written about as a core concept, popular culture is replete with discussions of the topic. Furthermore, those discussions are substantive, putting in narrative form the problematic, sometimes contradictory and evolving understanding of the term.

This chapter begins with a definition of loyalty that connects it to individual virtue and philosophical principle applied to institutions and communities. Trust and the need for individual loyalties to be transparent to others are elements of loyalty that are explored in multiple popular-culture artifacts. Because loyalty involves both self and others in community, the philosophical principle articulated in utilitarian theory can help pinpoint both the strengths and problems with making ethical choices based in loyalty. Finally, the chapter concludes with some research about how loyalty can be a building block of identity, including which groups we choose to be affiliated with, the goods and services we purchase, and how we evaluate people and groups who violate previously established loyalties.

Loyalty is an expansive concept that is capable of nobility and ignominy within the same sets of facts. Most of the time, loyalty is thought of as a virtue. "Our loyalties are important signs of the kind of persons we have chosen to become. They mark a kind of constancy and steadfastness in our attachments. . . . Real loyalty endures inconvenience, withstands temptation, and does not cringe under assault" (Bennett, 1993, p. 665).

Take this brief conversation from *Spotlight*, the 2015 Academy Award–winning film for best picture that recounts the *Boston Globe*'s investigative reporting that publicly revealed what many already knew: Catholic priests were sexually assaulting boys and girls, a way of life that had been covered up by the Catholic hierarchy for decades. The church's pedophile priests became a global scandal that has yet to be resolved; the problem itself has been "uncovered" in other Christian denominations.

UNNAMED POLICE OFFICER: Nobody wants to cuff a priest. I don't think I should talk about this shit.
SASHA PFEIFFER: Actually, I think you should.

Or this conversation, which occurs later in the film.

JUDGE: These records that you are asking for are very sensitive in nature. Where is the editorial responsibility in publishing records of this nature?
MIKE REZENDES: Where is the editorial responsibility in not publishing them?

These brief conversations let the audience know that the people involved—all members of professions that Americans call public servants—think about the story through entirely different lenses, each focusing on a different loyalty. For the police officer—and story source—declining to discuss the events of which he is personally aware means he remains loyal to a police force that has downplayed previous complaints to the point where many would accuse the various departments involved of condoning the church's cover-up. For the judge, it is making sure that the letter of the law is obeyed, even if private facts will be revealed in the process. For the journalists, the loyalty is to the story and to the potential public response that the story might provoke. Each believes they are being loyal to the common good, a foundational principle of utilitarian ethics that defines the greater good as the action that promotes the greatest happiness for the community at large, including many (but not always all) of its individual members.

However, the conversations reveal more. For most people, most of the time, there is an emotional component to loyalty. Loyalty is a building block of identity. People invest not just intellect but feelings in the people, causes, and ideas to which they chose to be loyal. Emotion can override logic—at least when loyalty is at the core of the emotion.

The focus of the *Globe*'s story, the institution-based cover-up of sexual predation, pushes a lot of emotional buttons. Sex is private, it's meant to be consensual. Some of the strongest religious strictures, regardless of specific faith, focus on sex. All societies, in one form or another, attempt to protect children from becoming sexual prey and to punish those who would behave otherwise. The police officer in the above conversation adheres to these loyalties in his "day job"; it is something he expects of himself and something that society expects of him. It is this loyalty—regardless of his previous actions— that has driven him to be willing to speak with a journalist about a story he knows through personal experience to be true yet unspoken. The judge faces a similar conflict: make something ugly public or disregard the law.

Discussion Question

What do you believe are essential virtues? How did *Boston Globe* reporters express these virtues in *Spotlight*?

Pfeiffer's response also reveals an important element of loyalty: for it to be the basis of ethical thinking, the focus of individual loyalties needs to be transparent. Transparency, in this sense meaning visible to others, suggests that loyalty can be discarded as well as affirmed, that facts as well as culture should have an influence on sustaining loyalty, and that it is possible for people to sustain—and to jeopardize—multiple loyalties with a single act or related set of actions. Loyalty conceived of as virtue includes an element of promise keeping, an important element of classical ethical theory exemplified in the work of W. D. Ross among others. Pfeiffer, in reporting the story, realizes it is so explosive that it may rupture her relationship with her Nanna (grandmother), a devout Roman Catholic. Matt Carroll, another of the *Spotlight* reporters, learns that a halfway house for abusive priests is in his neighborhood, a fact he wants to be able to share with his family and neighbors but cannot until the story itself is published. Loyalty, more so than most other virtues as philosophy defines them, carries within it the capacity for conflict; the kind person is kind to all, but loyalty by its definition means that I am loyal to some but not loyal to others. This conflict is not part of Pfeiffer's conversation with her source; what is transparent is her loyalty to the story itself. Her source knows—literally—"where she is coming from."

For these professionals, maintaining one set of loyalties is going to generate a conflict with another set of loyalties. Sifting among loyalties—making an ethical decision—is the focus of *Spotlight*.

LOYALTY AT THE INSTITUTIONAL LEVEL

The film opens with a scene at a police station—where a family has reported sexual abuse by a priest—only to have it hidden through the cooperation of those high in the police department with the Roman Catholic hierarchy.

This is institutional-level collusion, a loyalty that allows each institution to maintain its status in society with a minimum of friction. This institutional-level conflict of loyalties is articulated early in the film when the new *Boston Globe* editor, Marty Baron, speaks for the first time with Roman Catholic Cardinal Bernard Law, head of the church that has dominated the city since its founding.

> Law: I think you'll find that Boston is still a small town. . . . I find that the city flourishes when its great institutions work together.
> Baron: Personally, I'm of the opinion that for a paper to perform its function, it really needs to stand alone.

Of course, people are among the elements of institutions. Baron, who is Jewish and had never lived in Boston before he was named *Globe* editor, is perceived as an outsider throughout the film, including, initially, by his own newspaper staff. He reads books, talks to community—including religious—leaders, and attends the sort of functions "at which I am not my best" in order to better understand Boston. Because he is an outsider, Baron notices things others have not. To provide one example, it is Baron who notes that Cardinal Law "called down the wrath of God on the *Globe*" over allegations against a priest who did not serve in the Boston archdiocese. That one public act causes the outsider—in this case Baron—to question what the "insiders" knew.

In this case, individual perceptions—or refusals to question the accepted wisdom—were initiated at the institutional level and maintained by individuals within their own lives. Mitch Garabedian, the attorney whose life's work has been devoted to "outing" the pedophile priests, is also an outsider with a particularly relevant personal history. Garabedian is Armenian, a descendent of the Armenian diaspora that was the result of the first genocide of the 20th century. His legal practice reflects the personal impact of the genocide; he wants to speak for victims of institutions so strong that challenges to them can lead to the death of individuals and an attempt to stamp out a nationality or a race.

In *Spotlight*, "outsiders" can have an impact on insiders. During the initial weeks of the investigation, multiple *Globe* veterans, including senior editor Ben Bradlee Jr., insist that the story is "weak," "not there," or "already covered." However, as facts are amassed, minds are changed, in some part because skepticism is an accepted part of the journalistic process. The skeptical reporters and editors remain loyal to the story and the profession, allowing them to overcome other loyalties to church and community that, in light of the nature of this particular story, appear to be misplaced.

TRUST WITHIN A SINGLE INSTITUTION

As a plot point, it's almost a tangent. While the *Globe*'s reporting consumed more than a year of effort, it was paused by another news event: the September 11, 2001, attacks on New York City and Washington, DC. Journalists in the middle of a profoundly important story are asked to put it aside to cover an even more important one.

As the film itself demonstrates, the journalists had to explain the paper's reporting hiatus to their sources. Some of them understood; others did not take the news well. In one exchange, Pfeiffer tells the head of the organization SNAP, who has been a primary source throughout the project, that the paper will not publish as originally planned because of 9/11. He is distraught and accuses Pfeiffer—and hence the paper—of abandoning the story. He threatens to take the story elsewhere. Pfeiffer, in response, speaks to the emotional element of loyalty.

> PFEIFFER: I'm here because I care. We're going to tell this story, and we're going to tell it right. All we are asking for is a little more time.
> SAVIANO: You're going to do what you want. You always do.

Because *Spotlight* is a film and includes, as part of the ending credits, the number of places where Roman Catholic priests had been found to be pedophiles, the audience has a chance to see the impact of the story itself and to understand the goal of Pfeiffer's reasoning. However, at the time the decision was made, these facts were not available and could have been readily misunderstood. This potential misunderstanding is particularly true because this set of people had already been profoundly betrayed by a powerful institution—the church. It is reasonable that they would have been skeptical, even cynical, about another powerful institution—the *Globe*. Pfeiffer's request for more time from one of her main sources acknowledges that her source is a partner in the reporting of this story. The notion that journalists and their sources are "in it together" is never completely explored in the film, but it is a reality of professional life, for example when rape victims allow journalists to retell their experiences using their real names or when journalists protect the anonymity of their sources for fear of physical harm or professional retribution. Reporting, for both print and broadcast, on the COVID-19 epidemic includes multiple examples of this kind of partnership, from emergency room doctors who allow their video diaries to be aired on network television, to multiple stories in many national and local newspapers describing the economic impact of sudden job loss in the midst of a health crisis. Scholars have encouraged a more transparent acknowledgment of the need for such partnerships (Ward & Wasserman, 2010).

Placing trust in people, things, or ideas is an element of loyalty—at least, if popular culture's conceptualization of the term is accepted. Journalists operate by trust—first, of one another and then within ever-widening circles of people and institutions on which they report. Violating that trust can become a news story. Indeed, one explanation for investigative reporting is that it is a process whereby institutions are examined according to the public standards to which they subscribe (Ettema & Glasser, 1998). Journalists then ask whether the public face matches the private one, particularly when unstated motives are involved.

TAKING LOYALTY BEYOND VIRTUE

While many philosophers have defined loyalty as a virtue, others have argued that loyalty is a central ethical principle. Josiah Royce (1908) believed loyalty—which he defined as a social act that allowed the individual to develop and act on a "willing and practical and thoroughgoing devotion . . . to a cause"—could be considered the core of all morality. Royce believed that loyalty promoted self-realization; loyalty was about choosing, and even a failure to decide, in practical terms, reflected a decision and hence a loyalty.

Royce's articulation of the concept separated it from the field of virtue ethics. If loyalty is a virtue, as philosophers beginning with Aristotle and continuing through Alasdair MacIntyre (1987) and Philippa Foote (1977) have argued, then it is the virtuous individual who can be expected to understand loyalty and hence act in an ethical way. If loyalty is a philosophical principle, then even an unvirtuous person could reason her way into loyal—and hence ethical—choices. If loyalty is considered an ethical principal, as opposed to a quality of individual character, then the opposite would be equally true: a generally virtuous person, through a failure to think thoroughly about loyalty, could make choices that are unethical.

Spotlight, through its portrayal of lay members of the Catholic Church who through their actions aided in the church's cover-up, illustrates how good people, through a misapplication of loyalty, make ethical mistakes. Toward the end of the film, when it is obvious that the *Globe* has the story and is going to print it, *Spotlight* Editor Robby Robinson is asked to meet with the church's main public relations practitioner, Pete Conley.

CONLEY: You know a lot of people here respect you, Robby. People need the church right now . . . you know, you can feel it. And the cardinal, he might not be perfect . . . but we can't throw the cardinal out for a few bad apples.
ROBINSON: This is how it happens, isn't it, Pete? A guy leans on a guy, and soon the entire city is leaning away.

Figure 3.1. Pete Conley and Robby Robinson from *Spotlight*. Copyright 2015, Open Road Films

Loyalty is often connected to role. Role outlines how we will act toward others; role provides expectations in structured situations. Journalists, for example, are expected to have greater loyalty to truth telling than are other professionals; health care workers to have more loyalty to caring for others. The connection of loyalty and role emphasizes one of the weaknesses of Royce's thought—that most of us, most of the time, successfully maintain multiple loyalties because we all have multiple roles in life. Royce and many other philosophers who have written about the topic provide little guidance on how these decisions should be made.

Discussion Question

If you have a career in mind, what would your professional loyalties include? (If you do not have a career in mind, then make a list of your personal loyalties.) How much overlap is there between your loyalties and the loyalties espoused by characters in *Spotlight* and *Madam Secretary*? Where do you find the most serious conflicts?

Popular culture, however, has addressed important elements of these multiple, interrelated ethical choices. Balancing the various role demands in our lives is the focus of the television series *Madam Secretary* (2014–2019), where Secretary of State Elizabeth McCord routinely negotiates the demands of her public role with that of her role as spouse and mother. Furthermore, because the secretary of state has a political portfolio that spans the entire planet, she inevitably finds herself choosing between multiple worthy causes on behalf of the United States, which does not have unending financial or military resources. *Madam Secretary*, more than many popular culture artifacts that deal with politics, connects loyalty and ethics, in no small part because Elizabeth's husband is a professor of religion who, in multiple seasons, also works as an intelligence agent and ultimately becomes the "ethics advisor" to the White House. Unlike the academic writing about the topic, *Madam Secretary* infuses loyalty-based choices with emotion, including love of family and country, frustration and grief when choices produce unintended consequences, and sometimes a pervasive uncertainty about what the right action truly might be. In this, the television show probably reflects much of what many of us think and feel as we make decisions that require us to initiate and sustain loyalties and to make multiple decisions based on those initial choices.

In many episodes, Elizabeth McCord, the president, and others resolve these dilemmas by referring to "the greater good," the title of an episode in the second season where Elizabeth McCord must decide whom to back—and at what cost—in the murder of the president of Russia (itself a betrayal for power by his celebrity wife). As the fictional President Dalton explains, the "greater good" involves nothing but hard choices, "the greater good vs. individual harm." In this episode, Elizabeth McCord must balance a single, human life (a spy recruited to the CIA by her husband, Henry McCord) against a potential for nuclear war, all the while fielding questions from her family, the defense department, and the president. Although the precise meaning of the phrase varies somewhat from episode to episode—sometimes the phrase can mean family, sometimes political party, most often the nation-state, and routinely basic human rights—the phrase implies a decision that connects the individual to a community or multiple communities, what Royce called a "super-individual" quality. While Royce's discussion of loyalty never addresses how loyalty might guide citizens in thinking through questions involving majority views vs. individual rights—a political question that emerged before the U.S. government was founded—Royce's work implies that loyalties worth long-term devotion are to people, issues, and causes that others—those who are unlike the individual making the choice in important and meaningful ways—also could find both intellectual and emotional reason to support. For those who are unlike us to understand and accept decisions based on loyalty, the nature of the loyalty itself must be transparent. Others have to know, or be able to learn, what motivates our affiliations. Furthermore, that reasoning, at least in the popular culture of *Madam Secretary*, should take a long-term rather than a short-term view.

UTILITARIANISM ACCORDING TO *STAR TREK*

Star Trek, beginning with the 1960s television show that aired for three seasons, has had a profound impact on popular culture. Gadgets on *Star Trek*—cell phones, for example—are now part of our daily lives. In 2018, President Donald J. Trump called for a Space Force, a military version of *Star Trek: The Next Generation*'s Star Fleet. The original television series

Figure 3.2. Spock and Captain Kirk in *Star Trek*. Copyright Paramount Pictures and CBS Studios

was also noteworthy for the subject matter it sometimes focused on, including social justice and the role of care. However, the continuing narrative was one of community: how the captain and crew acted in such a way as to keep one another alive and flourishing, not just as individuals but as a crew of explorers with a scientific purpose (even if there was a lot of fighting and misogyny thrown into the mix). Without ever foregrounding it, the original *Star Trek* asked what is an essentially utilitarian question: how does one promote the common good?

When the *Star Trek* narrative rebooted on the big screen in 2009, perhaps what audiences were not expecting was a deepening lesson in utilitarian ethics. However, that's precisely what they received in the next two films, the first of which provides the backstory for how the spaceship *Enterprise* crew came to maturity and young adulthood. In the first of the films, *Star Trek* (2009), the very first words audiences hear the child Spock speak are "It is morally praiseworthy but not morally obligatory." What the audience does not hear is the question. However, Spock's lesson comes only after the film's opening sequence in which First Officer George Kirk sacrifices himself to save a starship crew that is under attack from an unknown assailant. Kirk's heroic act is ethically laudatory but not ethically obligatory. Philosophers have a name for this kind of heroism: supererogatory acts. However, the act itself, a fictional portrayal of the greatest good for the greatest number, sets a psychological path for Kirk's brilliant and semi-delinquent son, James Tiberius Kirk. Thus, by the time the movie is less than 20 minutes old, the two central characters have shown the practical impact of utilitarianism in daily life.

John Stuart Mill (1861/1998) and Jeremy Bentham (1789/1961) intended a practical, and for their time revolutionary, approach to ethics. They were the first philosophers to assert that the results of an act—the consequences—determine whether it is ethical. If an act produces more good than bad consequences—in their era Bentham and Mill talked of promoting "happiness"—then the act is considered ethical. Hence, utilitarianism has been crudely—and inaccurately—summarized as "the greatest good for the greatest number." Tally up the number of "good," subtract the number of "bad," do the math, and you can then determine whether an act is ethical. Living more than 150 years later, it is difficult to comprehend the revolutionary aspect of utilitarianism, for Mill and Bentham asserted that no one person's happiness (produced by good consequences) was any more important than any other person's happiness. The peasant's happiness was equal to the king's, an ideal that in the age of the "divine right of kings" was both revolutionary and profoundly democratic. However, what many contemporary authors—but not the screenwriters of *Star Trek* in its various incarnations—have missed is that

Bentham and Mill argued that happiness was a "community-wide phenomenon." Thus, if the happiness of a single individual made the rest of the community miserable, then that act, in utilitarian theory, is not considered ethical.

This concept of the ethics of an act being determined by its consequences is the motivating force behind every significant plot twist in *Star Trek: Into Darkness* (2013). In the process, all of the conceptual problems with utilitarianism are brought to the fore. Want to save a planet by squelching a volcano with a giant ice cube? That sounds like the greatest good for the planet, even if Spock has to die due to a technological failure. Rescue Spock in violation of "the prime directive"? Kirk's decision favors the minority of one—Spock—in defiance of the more generalized and initially far less consequential act of letting a primitive society glimpse a star ship. How does the greatest good for the greatest number balance minority and majority happiness? Mill and Bentham never say, but *Star Trek* does—the concrete action of saving a Vulcan life is balanced against the more ephemeral "bad" of a primitive society glimpsing something that might be in their future. The near-term good of saving Spock outweighs the diffuse and long-term common good. Making a choice that promotes short-term happiness and ignores long-term problems has bedeviled utilitarian philosophers for hundreds of years, and the *Star Trek* crew must confront the long-term and unanticipated consequences of their acts and those of others for the entire film. At its conclusion, Kirk decides to repeat George Kirk's supererogatory act. Here, the minority—Kirk—sacrifices himself for the larger *Enterprise* community. Does the price of Kirk's life outweigh the happiness of Star Fleet as it finally brings Kahn to heel? Does Spock's grief constitute happiness as Bentham and Mill conceptualized it? There is no math that adequately accounts for great, immediate harm with more widespread but far less deep happiness. At the end of *Into Darkness*, the screenwriters ask the audience members to decide for themselves what constitutes the greatest happiness in the 24th century. Emotionally, the answer is clear: the galaxy is better off with both Kirk and Spock in it. Utilitarianism, while a guide, has provided incomplete insight into consequences and the nature of ethical choice, all of them captured in the *Star Trek* narrative.

In academic and philosophical terms, Andrew Oldenquist (2002) has argued for the primacy of certain communal domains when human beings enact loyalty. In his view, all morality is tribal morality, and it is only within the tribe that considerations of impartiality may operate. "Our wide and narrow loyalties define moral communities or domains within which we are willing to universalize moral judgments, treat equals equally, protect the common good, and in other ways adopt the familiar machinery of impersonal morality" (Oldenquist, 2002, p. 31).

DOES LOYALTY TO TRIBE INFLUENCE HOW WE THINK?

Royce never considered the insider/outsider dynamic of loyalty. This is easy to understand; Royce was writing in the early 1900s, before both of that century's world wars, the rise of fascism internationally, and the flourishing of many sorts of human rights movements around the world. However, philosophers writing near the end of the 20th century have pegged the insider/outsider dynamic as one of the central "problems" for loyalty as either a principle or a quality of character. George Fletcher (1993) identifies the root of the problem when he writes that there are two distinct definitions of loyalty: "The first is: *do not betray me*. The second: *be one with me*."

Philosophers assert that for people to be considered ethical, they must have the ability to make decisions. The philosophical shorthand for this is the term *autonomy*, and philosophers connect autonomy with what it means to be human. Because autonomy speaks to our fundamental humanity, societies historically have protected groups of people who are assumed by qualities of role, age, or station in life to have less autonomy. We protect children in multiple ways because we assume—based on evidence—that children do not have the intellectual capacity to make independent, ethical choices. The same is true for some adults who suffer from ailments as distinct as traumatic brain injury or dementia. Cultures, the legal system, and role also can circumscribe choice. "I was just following custom . . . or orders . . . or the ways of my ancestors" are all reasons based in loyalty wherein autonomy appears to be circumscribed by external influences. Although both internal and external pressures regarding ethical choice are acknowledged to exist, autonomy allows for independent action. One can decide to betray one loyalty, most often for the sake of a different loyalty.

Not only does this definition of loyalty—do not betray me—accurately describe what some people mean when they use the word, but it also describes the enormous psychological costs of abandoning one set of loyalties to adopt another. Simon Keller (2007) notes that whistleblowers pay this sort of psychological price, something journalists are well aware of. Popular culture—as well as elite art—has employed this definition of loyalty with profound effect. Coming-of-age films such as *The Breakfast Club* (1985) or the many film versions of Spider-Man reflect the definition of loyalty that focuses on "do not betray me." The plots all hinge on loyalty, sometimes poorly understood, most often abandoned for another loyalty, or sometimes abandoned entirely. Popular culture in many forms understands that these distinct and in some ways conflicting definitions of loyalty require choice and must consider and face the consequences choices bring.

However, the second definition of loyalty, "be one with me," can be more devastating for the human psyche. Revolution is based on a refusal to "be one" with a current power structure, whether that is the Star War's film *Rogue One* (2016), the Amazon Prime series *Man in the High Castle* (2015–2019), or a novel such as *Fahrenheit 451* (1953). Understood in this way, loyalty helps human beings create an identity. Once that identity is in place, loyalty can make us not only willing to do harm but also to *be* harmed. "Be one with me" dismisses or greatly diminishes autonomy. In the 21st century, we sometimes summarize this definition—and its significant consequences—as "blind" loyalty or "unthinking" loyalty. Perhaps the best documented instance of this "dark side" of loyalty is the genocides of the 20th century that have been the subject of many films and television series. Genocide not only harms specific groups; it dehumanizes those who perpetrate the slaughter.

Discussion Question

How might social movements such as #MeToo or #BlackLivesMatter reflect loyalty? Which definition of loyalty do you think they encapsulate?

The film *The Killing Fields* (1984) provides a powerful examination of the impact of choices about loyalty on journalists under the most extreme of pressures. Protagonist Sydney Schanberg learns from his translator/fixer/colleague Dith Pran how loyalty to the human spirit—of which free speech and action is an essential part—can sustain people under life-threatening pressure. Schanberg begins the film (and book) as a journalist loyal to his career as it is reflected on the front page of the *New York Times*. But Schanberg learns that the front page cannot reflect the common cause he begins to feel with the people of Cambodia, whom he comes to know through photojournalist Pran. It is Pran, the nominal other, in his interior monologue to Schanberg who says that the Khmer Rouge has "forgotten love." He befriends the young son of a brutal Khmer Rouge commander in an act of human solidarity while demonstrating the sustaining value of loyalty to humanity itself. The horrifying brutality of Cambodia's civil war is matched against the vision of a journalist who wants to tell a human story with the subtext of "there, but for the grace of god, go I."

However, genocide is an extreme example of dehumanizing an outgroup to reinforce loyalty to *my* tribe. Scholars document the same phenomenon. Evidence shows that loyalty plays a role in shaping the influence of affiliations

on responses to ethical transgressions; however, the finding of partial media-
tion suggests that there may be other intervening forces at play. Evoking an
in/out group mentality may operate on judgment and punishment preferences
through psychological distance. Although "us" is psychologically closer and
"them" more distant to "me," consumers may be motivated to grant more
leniency to an in-group transgressor due to a shift in mental construal; psychological proximity decreases the weight of abstract, global elements and
increases the weight of concrete, contextual aspects (Liberman, Trope, &
Stephan, 2007).

This academic insight is reflected in the daily lives of the central characters in *Spotlight*. As the public relations practitioners for the Roman Catholic
Church attempt to redirect the journalistic efforts by the *Globe* reporters, they
note that the new editor of the *Globe* is not *one of us*. During a golf outing
with the *Spotlight* editor, one of those working for the church and with deep
knowledge of the extent of the pedophilia problem notes: "The new editor of
the *Globe* is an unmarried man of the Jewish faith who doesn't like baseball."
Clearly, the Boston tribe is married, Catholic, and a Red Sox fan. Others need
not apply, they will not be accepted if they do, and, most importantly, those
"others" cannot possible have *my* interests at heart.

Relationships that involve loyalty display what philosophers call epistemic
partiality. Because loyalty deals with questions of belief, knowledge, and justification, loyalties can influence the way that people form, adopt, and reject
beliefs. Add the element of emotion, and loyalty—once developed—can run
deep and be almost impossible to dislodge. Philosophers use the example of
how we feel about our friends. Not only are we more likely to defend friends
(say from unflattering gossip), but we will spend more energy defeating or
minimizing the impact of unfavorable information about a friend than we
would someone we consider an acquaintance (Jollimore, 2013, p. 19).

There may be "no crying in baseball," but in *A League of Their Own*, the
1992 film about the All-American Girls Professional Baseball League that
developed in the United States during World War II, there were tears about
friendship and love, overlooking "bad actions" by some for the health of the
team, and placing sisterly fulfillment above winning a baseball champion-
ship. The subtext of the film—that women should have equal rights and
opportunity in sports—emphasizes that loyalty to a group can have historic
meaning. *Hidden Figures* (2017) pits friendship against institutional tradition in the realm of overarching goals. Ultimately, the "out group" of Black
women become the key to success in the U.S. space program, in the process
forging a community with people who were unlike them but shared a common goal. In *Hidden Figures*, an initial loyalty (among three friends) allows
other, larger loyalties to emerge. The same is true in *A League of Their Own*

when they are given a permanent exhibit at the Baseball Hall of Fame, an acknowledgment that the league's "second-class status" was an ethical mistake.

If the insights of popular culture are taken seriously, then one test of whether loyalty is worth maintaining would be: does the initial loyalty generate second- and third-level loyalties that encompass more diverse groups of people; does the emerging and expanded loyalty touch all in the newly developed "group of us" equally? An institution that fails to allow loyalties to grow and flourish becomes itself suspect. It impedes flourishing. Applying this maxim might be one key to ethically based decisions that require us to choose among loyalties in our professional lives.

Failing to take this philosophically informed view is one of the themes of *Spotlight*. In Boston and among believers, the church is more than just a friend. It is a doorway to the divine. It makes human—if not logical—sense that, to defend the church, the faithful would be willing to tolerate acts that violate the core teachings of every religion. Instead of allowing new loyalties to emerge, the case of the pedophile priests illustrates that some choices demand a diminished set of loyalties. Royce called such loyalty wrongheaded; in more contemporary work, we wrestle with the problem of loyalty to unsavory causes.

THE COSTS OF RETHINKING "TO WHOM AM I LOYAL"

Philosophy only tangentially discusses the impact of "disloyalty." Political philosophy connects such choices with treason. However, our evolution as a human species illustrates why thinking about loyalty demands both rational analysis and a transparent acknowledgment of the emotions that are at work.

> Trust and sensitivity to betrayal thus become fairly basic components in the emotional structure of the human individual. We rely on people around us in a great many ways for a great many things, and in order to flourish, a human being needs the people around her to be people she can trust—to be, that is, people who will not be disloyal to her. That we rely on people in this way, that we need not be betrayed, is a deep fact about our social nature. . . . Understanding how much this matters in our own case, we find it easy to extend this understanding to others, and are naturally inclined to protect them, much as we desire to protect ourselves, from betrayal and abandonment. (Jollimore, 2013, p. 56)

Trust, once broken (or never forged in the first place), is difficult to rebuild. That lack of trust, whether it is in institutions or individuals, is both emotional and rational, a mechanism that protects us from what we perceive to be the "worst of others," whether justified or not. Trust also emerges from context;

history may not repeat itself act for act, but the context of history may continue to inform decisions even when a contemporary context has changed in profound ways.

Context matters, not just in terms of the brands we purchase, but in how we think about our professional responsibilities. If the lens of context is too narrowly focused, then troubling loyalties emerge from which poor choices may result. That's the takeaway from the film *Broadcast News* (1987), where ratings and becoming the on-camera star take precedence over quality journalism and the recognition that good work is really a team product. Only at the end of the film, when the on-air talent refuses the job of broadcast managing editor, is the audience allowed to understand that the central characters have recognized that ego alone is not enough to produce a quality national news broadcast seven days a week. Ratings don't make you smart; they can set you up for profound professional failures. *Broadcast News* is an "old" film, but substitute "clicks" or "likes" for the word *ratings*, and the same lessons still apply. However, in *Broadcast News*, the context also is important. In that film, there was a newsroom with countervailing voices and the belief that there was a professional community contributing to the program's success. In the current media environment of blogging and downsizing, those countervailing voices are fewer and the entire concept of a team may be subsumed by "my personal brand." When community becomes an abstraction, as the scholarly literature has found, evaluating loyalties both rationally and emotionally becomes more difficult.

Chief among those difficulties is what to do about those whom we perceive to be "disloyal," who, if the literature is to be believed, have a high likelihood to be somewhat unlike us or fail to provide the requisite credentials to become members of "my" tribe. That answer is punishment—unequally applied. In a marketing study, researchers found

> a biasing influence of group affiliation on ethical judgment and punishment preferences. Consumers judged an in-group marketer's behavior as more unethical when the marketer targeted fellow in-group members (as prospects for a harmful product) than when out-group members were targeted. Moreover, consumers selected less harsh, more lenient forms of punishment when the transgressing marketer was a member of their in-group. These findings document an important contextual influence on ethical judgment. When judging the ethicality of an act, it appears that people look beyond the nature of the act itself and implicitly consider their relationship to the parties involved: who is performing the act and who is being victimized. . . . A transgression by an in-group member against the in-group may seem more loathsome because it carries two offenses: the transgression itself is compounded by the sin of disloyalty. . . . Group affiliations activate loyalty, which biases consumers' perceptions of eth-

ics and reactions to ethically controversial business practices. It is particularly interesting to note that this effect appears to occur without awareness (or at very least without full admission) on the part of consumers (Wright, Dinsmore, & Kellaris, 2013, p. 206–207).

If loyalty has this impact on how we evaluate the behavior of marketers and the products they promote, how much more of an impact might it have on groups of people with whom we identify? Abandoning the group to which we emotionally and rationally belong is seldom easy, and punishment is often implied to reinforce conformity and assumed by those who are the focus of the act. This, too, is the focus of *Spotlight*, as the *Globe* reporters investigate not just individuals but the system—the community—that sustains them. As part of the public relations practitioner's effort to redirect the *Globe* reporters on the story, the head of the church's public relations arm notes that Baron will ultimately leave the *Globe* for another job (as of this writing he is the editor at the *Washington Post*) while the reporters and editors who work with him will remain in Boston—with the implication that they will be shunned by the community in which they have spent most of their lives.

However, *Spotlight*—and more importantly the *Globe*'s actual reporting—provides another and more optimistic response. On the day of the story's publication, the newsroom received hundreds of calls, almost all of them from the victims of predator clergy who were calling to affirm the difficult truth that the paper reported. This, too, was an act of loyalty.

4

Privacy in Public Places

Understandable Tradeoffs and Unforeseen Consequences

Central Concepts

- Historic definitions of privacy
- Technology's impact on defining privacy and the ethical questions that emerge from that shifting definition
- How the political state can employ "the media" as a control mechanism
- The role of journalists in supporting—and assaulting—individual privacy
- How celebrity and identity become public, political domain

For millennia, the concept of privacy was loosely linked with physical space. Peering over a garden wall or through a window or overhearing a conversation all required some physical proximity. Then, technology literally entered the picture. The telephoto lens, the hidden microphone, or the concealed camera made physical proximity less important. Instead, what became important was the intent of the person who was doing the "snooping" and the others with whom the information might be shared. There was a clear victim and a clear lack of consent to obtaining the information and sometimes to receiving it.

Almost every element of the concept is under pressure in the 21st century. Philosophy has defined privacy as retaining control over personal information and the context in which it is understood. The *New York Times* privacy project writes about it in this way: "You are losing control over your life. When technology governs so many aspects of our lives—and when technology is powered by the exploitation of our data—privacy isn't just about knowing your secrets, it's about autonomy," explained Matt Cagel, technology and civil rights attorney for the ACLU. "Privacy is really about being able to define for ourselves who we are for the world and on our own terms. That's not a choice that belongs to an algorithm or data broker and definitely not to Facebook" (Warzel, 2019).

This chapter is built on the most recent theorizing about the concept of privacy, theory that welds individual privacy to technology (Wilkins & Patterson, 2020). Because technology is implicated in how we understand—and what we expect when we think about—privacy, the fusion of the human with the metaphorical machine shapes what previously had been considered two exclusively human activities, psychological development and political participation. Privacy cannot take place outside of community, and it is this three-way connection—human beings, technology, and community—that inform contemporary thinking about the term.

Most theorizing about privacy before the latter part of the 20th century assumed that mechanical contrivances were a means to invade privacy. We suggest that technology allows one set of human beings to exploit other human beings for everything from selling goods and services to the creation of political myth and a willingness to participate in political activity. And politics is the original expression of ethical human activity, at least according to Aristotle.

Privacy is an instrumental concept that is best understood in relation to what it contributes to our well-being as people who live with others. There are many films, novels, and television episodes that deal with privacy, but relatively few of them take on the link between privacy, technology, and politics.

Figure 4.1. Katniss Everdeen from *The Hunger Games*. Copyright Lionsgate Entertainment

This chapter is devoted to an in-depth exploration of one set of them. Part of your challenge in considering it is to think of other popular-culture artifacts that provide insight into this triangular relationship all of us experience on a daily basis.

Katniss Everdeen lives our shifting understandings of privacy. Unwilling—but far from unwitting—star of reality television in the fictional Panem, Katniss trades away her privacy for her life. Author Suzanne Collins's popular young adult trilogy *The Hunger Games*, which became a four-film series of blockbusters, is a visual essay on our struggles with the concept of privacy and why—despite the assertions that privacy is dead—it remains a core component of our mediated lives—whether we are content producers or consumers. *The Hunger Games* also asks readers to think deeply about how and why privacy and politics are intimately connected.

Discussion Question

Throughout this chapter, privacy is defined in multiple ways. How would Katniss Everdeen define privacy? How does her definition of privacy incorporate the understandings of privacy defined in this chapter?

Collins grew up listening to and watching media, waiting for news of her father, who served in Vietnam during her childhood. The broadcasting of information, in other words the news, was a vast public arena that for her also was intensely personal. This consumption of news through a public-private realm could only be a passive, even helpless, undertaking (Dominus, 2011). The young Collins grew up to write Katniss, the girl who goes to war, leaving others—Primrose, Gale, her mother—behind to wait, forced to helplessly watch broadcasts of events as they play on television. Collins said the idea for the brutal nation of Panem came one evening when she was channel-surfing between a reality show competition and war coverage. "I was tired, and the lines began to blur in this very unsettling way" (Sellars, 2008).

The tension between the public and the private within a mediated political space is the central theme of the books; "the media" itself is a central character in the trilogy. Collins's specific contribution is the portrayal of the media as a control mechanism that can be employed by both those in power and those who seek to overthrow it. Prior dystopias—think *1984* (1949) or *A Clockwork Orange* (1971)—have framed the media exclusively as a tool for domination. However, in *The Hunger Games*, the human characters are so media savvy that they understand what will be mediated by the dominant culture and how to manipulate media content to their advantage.

In *The Hunger Games*, constructing an identity inside and outside the media spotlight is part of the accepted work of adolescence and of governing. This is precisely the central point of contemporary research on the impact of social media on young people (Gündüz, 2017; Eichhorn, 2019). *The Hunger Games* takes seriously the notion that truth—or at least the dominant meme—will be defined by those who capture both the image and the popular narrative. That image by necessity includes both public and private behaviors; it is a sort of forced authenticity that makes media content believable while it strips control and context from those who become the focus of the Games and by extension the autocratic political state. It is the mediated narrative that leads to public political power in Panem; how that public narrative is privately internalized provides the fuel to resist the contemporary regime.

KATNISS EVERDEEN: GIRL MEETS MEDIA

The Hunger Games plays out in large part through the interior monologue of Katniss Everdeen, a 15-year-old scarred by a pernicious political environment that is made more corrosive by personal tragedy and loss. Katniss's emerging identity mirrors the dialectic between individual and collective expression.

When the story begins, Katniss is just coming to know who she is and to have some sense of self in relation to others. She sees herself as fiercely independent, largely without friends, most certainly without parental nurture. Katniss's psychological pain over her father's death and her mother's resulting depression is real but enormously private: it visits Katniss only in frequent nightmares. She lives to protect her little sister, Primrose, and her hunting partner, Gale, from the omnipresent state that—through the televised reality of the annual Hunger Games and the application of brute force in the individual districts that are never allowed to connect—dominates and even scripts the front-stage lives (and many of the private thoughts) of Panem's citizens. This is Collins's recasting of the media as a control mechanism.

Throughout the trilogy, Katniss, like a real-life celebrity, encounters herself through the prism of media and is struck by the contrast between her inner life and her public image. In *Mockingjay* (2010), Katniss captures her "propo" or rebel propaganda image on a spare monitor during the filming and describes herself in third person: "Her body seems larger in stature, more imposing than mine. Her face smudged but sexy. . . . I don't know who this person is" (Collins, 2010, p. 70). Contrast the interior monologue above (from the third book in the series) to Katniss's use of media the first time she enters the arena:

"Move," I whisper to myself. I wriggle out of my sleeping bag. . . . I've been concealed by darkness and the sleeping bag and the willow branches, it has probably been difficult for the cameras to get a good shot of me. I know they must be tracking me now though. The minute I hit the ground, I'm guaranteed a close-up. The audience will have been beside themselves, knowing I was in the tree, that I overheard the Careers talking, that I discovered Peeta was with them. Until I work out exactly how I want to play that, I'd better at least act on top of things. Not perplexed. Certainly not confused or frightened. No, I need to look one step ahead of the game. So, as I slide out of the foliage and into the dawn light, I pause a second, giving the cameras time to lock on me. Then I cock my head slightly to the side and give a knowing smile. There! Let them figure out what that means. (Collins, 2008, p. 163–164)

Katniss, like all Panem citizens, has not just watched the previous Hunger Games, she has internalized previous tributes' strategies and tactics, a kind of intellectual alchemy that masks the horror of what the tributes do. The arena is a performance, a mediated cultural artifact of Panem through which collective cultural meaning and political control are prescribed.

If the fictional Katniss Everdeen had an intellectual grandparent, it would be Princess Ann, played by Audrey Hepburn in the 1953 film *Roman Holiday*. Princess Ann, who is so overwhelmed by her constricted royal life that she suffers a series of anxiety attacks, flees from her "handlers" only to be discovered asleep on a park bench by American journalist Joe Bradley, played by Gregory Peck. Ann is asleep because she's been given a sedative by her royal physician; Joe, uncertain of what else to do, takes her to his apartment to sleep off the effects of the drug. The next day, Ann borrows money from Joe so she can alter her appearance to look more like a commoner (and hence escape both the police and the news media now searching for her); Joe meanwhile realizes that the now publicly missing princess has become his companion for the day and arranges with a photojournalist friend to take pictures of her on "holiday." However, as Joe and Ann begin to fall in love, Joe lies to his editor about whether he knows Ann's whereabouts— despite the inducement of a $5,000 payment for the story. At the end of the day, the princess returns to her royal life and, at a press conference the next day, is surprised to see Joe and his photographer friend. They assure the princess that her secrets—and her photographs—are safe with them. The film ends with the protagonists thinking about "what might have been." Hepburn won an Oscar for her performance in this film, which, in a bit of political irony, also received the Oscar for the best screenplay, written surreptitiously by Dalton Trumbo, who had been blacklisted in the early 1950s American "Red Scare."

Figure 4.2.   Joe Bradley, Irving Radovich, and Princess Ann (left to right) from *Roman Holiday*. 1953, Paramount Pictures

The shifts in the thinking about privacy in the 60 years that separate *Roman Holiday* from *The Hunger Games* are striking, as is their common assertion that no one—even a princess—should be without it. This theme, that even royalty are due privacy despite media pursuit, is the focus of the 2006 film *The Queen*. That film takes the royals' point of view, fictionalizing the British royal family's attempt to deal with the political consequences of the tension between a need for privacy and public political response to Princess Diana's death. In *The Queen*, it is a monarchy that changes. Those changes, though, are forced by both the media and the political environment, and they cause clear distress. In *Roman Holiday*, Princess Ann must passively wait for the media to decide what to do with her private information. The journalists focus on what to *leave out* of the public discourse; for Queen Elizabeth, the issue becomes changing the media narrative, something that is accomplished only through the revelation of previously private emotions.

The central characters in *The Hunger Games* understand that capturing the media—more specifically the stories and memes that become mediated—is a multi-purpose tool. They focus on what to *leave in*. Initially, Katniss uses the media to help her survive the arena. However, the leaders of the rebellion—unknown to Katniss in the first of the books—are also ready to wield the media to seize power. The appropriation of media becomes a conscious rebel strategy. The rebellion elaborately appropriates media toward its own ends, through the rebel "propos," or propaganda broadcasts that echo war propaganda campaigns.

The rebels are equally intentional about what to omit. The roots of the revolution must not be televised. District 13 escapes the media glare, achieving a kind of peace in return for a sort of media death. The District literally takes its culture underground. This lukewarm tradeoff, for Collins, isn't presented as any sort of achievement. Instead, the sterile, off-camera existence of District 13 is almost a sort of death, a clinical-white, technology-centered culture reminiscent of Aldous Huxley's *Brave New World* (1932) with its sanitized, medicated conformity that comes off as impotent in contrast with the Capitol's technicolor world. District 13 seems to come back to life when it's back on air, participating in the rebel cause.

In the trilogy, Collins depicts a numb resignation, even a complicity, to the media and the entertainment of the Games. The spectacle—the broadcast—is itself rarely the target of public antipathy. Rather the public comes together around the spectacle, even though its immorality is abhorred and even though the viewing public's silent consent clearly empowers the Capitol. While this public hunger for the spectacle of violence-turned-entertainment is decried by Katniss from the trilogy's opening chapter, the only hope the characters have is to survive, perhaps even thwart, the Games. In *Roman Holiday*, the media—or at least two individual journalists—decide to keep Ann's "holiday" private. This is not possible in Panem. Hence, the audience in *Roman Holiday* is not complicit in the potential invasion of Ann's privacy. *The Queen* provides no clear indictment of the audience role, although there is pointed criticism of the media actions. But in *The Hunger Games*, there seems no alternative but to live with the spectacle. The public submits to the "show."

THINKING ABOUT PRIVACY:
VOCABULARY AND SCHOLARLY INSIGHTS

Just as the concept of autonomy and control permeate the plot of *The Hunger Games* trilogy, they also fund contemporary notions of privacy and moral development. Philosophy articulates that having privacy allows individuals to achieve, primarily through human dignity and human autonomy. Individuals need privacy in order to flourish—to become psychologically whole human beings who can interact in a community with the result that both the individual and the community prosper. In philosophy, privacy is deeply bound up with the concept of personhood (Fischer, 1980). The need for privacy, the compelling philosophical claim, is foreshadowed as early as Western medieval law. "Only citizens who respect one another's privacy are themselves dignified with divine respect" (Rosen, 2000, p. 19).

Privacy is not the same thing as secrecy—although we often confuse the two. Your doctor knows about your health; for example, your doctor knows whether you have had the measles or have been vaccinated against them. That information is private, and you expect your physician to keep it so. Your doctor isn't going to tell anyone else about your measles immunity and how it was acquired. On the other hand, let's say that—for whatever reason—you have not been vaccinated against the measles and you didn't have it as a kid. You decide not to reveal this information to anyone. In this instance, you have decided to keep this information secret. After all, it's your health information and no one can force you to divulge it. However, in this instance, secrecy about your immunity to the disease could harm the entire community while keeping the same information private could actually help it. In the modern era, we all live with "herd immunity"—if not enough people in the herd are immune, epidemics break out. If enough people in the herd are immunized, then the community, including the weakest among it (for example, infants or cancer patients whose immune systems are being deliberately compromised during chemotherapy), are protected. Communitarian philosophy posits that communities need to share an understanding of privacy, in some ways a rough parallel to the concept of herd immunity, in order to flourish. "A credible ethics of privacy needs to be rooted in the common good rather than individual rights" (Christians, 2010).

Retaining individual control over information about the self has been a constant in defining the term. Invasion of privacy occurs when the circles of intimacy are penetrated by the larger community (Westin, 1967) in ways that strip the individual of control over access to information about the self by others, the context in which that information should be interpreted, or both. Central to this notion of control and access is power: society needs privacy as a shield against the power of the state (Neville, 1980). Throughout history, totalitarian regimes have used extensive government surveillance—the near absence of privacy—as a major component of any attempt to create a uniformly subservient citizenry.

While there are many instances of mediated state surveillance in *The Hunger Games* novels, one of the most potent is realized for the films: the Games' arena command post. The command post is reminiscent of drawings of Jeremy Bentham's "panopticon," a thought experiment Bentham created to rehabilitate criminals by having them live in an environment where they would be continuously observed (Wezner, 2012). In the films, the arena "panopticon" is media saturated; virtual reality births actual weapons aimed at specific contestants. Contemporary empirical work (see Larson, 1995) supports what Collins details as the central, potent mechanism of government control in Panem: constant observation strips humanity of almost everything but a desire to survive.

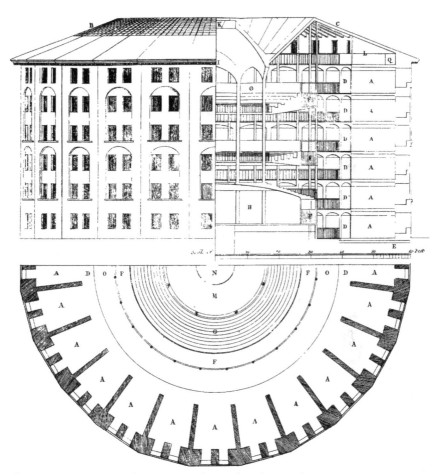

Figure 4.3.   Jeremy Bentham's "panopticon" thought experiment.

What the state in *The Hunger Games* is trying to forestall is the development of autonomy; in *Roman Holiday*, some autonomy is required so that the function of government—in this case a monarchy—can continue. "Communitarians see the myth of the self-contained 'man' in a state of nature as politically misleading and dangerous. Persons are embedded in language, history, and culture, which are social creations; there can be no such thing as a person without society" (Radin, 1982). Narratives are what a culture and history build—the social context. Thus, the thirst for control over the narrative of Panem is also a battle for individual autonomy and the ability to define the self as, among other things, a political actor.

Responsibility for keeping things private is shared; individuals have to learn when to withhold information, and the community has to learn when to avert its eyes completely or to narrow its gaze:

> Jewish law, for example, has developed a remarkable body of doctrine around the concept of *hezzek re'iyyah,* which means "the injury caused by seeing" or "the injury caused by being seen." This doctrine expands the right of privacy to protect individuals not only from physical intrusions into the home but also from surveillance by a neighbor who is outside the home, peering through a window in a common courtyard. . . . From its earliest days, Jewish law has recognized that it is the uncertainty about whether or not we are being observed that forces us to lead more constricted lives and inhibits us from speaking and acting freely in public. (Rosen, 2000, p. 18–19)

In the fictional world of Panem, the injury caused by seeing is deliberate, interactively mediated with an audience, and one of several tools of political control. In Panem, citizens in the outlying districts are required to watch the Games; they have no autonomy even though many would prefer to avert their eyes. Forcing one to injure another—as is the case of the required viewing for the citizens of Panem—injures both those who are seen and those who are doing the seeing. It is a calculated assault on individual human dignity enforced by the state. However, the required viewing undermines the development of authentic community in Panem, a fragility that President Snow alludes to throughout the trilogy and one that leads to the dissolution of the political confederation once autonomy (through the person of Katniss) and authentic communication take hold.

Historically, American understandings of privacy have been governed by a legal understanding of the term first articulated by Samuel Warren and Louis Brandeis (1890/1984). However, with the digitization of so much information, philosophers have begun to suggest privacy standards rooted in philosophic as opposed to legal theory are more appropriate (Nissenbaum, 2010, p. 78–84). When the issue is information, invasion of privacy philosophically can be encapsulated in the following harms:

- identity theft, which most of us understand as stealing specific sorts of information—your social security number or your various access codes—to be used by another human being for their own purposes without your permission. In Panem, identity theft has a less technological edge. The tributes are required to participate in television interviews, smiling, funny, innocent, all on the eve of the annual slaughter—a sort of identity perversion. No one believes that these interviews are anything other than performance; the tributes authentic identities have been appropriated by the state.

- information inequality, such as governments and corporations amassing large amounts of data about individuals. In *Mockingjay*, President Snow tells Katniss, "I can find you. I can reach you. Perhaps I am watching you now" (Collins, 2010, p. 15).
- encroachment on moral autonomy, "the capacity to shape our own moral biographies, to reflect on our moral careers, to evaluate and identify with our own moral choices, without the critical gaze and interference of others" (Hoven, 2004, p. 439). The shaping of Katniss's moral biography is her response to the information inequality imposed by the state. However, there is also a tool of collaboration at work: television and the world of the visual image.

Tools of collaboration are not limited to political purposes. In this century, it is difficult to escape the realization that tools have an economic goal. Elderly and seemingly out-of-touch former U.S. Senator Orrin Hatch, in 2017, asked Facebook founder and CEO Mark Zuckerberg how Facebook made its money. Zuckerberg replied, "I sell advertising." A more fulsome reply would have included that Zuckerberg sells information about individuals with seeming user acquiescence on a platform that has been plagued with privacy scandals since its inception. The problem, as noted above, is that algorithms are not the equivalent of autonomous human beings, that people do not have the sole purpose of buying "stuff," and that the "market" is not a community. Users who are sold to corporations and political candidates via Facebook are not so distinct from the passive citizens of Panem, so enraptured by the Games that they ignore their moral core. An important distinction between the fiction of Panem and the facts of Facebook is that, in the fictional world, the technology and the narrative are repurposed in favor of political authenticity. In our current world of Facebook, we have not yet come up with a remedy for those who would use the platform as a mechanism to broadcast the slaughter of worshipping Muslims in Christchurch, New Zealand, or the willingness to avert our eyes or to demand a tool that is less susceptible to lies and mayhem (Zuboff, 2019).

CELEBRITY—OR IDENTITY—AS PUBLIC POLITICAL DOMAIN

Panem, of course, is amusing itself to its political death (Postman, 1985). While Neil Postman anchors the fault for such political nihilism in the televised image that numbs the audience, others have lodged the responsibility in mediated political spectacle (Edelman, 1988) in which political acts are reduced to mere "circus" attendance that enforces and narrows the interaction between homogenous media content and the image-fixated audience (Herman & Chomsky, 2002). It is only in her non-public thoughts that Katniss questions the underpinnings of the dominant political narrative. She is not alone, but the initial passivity of Panem's citizens is palpable in the world where moral, personal, and political/military lines are blurring.

While Collins would probably accept the foregoing analysis, she also draws from contemporary culture's fascination with celebrity and the construction of an exclusively public identity by individuals as part of the oppression. For Collins, it is not just the entertainment but internalized and unexamined mediated narrative that produces the political result.

Discussion Question

In the film *Back to the Future*, Doc Brown exclaims to Marty that in order to be a president you have to be good on television. Update Brown's insights to the latest national and local elections, expanding beyond television to include Twitter and other social media platforms.

Katniss doesn't seek political power or attention; rather it's earned through heroic actions and reactions to the awful events controlling Panem's districts. This passive reluctance is important. The symbol of the rebellion must be a quiet, helpful Ariadne, accepting her role in slaying the Minotaur and only reluctantly taking on the role of Theseus as well. "What they want is for me to truly take on the role they designed for me: the symbol of the revolution. . . . They have a whole team of people to make me over, dress me" (Collins, 2010, p. 10).

As important as heroic action becomes to Katniss's identity, achieving moral autonomy is a struggle in the first two books/films. In *Mockingjay*, after the District 2 skirmish where Gale and Katniss disagree about the morality of killing the flushed-out mountain workers in an act reminiscent of the mine collapse that killed their fathers, the actions as rebel fighters reinforce their own victimization. Katniss is again reduced to passive spectating of a horror show. Gale reports to Katniss "the whole country just sat back and watched." "Well, that's what they do best," replies Katniss. It is this same choice—to watch or to act—that confronts Katniss at the end of the novels and films. At the end, the reader/viewer knows Katniss's private thoughts only through her public and political acts.

In *Mockingjay*, Katniss provides a list of the ways she has been passively used, first by the Gamesmakers, then President Snow, now the rebels and Coin, each of whom discover that she has her own active will that makes it "even harder to groom a Mockingjay than to catch one" (Collins, 2010, p. 59). The dialectic between heroic fighter and passive symbol allows others to project their hopes onto the character of Katniss, the essence of political symbolism. Although it is not a central point of the books, it is worth noting that the focus of this makeover effort is a young woman, just as it is in *Roman Holiday*, and that the makeover would be impossible without the initial invasion of the circles of intimacy that Princess Ann and Katniss create as they work through what they want others to know about their "public" selves.

Not only is Katniss's "Mockingjay" constructed on the public stage, her evolving personal relationships also play out in the media glare, courtesy of the "Flickermans" of the world. Peeta, in a television interview with Flickerman, says, "Everything in the arena becomes your final reality," "everyone important to you" fades into the distance, and killing people destroys "everything you are." "Everything you are," parrots Flickerman (Collins, 2010, p. 22). Peeta has been aware of this horrible outcome since the first novel: it is he who wants to die in the arena as himself. Peeta understands the dehumanizing impact of state-forced media exhibitionism (Nissenbaum, 2010, p. 106).

Dehumanization is at the heart of the 2014 film *Nightcrawler*. Louis Bloom is a petty criminal who becomes a citizen journalist when he discovers that he can videotape violent events and sell the footage to a local news station. The resulting footage, which often centers on the most private matter in humanity—the dying moments of car crash, carjacking, and other accident victims—shows the balance between compelling television, consumer demand, and unethical journalism. Bloom tampers with criminal evidence, even moving a body at one point, in order to get better footage. The movie culminates in a home invasion; Bloom arrives on the scene before the police, capturing footage of the gunmen leaving the house and then entering the home to record footage of the dead inside. Journalists in the television newsroom debate the ethics, but the producer wants to air the footage immediately because it will garner great ratings. After the footage airs, Bloom hands over an edited version to the police that does not include the gunmen leaving the house. Instead, Bloom tracks down the gunmen, calls the police, and gets another exclusive when the arrest turns violent.

The point that both Collins and the filmmakers are making is clear: in a society where media messages are reduced to mindless entertainment, the future is subordinate to the interests of the broadcast and its entertainment function.

All the personal dramas, and those of humanity, are really best consumed in neatly produced episodes between segments. Reality doesn't exist off camera; in Panem, privacy truly is dead. The only political truth worth knowing is the mediated version. Most of us in this century would add that the neatly produced episodes would be separated by commercial messages.

PUBLIC AND PRIVATE COLLIDE IN POLITICAL ACTION

Of course, Collins also is telling a love story, and the connection between Katniss's private, emotional inner world and her public-yet-private face is Peeta who, unnoticed, has loved her since first grade. Katniss sees little connection between her private world and the role she must play in the Games, but Peeta's public acts connect to a private emotion. He loves Katniss enough to ask Haymitch, their alcoholic mentor, to do everything he can to make sure that Katniss wins the Games, a suicidal strategy that must be played out on television. Katniss accepts the love affair for the cameras but privately remains conflicted over her feelings for Gale, whose political worldview is never in doubt. It is Haymitch, who is as insightful as he is drunk, who tells Katniss that she has no choice but to marry Peeta: a triumph of the public over the personal. After all, they've been in love on television; the mediated narrative demands it, and the state is counting on it.

Yet this public revelation of private facts is strategic and consciously framed for mediated consumption by Katniss and the Rebel propaganda team. Peeta, too, makes what was private public—as when he confesses on camera that the girl he's had a crush on since childhood came with him to the Games. He later inverts public and private in the televised arena when he uses his declared love of Katniss to fool other tributes into thinking he has turned against her in order to lead them away from the place Peeta knows Katniss is hiding. In this mediated environment, privacy is entirely instrumental, but it is an instrument of the rebellion as well as of the controlling state. In philosophical terms, this negotiation between public and private illustrates that privacy is not an a priori right—rather, the need for privacy can be overwhelmed by the needs of the community or, in Peeta's case, the need of a single individual. However, the needs of the community and the individuals within it are not always benign.

In the third book, as both protagonist and pawn, Katniss decides to kill Panem's new would-be ruler for much the same reason that she refused to conform in the arena initially. However, in the third book, Katniss commits a self-aware political act: she kills the new political boss, Coin, who was only too willing to reinstate the arena for her own political purposes. That act represents the fusion of public politics with a private understanding of them and the resulting willingness to act on that understanding in a way that risks individual safety for the common good—what Katniss, Peeta, and Gale had always believed was the original goal of the rebellion. Public and private morph into a single self-aware political moment. It is a demonstration about how privacy must first consider community in order for an individual to make an autonomous choice among multiple options.

CATCHING FIRE: PRIVACY WITHIN COMMUNITY

It begins on screen. "So instead of crumpling to the ground and weeping, I find myself standing up straighter and with more confidence than I have had in weeks. My smile, while somewhat insane, is not forced. And when President Snow silences the audience and says, 'What do you think about us throwing them a wedding right here in the Capitol?' I pull off girl-almost-catatonic-with-joy without a hitch" (Collins, 2009, p. 76–77).

For the first time, Katniss consciously chooses to defy Panem's rulers by broadcasting a public self separable from the "private" girl. What Katniss has discovered is a sense of agency, a belief that she has the power to act rather than simply react. Not only does she go to war, she learns that she can prosecute its outcome. But this awareness is progressive. For Katniss, agency is "bounded," not just by the traditional strategy and tactics of political ferment but by how those mediated tactics will be understood by various audiences.

Discussion Question

How complicit are *Hunger Games* audiences—and communities—in the invasion and maintenance of privacy? What are possible remedies when "things go too far"?

Katniss discovers two distinctive privacy constraints as she unwillingly prepares for the Quarter Quell. The first boundaries are personal: Katniss thinks she has a private bargain—save Peeta—that both Peeta and the other contestants circumvent for the larger cause. Personal agency doesn't mean much outside of community. "I've spent all these weeks getting to know who my competitors are, without even thinking about who my teammates are. Now a new kind of confidence is lighting up inside of me, because I think I finally know who Haymitch is. And, I am beginning to know who I am" (Collins, 2009, p. 203). Katniss, however, is only haltingly aware of her capacity for choice.

The second boundary about privacy that Katniss must understand is that even personal agency within the larger culture must take others into account. "My private agenda dovetails completely with my public one," Katniss says. "And, if I really could save Peeta . . . in terms of a revolution, this would be ideal. Because I will be more valuable dead. They can turn me into some kind of a martyr and paint my face on banners, and it will do more to rally people than anything I could do if I were living. But Peeta would be more valuable alive, and tragic, because he will be able to turn his pain into words that will transform people" (Collins, 2009, p. 283).

In *Mockingjay*, it's a grown-up world. Symbol and metaphor merge into reality—the public and the private fuse. The Games, always a symbol for the arena of war, are swapped for an actual arena of war. Reality in the world of Panem takes over the fantasy of violence. At the same time, the lines demarcating Katniss's image of Mockingjay and her real, inner self-identity merge. Passive objectification is transformed into agency; image is shed and replaced by a final, clarifying act.

In *The Hunger Games*, Katniss's political development is made possible predominantly by her ability to first separate self from public symbol, from community—and then to forge connections among the three that work for all involved, although it always feels preliminary to her. In the last lines of the books and the film, the readers/viewers share Katniss's private thoughts: "I'll tell them how I survive it. I'll tell them that on bad mornings, it feels impossible to take pleasure in anything because I'm afraid it could be taken away. That's when I make lists in my head of every act of goodness I've seen someone do. It's like a game. Repetitive. Even a little tedious after more than twenty years" (Collins, 2010, p. 398).

Political philosopher James C. Davies (1963) theorized that full-blown political action, and particularly leadership, required the development and understanding first of community and only then an understanding and actualizing of the self. Collins's work provides an important contemporary vantage point: how does development happen in a heavily mediated environment—not merely from the point of view of the state but from the point of view of the individual? In Davies's terms, self-actualization constitutes what for Collins and her characters is the creation and maintenance of an authentic narrative of what it means to be a member of a political community in both public and private. And, unlike its predecessors, in Collins's world, the media has much to do with acquisition and maintenance of institutional and personal power—a significant contribution to the understanding of dystopia as well as a critique of current political culture. In every instance, shifting definitions of privacy fuel the plot while providing the basis for the central themes of the books and the films. While the transformation is fantasy, it also lifts a veil to show the effort behind the seemingly effortless phenomena of what audiences see on screen and on the web. A media-rich environment provides as many opportunities for self-delusion as it does for political control—a notion that past dystopias have only incompletely realized. It is only in the final pages of *Mockingjay* that Katniss seems to acknowledge that the characteristics of quality life are achieved at once and inseparably: privacy, personal liberty, and freedom.

5

Journalism and Public Relations as Public Service

Central Concepts

- How public service is linked to professionalism
- The normative roles for the media
- The theory of virtue ethics
- The distinction among free, responsible, and courageous speech
- How professionals fulfill multiple normative roles simultaneously

> The pitch was about helping other people. This was always the truest, best reason to talk to a journalist, and one of the only potent answers to "I don't want the attention" or "I don't need the stress." (Kantor & Twohey, 2019, p. 26)

Public service means many different things in many different contexts. However, in almost all of them, it reflects this dictionary definition: "something that is done or provided for the public because it is needed, and not in order to make a profit." This dictionary definition also reflects the contemporary stresses in the concept. Does doing something because it is needed mean there should never be profit? Can doing something have multiple motivations? In order to become a doctor, medical students need to run an academic gauntlet that, at the end, will allow most of them to save lives *and* become wealthy. And just who is "the public"? A single entity? A subgroup—say the people who live in my neighborhood or who friend me on Facebook? Citizens of a nation-state? In some contexts, the phrase "public service" is used to cover such a vast array of activities by individuals, organizations, and professions that it's lost the advantage of a narrower meaning. So, before thinking about how popular culture has visualized and storified the term, perhaps a little definitional work is necessary.

In order to think about the ethics of public service, the term itself needs to be defined and connected with ethical concepts. The chapter then explores the institutional goals of public service, including a review of the extensive literature on the normative theories of the press. As noted in the definition of public service, not only institutions but also individuals have duties connected to public service, and that individual focus introduces readers to the concept of virtue ethics—first outlined more than 3,000 years ago. Finally, the chapter uses the film *Contagion* (2011) to explore how individuals and institutions can fulfill multiple—and sometimes conflicting—roles in an effort to serve the public.

The first known use of the phrase "public service" dates to 1576, where it was linked to health care and garbage collection. Add 300 years, and the notion of public service was linked to the aims and qualities of professionals and to the concept of profession itself. Indeed, the three ancient professions—the clergy, law, and medicine—historically have incorporated the concept of public service into the definition of what it meant to do a particular kind of work. Thus, Denver Broncos quarterback Drew Lock is a highly paid professional (he possesses the skills and knowledge to play in the National Football League), but football is not itself considered a profession. Instead, the concept of profession has been defined—for at least the past 200 years—as a group that possesses special knowledge and skills in a widely recognized body of learning derived from research, education, and high-level training and is recognized by the public as such (Craft, 2017). Many professions require licensure: lawyers have to pass a bar exam, doctors their medical boards, engineers a variety of knowledge-specific tests. Licensure is the most common form of public recognition that an individual is a professional. Failing to pass such exams can make a great difference in the lives of individuals. Mao Zedong, for example, failed to pass his required exams for entrance into the Mandarin class (ancient China's version of the contemporary civil service), one of the many things that scholars believe helped motivate him to lead the Communist revolution in China (Snow, 1937). Becoming a professional in the 21st century generally means employment stability, a living wage, higher social and class status, and the possession and mastery of a specific body of knowledge. Most professions also have codes of ethics, and whether you are an attorney, a physician, or an architect, those ethics codes almost always refer to the concept that professionals exist to serve the public among other constituencies.

Public-sector values, regardless of specific profession, are generally agreed to include: responsiveness, integrity, impartiality, accountability, respect, leadership, and human rights (Molina & McKeown, 2012). Such values are most often associated with individuals and include the idea that professionals have a wide range of possible choices to make when exercising their professional roles. Some values (e.g., integrity and responsiveness) may be considered individual virtues. Other values (e.g., leadership) most often reflect a series of actions over time. Others (e.g., accountability) suggest that individual acts have a larger, social role—one that implies not just action but evaluation of its appropriateness and consequences. Still others (e.g., human rights) link professionalism to a philosophically informed definition of what it means to be human; without human rights, the species in community cannot flourish. Sorting between and among values requires ethical thinking.

THE PUBLIC SERVICE ROLE OF JOURNALISM

Civic engagement and democracy have been linked historically through journalism. This link is far from modern. During the Enlightenment, the philosophical concept of objectivity began to form when the British House of Lords allowed journalists—who then functioned more as stenographers than reporters—to be present and then write about its deliberations (Ward, 2004). The founders of the American republic believed that citizens must be informed and then participate in politics; doing so required that the citizen receive information from the "media" of the day. However, in 1776, the "media" was highly partisan, privately owned, and sometimes written by those who chose to remain anonymous, including, among others, Benjamin Franklin. Alexis de Tocqueville (1835/1985) in his analysis of the American experiment in 1835 noted that newspapers of that day were essential to citizens' ability to learn about community concerns. Indeed, de Tocqueville saw newspapers as a necessary antidote to Americans' tendency to focus on the self before community.

About 70 years later, John Dewey (1954) suggested that politics, particularly a politics that centered on solving community-wide problems, met at the intersection of elites, citizens, and experts through the mass media. In 1890, Dewey wanted to spread his ideas beyond the classroom and began to work with eccentric journalist Franklin Ford. Ford had quit his New York newspaper job to found a national "sociological newspaper" that would focus on the reporting of social trends, replacing the sort of scattershot, event-oriented journalism common in his (and frankly, our) time. Dewey signed on in the belief that such a publication would promote social justice and that the beginnings of such a movement "rested on the ability of individuals to become conscious of their 'function' in an interdependent community. Consciousness is social in so far as any individual consciously directs his own activities in view of the social relations involved" (Dewey, in Westbrook, 1991, p. 53).

Thus, the notion that in order for a people to be self-governing, journalism—whether it is the licensed press of Enlightenment Britain, the partisan press of the founding of the United States, or the emerging mass and sensational press of the early 20th century—is essential to democratic functioning. Writing at about the same time as Dewey, Walter Williams, the first dean of the first U.S. school of journalism, opened his Journalist's Creed with the statement: "I believe that the public journal is a public trust, that all connected with it are, to the full measure of their responsibility, trustees for the public; that acceptance of a lesser service than the public service is a betrayal of this trust" (Ibold & Wilkins, 2008). More than 100 years later, research that asks journalists what motivates their work has repeatedly found that individual journalists believe they are in a profession—much like medicine or teaching—that focuses first on public service. The preface to National Public Radio's ethics code notes that journalism is a public service. Similarly, the ethics code for public information officers (PIOs) asserts that all PIO activities must be conducted in the public interest.

THE NORMATIVE ROLES OF JOURNALISM

These broad statements are consistent across more than 400 years and have survived massive changes in technology and the sorts of jobs that journalists and their first cousins, public information officers, perform. Just how they perform those roles also has been the focus of scholarship (see Christians, Glasser, McQuail, Nordenstreng, & White, 2009), as well as scripts for both the small and large screen.

The first journalist most Baby Boomers encountered was the mild-mannered reporter Clark Kent, literally Superman. In the televised *Adventures of Superman* (1952–1958), Kent, in his role as a journalist working for the *Daily Planet*, monitored the activities in his city and intervened to right wrongs. The journalist here was literally a superhero, and he fought for "truth, justice and the American way," a slogan that in the 1950s contained not a hint of irony and might certainly have pleased Dewey with its emphasis on justice in pursuit of a better, happier community. *Superman* the television show, which was based on the 1930s comic-book character, also was noteworthy because a woman, Lois Lane, also functioned as a journalist—not a secretary—at the paper. Lois Lane, the television screen character, certainly was in the vanguard of women in a profession that, at the time, was dominated by men. Decades later, Jane Fonda, who played a television journalist in the film *The*

China Syndrome (1979), dyed her hair red—like Lois Lane's—in homage to that first onscreen woman journalist. In his journalistic guise, Superman remains an example of the monitorial role—bringing injustice to the attention of those who have the capacity to do something about it.

Discussion Question

Look at your local newspaper, listen to news on your local radio station, or watch a local television newscast. (Of course, you can do all of this online.) Which normative role(s) do you think your local news outlet is playing? How do those role performances compare to those of Clark Kent and Lois Lane in *Superman*, C. J. Cregg in *The West Wing*, and Woodward and Bernstein in *All the President's Men*?

Because democracies are linked so closely to journalism, they require that citizens learn about various activities so that they can discuss, participate, and respond to them. Scholars have labeled this the facilitative role of the media. In this century, facilitation is also the role of public relations, specifically public information officers. On the small screen, perhaps the best example is White House Press Secretary C. J. Cregg, who for most of the seven seasons of the show *The West Wing* (1999–2006) acted as an information conduit between the executive branch of the government and the White House press corps. Cregg's ultimate goal was to provide news, admittedly from the administration's point of view, to journalists so the information could be shared with the wider public. In multiple episodes, Cregg defends the role of journalism—and of specific journalists—when their jobs can, and sometimes do, include publishing or broadcasting unflattering news stories. This is the symbiotic relationship between public information officials and journalists; one element of the relationship could not exist or function effectively without the other. Facilitation is both an accurate and deep expression of this relationship. When the public information officer is in the White House, the facilitative role takes on marked political overtones, but today, local and state governments, agencies within those governing bodies, health care providers, and many nonprofits employ public information officers to work with journalists to facilitate an enormous number of various activities, all of which require public awareness and often specific actions. In these contexts, and in most instances, the facilitative role is noncontroversial, is reciprocal, and adheres to the same standards of truth, impartiality, and accountability that characterize journalism as a profession. Indeed, in the last decade, while the number of journalists has declined, the number of public relations professionals has significantly increased; currently there are about four to five "public relations professionals" to every single person who works as a journalist.

Normative theory also has outlined a collaborative role of the media, which implies a partnership between the media of the day and powerful political and economic institutions. In the 21st century, the term *collaboration* has an authoritarian edge; people as well as institutions can collaborate to keep dictators as well as duly elected rulers in power. Sometimes it is difficult to know the difference because whether power is used for public as opposed to private ends is difficult to determine. This darker version of collaboration is a subplot of the television series *House of Cards* (2013–2018), where journalists are easily and sometimes willingly manipulated by Senator Frank Underwood in his unceasing and entirely sleazy drive for political power. Unwitting collaboration is the focus; the public interest is replaced by the interest of individuals in the short term. The documentary film *Control Room* (2004) provides viewers with a vision of collaboration between journalists and public relations professionals representing nation-states, in the context of the fog of war. In *Control Room* culture is a major element in determining what the story is and how facts will be interpreted. The filmmakers leave viewers with an important question: is some form of political collaboration between the media and government inevitable, particularly in times of crisis? The collaborative role of journalism is also a continuing subtext for the HBO series *The Newsroom* (2012–2014). Collaboration in this series is also dependent on media ownership and industry economics; the series foregrounds that it is not merely political power that can demand professional acquiescence.

Discussion Question

The examples of normative roles provided here all involve the news. Examine the music you and your friends enjoy. Which of the normative roles does this form of entertainment fulfill? How would you respond to the same question regarding the films *Bohemian Rhapsody* or *Rocketman*? How about films such as *Yesterday*?

The final normative role that scholars have outlined is that of the radical media. This role assumes that most existing media outlets are part of an elite power structure that minimally needs to be contested and maximally should be overthrown. The radical media serve as an oppositional voice to much media content. In many ways, one role of the radical media—the realignment of political and economic power—is served by investigative reporting. That activity has been the subject of multiple films that have focused on investigative reporting as a process of unearthing the truth. Probably the best known of those is *All the President's Men* (1976), based on the book by Watergate reporters Bob Woodward and Carl Bernstein, who are both still profession-ally active today and at that time were working for the *Washington Post*. *All the President's Men* (which took its inspiration from Robert Penn Warren's Pulitzer Prize–winning novel *All the King's Men*) essentially recounts the steps "Woodstein" and their editors took to uncover then President Nixon's attempt to steal documents from the Democratic Party headquarters in the Watergate Hotel and subsequently to sabotage the campaigns of his Demo-cratic Party rivals in an effort to ensure his re-election in 1972. Watergate birthed a generation of journalists, many of whom entered the profession to provide a check on political power. The film itself has become iconic, in part because of the visual imagery the filmmakers employed to explore the con-nections among "the president's men" who first planned and then covered up the election skullduggery.

Figure 5.1. Carl Bernstein and Bob Woodward from *All the President's Men*. Copy-right 1976, Wildwood Enterprises

While the films came out literally decades apart, *The Post* (2017) explores how newly widowed *Washington Post* publisher Katharine Graham found her managerial footing while also emphasizing the role not just of individual journalists but of the for-profit institutions that employ and enable them. In this film, director Steven Spielberg recounts how Graham withstood significant pressure, much of it because she was a woman in the publisher's office, to allow the paper to report the Pentagon Papers in a journalistic race between what was then the upstart *Post* and the *New York Times*. The film, which lacks some of the dramatic punch of *All the President's Men*, makes a subtle point that academic research has confirmed: good journalism is more profitable than mediocre professional performance. There is also a journalism history lesson embedded in *The Post*; just as the paper was weathering the Pentagon Papers crisis, the police uncovered the Watergate break-in.

Roles are the purview of institutions and individuals, and institutions represent collections of individuals. Individual people may subscribe to one role or the other, but in real life and the real world of journalism, roles shift. Taken as a unit, the seven seasons of *The West Wing* provide multiple illustrations of how roles shift over time. Public service is not just one easily categorized act. People need different sorts of information—about different elements of their lives—in order to make the informed political and economic decisions contemporary democracies require.

Performance of a role, however, does require a balancing of obligations. Balance among competing demands requires virtue, and the field of virtue ethics—that the ethics of a specific action is intimately connected to the character of the actor—is one of the oldest insights in the field. Aristotle's *Nicomachean Ethics* (1947) outlines the four virtues that equated with ethical action for the ancient Greeks: courage, justice, and wisdom all balanced through temperance (moderation in contemporary English). For Aristotle, and the virtue ethicists who have written in the 3,000 years since, virtue is lodged in individual character. Character, in turn, is built through repeated, consistent ethical choice—the metaphor of character being like a muscle that must be exercised to remain strong is apt. For the Greeks, and particularly for Aristotle, virtue is the mean between extremes. Courage, thus, would be the mean between cowardice on the one hand and foolhardiness on the other. Less obviously, courage for one individual might not be the same act as courage for another, even in similar circumstances. Thus, virtuous action is not one single approach in all circumstances. Rather, as the Greeks conceptualized it, virtuous acts represented a range of choices. One of the most useful insights from the field of virtue ethics is that, while it is not always possible to agree on the single, virtuous act, it is usually possible to agree on those acts that are unethical. Eliminating the unethical from potential options can be a terrific first step in "doing the right thing."

The normative roles outlined above each reflect a different balance of the virtues of public service, but they all do reflect that effort. *The Post*, for example, is a fictional account of the fact-based need for courage in the face of adversity; *All the President's Men* is a cinematic essay on impartiality and integrity. Superman—superhero or not—epitomizes responsiveness. Similarly, a lack of these virtues is one of the major plot points through multiple seasons of *House of Cards*.

FREE SPEECH, RESPONSIBLE SPEECH, COURAGEOUS SPEECH

In the otherwise undistinguished film *Born Yesterday* (the 1993 remake of the critically acclaimed 1950 film of the same name), the screenwriters voiced an utterly American approach to speech. Las Vegas showgirl Billie visits Washington, DC, for the first time with her unscrupulous but wealthy boyfriend Harry Brock. In Washington, she makes a series of public gaffes. Determined to "smarten her up," Brock hires journalist Paul Verrall to give Billie civics lessons, which change her life in many ways. Among the things she has to learn is the Bill of Rights, which Verrall and Billie turn into a song, as a mnemonic device. The First Amendment is reduced to "You can say any damn thing you want." For most Americans, this impulse summarizes their initial understanding of political speech—even though most would acknowledge that saying "any damn thing you want" in private life has significant interpersonal and professional risks.

Those risks are what philosophers refer to as harm. Even in this age of social media, what many people fail to realize until their decisions have produced unintended results is that most public communication is capable of causing harm to someone. Journalists know this potential for harm as part of their professional universe, and the desire to minimize harm is one reason for adopting a variety of professional norms. Entire chapters of this book, for example privacy and truth telling, focus on the harm to others that journalism and strategic communication can do.

The U.S. Supreme Court, in *Schenck v. United States* (1919), ruled that "you cannot falsely shout fire in a theater." Schenck, however, is one of the most controversial Supreme Court rulings of the past century because the court ruled that individual Americans did not have the right to protest the nation's participation in World War I. So, in the process of telling Americans that some forms of speech could be harmful, the court also made it more difficult to protest what some citizens might see as the hurtful actions of their government, a ruling that stood until 1969 and the protests over the Vietnam War.

Schenck encapsulates how Americans feel about political—and some commercial—speech. We believe we should be supportive of our form of government, yet we also believe we have the right to protest that same government. We believe speech should not deceive, hence, advertisers are legally prohibited from substituting mashed potatoes for ice cream in television commercials, but we allow—and sometimes believe—political commercials that include outrageous and defamatory claims. We believe speech that hurts people is wrong; however, we patronize websites that support conspiracy theories, and we elect people to public office who support such theories. We believe that social-media sites should take down posts and websites that are based on lies and conspiracy theories even though they have tens of thousands of followers and likes. Finally, we believe for-profit corporations can purchase political advertising for candidates and causes (see the Citizens United ruling), including of social media.

Not only do we legally, professionally, and culturally confound different categories and purposes of speech, but as citizens we appear to hold multiple and contradictory opinions about what is the same act. When it comes to speech, we do not have a two-sided debate; we have a political and cultural octopus. This complex calculus means that, in the world of ethics, free speech is more problematic than responsible speech. The difficulty is distinguishing between the two at the time the words are written, spoken, or broadcast.

The Fifth Estate, a 2016 film about the early days of WikiLeaks and its initial cooperative relationship with four journalism organizations worldwide, and the 2010 film *The Social Network*, about the beginnings of Facebook, both provide insight into the debate about if—and whether—unfettered free speech is also responsible speech.

In the case of WikiLeaks and its initial publication of more than 90,000 classified documents primarily from various U.S. government agencies, the organization was viewed as a journalistic whistleblower. The initial document dump included what has become known as the "war logs" and included video of U.S. troops attacking civilians as part of the invasion of Iraq. However, as the website expanded, and the site's creator Julian Assange espoused a more radical understanding of transparency, many of his early supporters—including journalistic organizations—withdrew from cooperating with WikiLeaks because they could not assure themselves that the revelations did not cause harm to individuals and some institutions. For some, at least as portrayed in the film, radical transparency did not always constitute responsible speech. In certain instances, the news organizations viewed what Assange was proposing as unethical.

The Social Network raised much the same question: Is it responsible to communicate among a small group of misogynists a system rating women on their physical attractiveness under the guise of providing connection? Or, does the practice become problematic only when it starts to make money? It's hard to view the film—which is really about the origins of social media—without our current understanding of the role social media plays in our political, personal, and professional lives. However, at some point, whether it's during the litigation over ownership and profit sharing or the general discussion of Facebook's early content, the audience is asked whether free speech equals responsible speech.

Finally, there is courageous speech. In *Good Night, and Good Luck* (2005), Edward R. Murrow employs the relatively new medium of television to facilitate public discussion of the abuses and demagoguery of Joseph McCarthy, a Republican senator from Wisconsin who, in the 1950s, bludgeoned civil servants and political foes alike by linking them to the Communist Party without evidence. Much of Murrow's career, which began in radio with on-the-scene reporting of World War II in Europe, was designed to facilitate public discussion of important issues. Murrow is remembered for documentaries such as *Harvest of Shame* (1960) about hunger in America in the 1960s, as well as for his professional courage in taking on McCarthy at a time when the television industry was neither the political nor the financial behemoth it is today. Murrow's journalism was a model of professional leadership and respect for the television audience and a service to those who were governed, not those who did the governing.

Murrow's "Wires and Lights in a Box" speech to the 1954 meeting of the Radio and Television News Directors Association—which is recreated in the film and available in full at rtdna.org—reads as if it could have been written today. It is about the need for courageous speech and the forces arrayed against it. Murrow closes his speech by saying,

> This instrument can teach, it can illuminate; yes, and even it can inspire. But it can do so only to the extent that humans are determined to use it to those ends. Otherwise, it's nothing but wires and lights in a box. There is a great and perhaps decisive battle to be fought against ignorance, intolerance, and indifference. This weapon of television could be useful.

Professional journalistic virtue in real life is complicated. Public service is complex. One of the best onscreen explorations of the complexities of virtue in a time of crisis is the film *Contagion* (2001), which explores the role of the media in a 21st-century public health crisis.

CONTAGION: THE COMPLEXITY OF NORMATIVE ROLES

Bat meets pig meets human indulging in recreational gambling in a Hong Kong casino: the result is a worldwide, Ebola-like pandemic. That's the premise of the 2011 film *Contagion*, produced by Steven Soderbergh and starring Jude Law (as a San Francisco–based blogger), Matt Damon (a citizen immune to the disease), Gwyneth Paltrow (patient zero), and Laurence Fishburne (public health official), among others. While *Contagion* was not a blockbuster, it continues to provoke conversations about public health, risk perception, and the normative role of the media almost a decade after it was produced. One reason for its longevity was that the filmmakers got the "science" of a pandemic right. Briefly, the science-based subplot of the film follows a chronology of how modern public health institutions would most likely respond to any potential pandemic, both in terms of identifying the pathogen, attempting to produce a vaccine for it, and distributing the vaccine worldwide. Ultimately tracing the origin of the pathogen itself—in the instance of *Contagion* what scientists refer to as a zoonotic disease, or a disease that "jumps" from animals to humans with lethal results—is the scientific backbone of the film. It is not science fiction; AIDS is believed to have zoonotic origins. A pandemic of the sort described in the film did occur in 1917–1918 when the Spanish Flu swept the globe, infecting an estimated 500 million people and influencing the outcome of major world events, including which side was victorious in World War I.

Figure 5.2. The film *Contagion* might seem eerily familiar to audiences living through the COVID-19 pandemic. Copyright 2011, Warner Bros.

But the science of a potential lethally virus is not the only thing the filmmakers got right. The film also focuses on the role of the media in its normative complexity and demonstrates how the various normative roles interact and sometimes conflict.

M-1, the name for the fictional *Contagion* virus, first strikes in private when businesswoman Beth Imhoff (Paltrow) returns from a trip to Hong Kong at the beginning of the Thanksgiving holiday with what initially appears to be a horrible cold only to die as a result of seizures and hemorrhaging less than 48 hours later. Imhoff herself is a complicated character; on her return flight home, she has a layover in Chicago where she renews a love affair that predates her marriage. Symptom free at the time, she nonetheless transmits the virus to her lover, thus spreading it in the United States before the first symptoms even appear. Her Minneapolis-based husband, Mitch (Damon), who is unaware of his wife's infidelity, is the person who ferries her to the local hospital and who ultimately finds one of their two children dead from what appears to be the same disease. Mitch, although exposed to the virus for much longer than Imhoff's lover, appears to be immune, a biological accident that ultimately results in him being placed in quarantine while medical personnel determine his prognosis. In the film, Mitch represents the average American trying to learn about the disease and to protect himself and those he loves against a disease that devastates not only the United States but also the rest of the world.

Because the cause of the illness is illusive and the symptoms both bizarre and terrifying, hospital doctors send a sample of Imhoff's blood to the Centers for Disease Control, and the race begins to identify what appears to be both a novel and lethal virus. There Dr. Cheever (Fishburne) begins not just the work of identifying the genetic makeup of the virus, which involves determining where it originated, but also of communicating what the CDC is learning to the larger public.

Discussion Question

There are obviously parallels between the fictional M-1 pandemic in *Contagion* and the very real COVID-19 pandemic. How are the media reports in *Contagion* similar and dissimilar to media reports you have seen about COVID-19? How are the actions and reactions of public information officers, such as the fictional Dr. Cheever, similar and dissimilar to those of their real-life counterparts, such as Dr. Anthony Fauci? What normative roles have journalists and public information officers fulfilled in reporting on COVID-19?

The first news reports of the illness also initiate a political response. The Chinese deny that the virus could have originated in their country. This is the beginning of a continuing news story, the monitorial role of the media, that has consequences for the real world: it postpones the ability of the CDC to thoroughly track the virus's origins, thus slowing efforts to identify and then combat it. This portion of the plot also emerges from real-world events. The 2003 SARS epidemic originated in Asia, but government officials there originally denied that the disease came from that geographic locale. While SARS was deadly, it did not kill anywhere near the number of people who die as a result of the M-1 virus in *Contagion*. This political wrinkle demonstrates that the monitorial role of the media is only as good as the information provided. In the first week after onset, the film includes Mitch watching Minneapolis television coverage of the disease that notes, "In response to the recent outbreak of a still unknown disease that has so far taken the life of a school nurse and two students," parents are asked to keep symptomatic students home from school. The broadcast notes that initial reports of the disease may be tracked to a 34-year-old Minneapolis woman. Ten days later, international media coverage of the epidemic notes that 8 million people worldwide have contracted the disease.

Here is another thing the filmmakers got right: U.S. news reports have a worldwide audience, including authorities in Hong Kong—who do not want to be publicly identified as the geographic source of the disease. That lack of willingness to be forthright about the virus's potential origins also influences communication with and among scientists trying to study the virus. These decisions, in turn, have profound consequences. Hong Kong is the most densely populated geographic area on the planet; the disease spreads from Hong Kong into China, the most populated country on earth.

In the early stages of the film, Cheever has to respond to questions about whether the CDC is being alarmist about the new virus as journalists point out that its warnings about the swine flu appear to have been greatly overblown. Cheever not only has to respond to questions of consistency but also to provide a basic scientific education to the reporters he begins to work with in the early stages of the crisis. In these scenes, journalists are performing not just the monitorial role but also two others: they are collaborating with the government agency (the CDC) to get the word out about what becomes an enormously deadly and consequential epidemic; journalists also are investigating whether the government is doing its job—in this case whether the government is sensationalizing the possible impact of the virus, something there is a track record for in the film as well as in real life. "Dr. Cheever, are you concerned that the CDC has a credibility issue?" one journalist asks. The monitorial role of the media overlaps significantly with the collaborative role in the film, sometimes to the consternation of government officials who also do not want to be the ones to "get something wrong." "We can't even tell people what they should be afraid of," says one government official at an initial meeting with CDC investigators. "We tried that with swine flu, and all we did was get healthy people scared." By the end of the film, Congress is working online to avoid the disease, and the president is speaking to the American public from an undisclosed location. The media chronicles these political changes as well.

Dr. Sussman, a researcher in San Francisco who ultimately identifies the virus and its chimeric origins, is tackled outside his lab by the hard-charging blogger Alan Krumwiede. Blogging represents the radical role of the media, less bound by fact and more bound by "getting it out there first." Sussman characterizes blogging as "graffiti without punctuation" and dismisses Krumwiede. Unfortunately, Krumwiede does not feel bound by journalistic norms; his early work is based on conspiracy theories, he is personally greedy, and he ultimately decides to use his blog to make the news rather than merely report it. Krumwiede is all about upending the existing power structure—what could be a version of the radical media role and which certainly reflects the impact that the Internet has had on "legacy" journalistic organizations—but in the film, Krumwiede twists that radical role to his own, unethical ends. He decides to ignore the slow pace of science and sees the potential for quick profit by lying, in this case by suggesting to his two million unique viewers that a natural substance, forsythia, is cure for the disease. This lie spreads, making a lot of money for Krumwiede but also prompting runs on the substance at pharmacies and homeopathic shops worldwide. Normative scholarship has always assumed that the radical role of the media would be based on truth. Krumwiede's use of the Internet for radical but unethical purposes poses an important philosophical question: how culpable is the audience for believing unsubstantiated claims found on the Internet? In *Contagion*, two individuals who die from the pandemic despite taking the homeopathic remedy pay one sort of price for a lack of critical thinking. Society pays another by having to direct scarce resources to investigate this "rabbit hole" and to maintain social order in the face of the irrational and hostile demand for the substance. Most importantly, the film asks viewers to consider whether truth is a necessary foundation for the normative, radical role of the media.

However, the blogger also performs multiple roles, including that of investigative reporter. He is the person who "catches" Cheever in an ethical breach of his own—in this instance, the doctor warns his fiancée to leave Chicago (where the disease is rampant) for Atlanta (which has yet to be as infected). When Cheever's personal communication (his fiancée posted the warning on her Facebook page) becomes public, he loses credibility, both with journalists and within the CDC. "We just need to make sure that nobody knows until everybody knows" was the CDC communication "best practice" that Cheever violated; the result is not only professional catastrophe but additional domestic consequences, an illustration of how media coverage both reports on and prompts responses from a variety of government and private actors, among them governments, banks, and law enforcement at multiple levels, and, of course, at the individual level. Cheever has violated the basic public service norms of impartiality and respect; his actions constitute legitimate news, but the way they are brought to public attention not only distorts the media's ability to monitor events but also denies journalists access to a knowledgeable source who made a very human mistake.

The role of social media, whether blogging or Facebook posts, confounds events; neither are easily categorized into the traditional normative media roles scholars have written about for decades. Krumwiede's actions are not mistakes; they are deliberate ethical choices that are confounded, at the end of the film, by the strictures of the First Amendment. As a journalist, Krumwiede cannot be prosecuted for lying even though his choice costs thousands of lives. He can be prosecuted for fraud and illegal profiteering from the homeopathic non-remedy, but as one would expect, about 12 million of Krumwiede's followers (his audience grows geometrically during the epidemic) have given $1 each to post the $12 million bail bond. In Krumwiede's world, truth has become a mashup between reflecting reality and helping to create it. In the span of the film, Krumwiede has exercised at least three of the media's normative roles in his work as a blogger; normative implies ethically based, a concept that Krumwiede's actions turn on its philosophical head.

Once a vaccine has been developed, the government must implement a policy to allow for distribution of this scarce resource over time. Again, the media performs both a monitorial and collaborative role, covering the lottery drawing that identifies when citizens will receive the vaccine based on their date of birth (but not year of birth). The media coverage here assures governmental transparency and demonstrates how different professions require the effective functioning of other professions in order to achieve the public good. This lottery, of course, also has historic precedent; it was last used in the 1960s and early 1970s to determine which young men would be drafted in the armed forces to serve in Vietnam. In *Contagion*, the media and the federal government remain in a mutually beneficial relationship made possible, in no small part, by the virus itself, which has a biological—not a political— agenda. The same could not be said of the draft lottery of an earlier era, one reason that the practice was replaced by the current "all volunteer" system.

The film, because it is focused on science and risk, leaves an enormous number of questions unasked and unanswered: How do we rebuild a society that has suffered staggering human loses and their concomitant economic impacts? How does the United States integrate its political and economic system with that of others founded on different principles? What should humanity do about Internet content—both truthful and fallacious? The one question the film does make sure the audience asks is: how will society respond to the certainty of another pandemic? These questions, of course, have all been raised in various news accounts, but the vivid portrayal of them in a film with its immersive narrative makes them stand out in a way that most traditional journalistic reports do not.

PUBLIC SERVICE IS NEITHER EASY NOR SAFE

Public service is not meant to be easy, but neither is it meant to be lethal. Most of the time, for most professionals, it is not. While people make jokes about lawyers, few of them die in the service of the law. When doctors are targeted for the sort of medicine they practice, it is news. Of the ancient professions, only the clergy has a history of violent death for serving the public. During the Middle Ages, the Reformation, and the Enlightenment, clerics were tortured, killed, and imprisoned for their beliefs. In some parts of the world, this sort of systematic repression continues. Being a professional means many things, but in some historic times and in some contemporary contexts, it also has meant having a target on your back.

If lethality is a measure of difficulty, then journalism is a difficult profession. According to the Committee to Protect Journalists, more than 1,891 journalists have been "killed on duty" since 1992—and while you are reading this book. Many of them were covering war or other conflicts. Some have died horribly: Daniel Pearl's beheading was posted on the web. In the United States—a country that has enshrined the press in its Bill of Rights—more than 39 investigative journalists have been killed since the committee began keeping records. Indeed, IRE (Investigative Reporters and Editors) was founded after Arizona journalist Don Bolles was killed with a car bomb in 1976. Covering war and conflict also takes an internal toll, a sort of cumulative post-traumatic stress that is chronicled in *A Private War* (2018) about war correspondent Marie Colvin. News organizations have responded; most now screen access to their physical newsrooms, something that the film *Contagion* portrays in its opening scenes and which is certainly part of the *West Wing* with a security-minded country. The Dart Center now advises journalists at all levels about how to cope with the psychological stress, including the physical threats, that come with doing journalism.

While loss of life or imprisonment is a high cost to pay for any professional choice, being stymied from doing your job by others is a much more familiar phenomenon. Physicians know that their patients lie, sometimes by omission, others times through exaggeration. Attorneys are taught that their clients are likely to withhold some or all of the truth. Both physicians and lawyers have legal protection to promote honesty: doctor-patient confidentiality and attorney-client privilege. Journalists have no such recourse. In the United States, shield laws differ from state to state and few other nations have even this sort of protection.

However, in more recent years, journalists also have had to face the concerted and well-funded opposition of the focus of their investigative work. In the 1980s, lawyers for the tobacco industry sued to recover journalists' travel records in an effort to learn who confidential sources on tobacco-related stories might be. It is common professional practice today for journalists—not just investigative reporters—to mask their phone calls and texts through a variety of encryption programs. Among the best documented efforts to thwart reporting are the actions of Harvey Weinstein, as he attempted to sidetrack, bully, and threaten *New York Times* reporters Jodi Kantor and Megan Twohey as they reported the story of his sexual harassment through the decades. Weinstein used the legal system to try to intimidate both the journalists and their potential sources; at one point, he hired a "black ops" firm from Israel to attempt to deflect their work. At multiple points during the investigation, the *Times*'s legal staff and editor Dean Baquet, himself an investigative journalist, had to speak with Weinstein or his lawyers in support of the journalists who had spent months on the story. Ronan Farrow, who also was reporting the same story, first at NBC and then, finally, in the *New Yorker*, has detailed how NBC attempted to shut down his reporting, a charge that has been vigorously denied by the network.

What happens in the national spotlight also trickles down to the local level. It is common for elected, public officials to refuse to answer journalists' routine as well as investigative questions. Local news outlets do not have the financial, legal, or experiential resources of news organizations such as the *Times* or NBC to combat such tactics. The forces that oppose reporting can be economically and politically powerful. The result, at least from the journalists' perspective, is that it is the public that is shut out from information that might—and in many cases does—have a bearing on the choices people make in their daily lives.

NORMATIVE ROLES AND THE ALIGNMENT OF VALUES

In their book *Good Work: When Excellence and Ethics Meet*, Howard E. Gardner and his colleagues (2001) focus on the concept of alignment. In the professional world, alignment means that the rewards that accompany good work—from public approval to financial remuneration—match the ethical values associated with the work itself. Professions that are aligned—that is when the concept of excellence that is rewarded matches the ethical values that undergird it—are relatively stable. The professionals that practice in those domains know what is valued and what actions will be rewarded.

Professions that are out of alignment are ripe for change. That change, however, does not necessarily mean that emerging definitions of excellence will match their professional antecedents. Two of the professions examined in *Good Work*, biological science and journalism, are evaluated as out of alignment—and in the same way. Biological science, once the domain of academic research and medicine, in the 21st century has become the locus of startups, patents, and profit. Journalism faces the same sort of economic challenges, in this case through the disruption of the Internet on the one hand and the impact of media conglomeration and ownership patterns on the other. This emphasis on profit, and on the individual fame that may be necessary in order to monetize content, has made journalistic choices much more subject to influences that are incompletely accounted for in the values that support public service. The changing values also reflect changing roles or, at the minimum, a rebalancing of the traditional roles and values that have characterized the profession in the 20th and early 21st century.

Contagion puts the question of what constitutes good journalistic work within the context of public service on full display. The actions that various individuals and institutions take reflect the shifting nature of professional work in this century. Journalists and public relations professionals enact multiple, normative roles simultaneously. The contradictions between and among them have real-world consequences. The contemporary media environment is no longer the world of Superman, but neither is it the world of a blogger for whom unique views replace integrity, accountability, and respect for the audience. In a democracy, journalism as public service is a means to an end: self-government. Whether professionals live more in the world of *House of Cards* or the idealism amid realpolitik of *The West Wing* is as much in play in the real world as it is on the large and small screen.

6

Authentic Alignment

The Tension between Big Profits and Good Work

Central Concepts

- Balance between profit and social responsibility of the media
- Hutchins Commission
- Conglomeration and consolidation of legacy and internet media
- Stakeholder vs. stockholder theory

The American media system is an unusual one, for since its inception, it always has been required to pay its own way. In the early days of the republic, printers supported themselves by printing—among other things—political tracts. It wasn't much of a living, but it established an initial connection between financial support of media content and achieving a desired result.

The focus of this chapter is the balance between the public service role of a socially responsible press (the realm of ethics) and the need for profitability of media organizations that are privately, not government, owned (the realm of economics). Issues of consolidation and conglomeration, market-driven journalism, and shrinking newsroom budgets are explored in *Network*, *The Insider*, *The Newsroom*, and *The Wire*—four newsrooms in crisis for four different but related reasons. Finally, we discuss the limits of economic thinking: those times when market language crowds out moral thinking, when adherence to stockholders supersedes necessary thinking about multiple stakeholders.

Financial support of media content has provided a spectrum of ways to make money, among them traditional advertising, subscriptions, or the purchase of individual media products. Each has found a niche in the 21st century, whether it's buying a movie ticket, subscribing to a publication online, or allowing various social media platforms to sell personal information about you to advertisers in exchange for access to an enormous variety of media content—much of it mistakenly thought of as "free." Those who *own* media outlets today make a very good living. In this framing, the word "media" can imply more than a single media outlet and more than a single medium existing in a culture with other, powerful institutions—government, the church, business. Used in this way, the word "media" implies both multiple media outlets and many forms of content acting as a single institution, which collectively contributes to a culture and a social and political community.

Achieving a desired result has had an equally complex history. Whether it's getting consumers to purchase a particular product or providing political content that promotes a specific sort of action, achieving a desired result—media effects—focuses more on individual responses to media content. But achieving a desired result can have systemwide impact, too. Using the word "media" when talking about achieving a desired result can include public response to everything from a single news article or advertising campaign to the impact of many, sometimes thousands of media messages that provide a particular point of view about something in the culture to the exclusion or amplification of other views about the same thing.

From the beginning, there also has been a tension between the two goals. That tension is the root of many contemporary questions in the subfield of media economics. There is no better place to start than a bunch of college professors trying to make sense of something as complicated as the media as an institution having a simultaneous but not identical impact on the culture and the individuals who comprise it.

In the 1940s, a panel of scholars, none of whom were journalists or media practitioners, led by University of Chicago President Robert Hutchins and largely funded by *Time* magazine owner Henry Luce, developed what later came to be known as the social responsibility theory of the press. According to the Commission on Freedom of the Press (1947), commonly called the Hutchins Commission, the press has the following five functions in society:

1. to provide a truthful, comprehensive, and intelligent account of the day's events in a context that gives them meaning;
2. to serve as a forum for exchange of comment and criticism;
3. to provide a representative picture of constituent groups in society;
4. to present and clarify the goals and values of society; and
5. to provide citizens with full access to the day's intelligence.

The Hutchins Commission findings were quickly ignored by journalists but embraced by media ethicists. However, there was a fundamental flaw at the heart of social responsibility theory: it largely ignored the impact and influence of media economics. This omission means that social responsibility theory does not address the realities of concentrated economic power, market-driven journalism, stockholder theory, or many of the myriad other economic influences on a media system that at times acts socially responsible but at other times acts anything but, especially in an era when information has become a valuable commodity. It ignored the potential connection between paying for something and exercising either straightforward or subtle control over the "content" of that same commodity.

PUBLIC SERVICE MEETS THE BOTTOM LINE

The struggle to balance good journalism and profitability is at the heart of the 1976 film *Network*. Max Schumacher, the news division president at the fictional network UBS, is losing a battle for journalistic respectability. The network's news anchor, Howard Beale, either has had a nervous breakdown or has heard the voice of God. Regardless, he is a journalistic disgrace but becomes a ratings bonanza as he descends into madness. The increase in ratings attracts UBS Vice President Frank Hackett, who reorganizes UBS so that "the news division would be reduced from an independent division to a department accountable to network."

Discussion Question

In this chapter, we discuss the tension between the monetary needs of a conglomeration versus the public service orientation of a socially responsible newsroom. How do UBS, Howard Beale, etc. balance these tensions? Do they err too far to one side? Should news organizations strive for a balance, or should one side take precedence over the other?

Schumacher's major nemesis, however, is Diana Christiansen (though the two also have an affair throughout the film). Christiansen, as Schumacher calls her, is "television incarnate." Her entire being is dedicated to better ratings, and she is ready and willing to take any shortcut to get there. For example, she spearheads production of a show about a terrorist group that shoots footage of its illegal acts, reminiscent of the Symbionese Liberation Army kidnapping of Patty Hearst in 1974. The idea behind the show, dubbed the

Mao Zedong Hour, is that each episode would lead with the raw footage shot by the Great Ahmed Khan's terrorist group, and then network writers would craft a narrative, dramatic backstory. The show illustrates what Christiansen is willing to do to get good ratings, a theme that surfaces again when she pitches a novel concept for a news show featuring Beale that is much more about flash and entertainment than it is about news. *Network* foreshadows the well-documented approach of "if it bleeds, it leads" that was common during the 1990s, particularly in local television news.

Early in the film, Beale is told that he is being replaced as network anchor because of his low ratings. He then announces on air that he will commit suicide, saying that such a stunt surely will increase ratings. Beale's fictional threat mirrors the nonfiction on-air suicide of Christine Chubbuck, a local Florida news reporter who did kill herself on air in 1974, although not over ratings. Schumacher tells Beale that he's taking him off the air immediately, but he relents when Beale says that he doesn't want his outburst to be the public's lasting memory of him.

Beale, however, does not return to normalcy. Instead, he rants on air that he "just ran out of bullshit." Christiansen argues that UBS should retain Beale because he's getting great ratings. She frames him as "a latter-day prophet, a magnificent messianic figure, inveighing against the hypocrisies of our times, a strip Savonarola, Monday through Friday." Notice the juxtaposition of the words "prophet" and "profit." Beale could be a prophet, or he could be insane. However, he definitely will create profit if his rantings create high ratings.

Figure 6.1.   Howard Beale from *Network*. Copyright 1976, MGM

Christiansen envisions a "news" show as part of the network's primetime TV programming. In addition to Beale, who is dubbed "the mad prophet of the airwaves," the show includes a soothsayer, live audience, and an announcer, as well as running segments such as the "Endless Truth Department," "Skeletons in the Closet," and "Vox Populi." *Network* is the amalgam of all television news, from local to national, in an era when, for the first time, news was found to be a profit center.

Neil Postman (1985) wrote that Americans are the best-entertained but least well-informed people in the Western world. He argued that important matters—politics, religion, news, athletics, education, and commerce—had been subsumed by and transformed into entertainment. His thesis was that television made entertainment itself the natural format for the representation of all experience, so these other types of experiences were no longer distinct entities but merely adjuncts to show business. That subsumption and transformation are happening at UBS. Beale and Schumacher repeatedly talk about how they are "Murrow Boys," a reference to the group of CBS journalists closely aligned with Edward R. Murrow before and during World War II. Such references are an attempt to contrast sideshow hustlers such as Christiansen and respectable journalists such as Murrow. For a film-based version of Murrow's influence on television journalism, *Good Night, and Good Luck* (2005) summarizes Murrow's political impact—and the risks he took to achieve that result—and his legacy in broadcast news journalism.

In *Network*, however, Christiansen sees that even credible journalism has traded respectability for ratings, telling Schumacher,

> I watched your six o'clock news today—it's straight tabloid. You had a minute and a half on that lady riding a bike naked in Central Park. On the other hand, you had less than a minute of hard national and international news. It was all sex, scandal, brutal crimes, sports, children with incurable diseases, and lost puppies. So I don't think I'll listen to any protestations of high standards of journalism. You're right down in the street soliciting audiences like the rest of us. All I'm saying is, if you're going to hustle, at least do it right.

Other films from *Good Night, and Good Luck* to *Morning Glory* (2010) show the need to balance ratings with credible journalism, especially in network television. When Murrow isn't attempting to take down Senator Joseph Mc-Carthy, he's doing puff-piece interviews with Liberace. These interviews get good ratings for the network, which in turn allow Murrow to research and run public service journalism at a financial loss to the network. Similarly, in *Morning Glory*, the fictional Mike Pomeroy, a respected television journalist in the mold of Mike Wallace, is forced to co-host a network morning program that has more fluff than substance. He initially balks at doing the typical morning show fare such as cooking segments, instead concentrating his efforts on breaking a story that leads to a governor being arrested on racketeering charges. However, when Pomeroy fears that a producer he has grown to respect might leave for a competitor, he puts on an apron and cooks a frittata. The message is clear: even respected journalists who break major stories will do almost anything for ratings if it helps the show and their career.

Network's Beale takes his "mad prophet" shtick to another level when he enters the studio soaking wet, wearing pajamas and a raincoat, to give his "witness" to the television audience:

> I don't want you to riot. I don't want you to protest. I don't want you to write your congressmen because I wouldn't know what to tell you to write. I don't know what to do about the depression and the inflation and the defense budget and the Russians and crime in the street. All I know is first you got to get mad. You've got to say: "I'm mad as hell, and I'm not going to take this anymore. I'm a human being, goddammit. My life has value." So I want you to get up now. I want you to get out of your chairs and go to the window. Right now. I want you to go to the window, open it, and stick your head out and yell. I want you to yell: "I'm mad as hell, and I'm not going to take this anymore."

The next several scenes show the aftermath; people around the country are following Beale's lead and shouting in the streets. The show is a hit, and Beale is a star who can garner huge ratings.

SAME MESSAGE, INDIVIDUAL INFLUENCE

Network was released in 1976, a time when scholars were rethinking media effects. In the 1920s and 1930s, researchers used the metaphors of a hypodermic needle or magic bullet to argue that mass media had a direct, immediate, and powerful effect on audiences. Those ideas started to shift in the 1940s and 1950s, when a limited-effects model came into vogue. The basic idea was that media effects were more complex than previously assumed, and effects were mitigated by networks of parents, friends, and teachers, as well as informational diets. The pendulum began to swing back a bit in the 1970s when the first studies on agenda setting and cultivation signaled a return of powerful mass media, though not as unidirectional as the hypodermic needle model.

Beale, eventually, takes his "mad prophet" bit a bit too far when he does a diatribe about conglomerations, truth, and entertainment. He is upset that the Communications Corporation of America, the parent company of UBS, is being bought by "Arabs." He does a monologue centered on the idea that the Arabs are buying "every" company in America and tells his now sizable audience to send telegrams to the White House to stop the CCA deal. Reflecting the hypodermic needle model of media effects, his viewers follow his command, and the White House mailroom is inundated with telegrams. One important listener, however, is furious. Arthur Jensen, the CEO of CCA, demands to meet with Beale. During their one-on-one meeting, Jensen, in almost biblical terms, tells Beale that he is disturbing the "primal forces of nature" by thinking in terms of nations and people instead of about money, businesses, and corporations:

> You get up on your little 21-inch screen, and howl about America and democracy. There is no America. There is no democracy. There is only IBM and ITT and AT&T and Dupont, Dow, Union Carbide, and Exxon. Those are the nations of the world today. What do you think the Russians talk about in their councils of state? Karl Marx? They pull out their linear programming charts, statistical decision theories and minimax solutions and compute the price-cost probabilities of their transactions and investments just like we do. We no longer live in a world of nations and ideologies, Mr. Beale. The world is a college of corporations, inexorably determined by the immutable bylaws of business. The world is a business, Mr. Beale. It has been since man crawled out of the slime, and our children, Mr. Beale, will live to see that perfect world in which there is no war and famine, oppression and brutality—one vast and ecumenical holding company, for whom all men will work to serve a common profit, in which all men will hold a share of stock, all necessities provided, all anxieties tranquilized, all boredom amused. And I have chosen you to preach this evangel, Mr. Beale.

Beale asks Jensen why he must deliver this message. Jensen's response: "Because you're on television, dummy. Sixty million people watch you every night of the week, Monday through Friday."

Its influence at the individual level is what has made CCA an economically powerful institution, one that political scientist C. Wright Mills (1956) would describe as part of the "power elite" ruling class within a democratic society. Jensen says that there are no nations, but CCA uses its power over information distribution in the same way that a monarch would use his army. CCA is a multinational corporation engaged in the information business, and Beale, because he reaches 60 million people nightly, can serve the corporate financial interests by promoting the company line.

Beale does promote the company line, changing his spiel from a fire-and-brimstone call to thwart corporate interests in the name of America and democracy to a eulogy for a dying democracy and a rise in dehumanization. While the change pleases Jensen and helps CCA's financial interests, it does not resonate with viewers, so Beale's ratings start to tank. Christiansen wants to fire Beale, but Hackett tells her and a roomful of other television executives that Jensen has ordered Beale to remain on the air. Hackett then says that they have no choice but to kill Beale, and as if to prove that Beale is correct in his talks about dehumanization, no one flinches. Christiansen pitches an idea for Ahmed Khan's terrorist group to assassinate Beale on air as a perfect opener for the new season of the *Mao Zedong Hour.* After Beale's assassination, the movie closes with this recap: "This was the story of Howard Beale, who was the network news anchorman of UBS-TV, the first known instance of a man being killed because he had lousy ratings."

Much like UBS, most news organizations today are corporate owned and publicly traded. Indeed, media conglomerates are among the largest and traditionally most profitable corporations. A handful of corporations—Walt Disney Company, NewsCorp, AT&T/Time Warner, Comcast, and Viacom/CBS—own the vast majority of newspapers, broadcast and cable television networks, radio stations, movie and music studios, and book publishers in the United States and worldwide. Other conglomerates—from Sinclair Broadcast Group in television and iHeartMedia in radio to Gannett/Gatehouse in news-papers—have a nearly total stranglehold on specific mediums. The situation is not much better online, as the FAANG corporations (Facebook, Apple, Amazon, Netflix, and Google) control the vast majority of online traffic, advertising, and commerce.

Such consolidation might limit the marketplace of ideas, especially when ownership has a defined partisan or political bias. Corporate owners, unlike local owners who live and work in the community in which their news or-ganizations report, also typically are more insulated from contact with news consumers than virtually any other business owner in America. Ultimately, the organizational-level power in a newsroom lies with owners, who con-trol content indirectly through hiring and promotion practices and directly through self-censorship (Shoemaker & Vos, 2009; Shoemaker & Reese, 1996). Indeed, the combination of the size, concentrated ownership, owner wealth, and power orientation of the dominant mass-media firms constitutes one of the five filters outlined by Herman and Chomsky (2002) that narrows the range of news and limits what can become "big news." In other words, "news" often is what the ownership of a media conglomeration wants it to be; the interests of a conglomeration trump the obligation for public service (Hendrickson & Wilkins, 2009).

CONTENT THAT ALIGNS WITH THE GOAL OF PUBLIC SERVICE

This conflict between the monetary needs of a conglomeration and the public service orientation of a socially responsible newsroom is at the heart of the film *The Insider* (1999). Jeffrey Wigand is the ultimate insider—the top research scientist at the big tobacco company Brown & Williamson, though he recently was fired by the company. *60 Minutes* producer Lowell Bergman convinces Wigand to serve as a whistleblower, exposing the lies of big tobacco on the program. Specifically, Wigand calls the cigarette industry a "nicotine delivery business," saying that nicotine is addictive and that the seven big tobacco companies consciously put profits before health. While these statements are not groundbreaking today, they were major news in 1996 when Wigand acted as a whistleblower.

Figure 6.2. Jeffrey Wigand and Lloyd Bergman from *The Insider*. Copyright 1999, Touchstone Pictures

The corporate and legal side of CBS, however, kills the story because of potential legal liability. Bergman is apoplectic, but *60 Minutes* producer Don Hewitt and correspondent Mike Wallace ultimately support corporate's decision. Brown & Williamson, Wigand's former employer, had threatened a lawsuit because Bergman, and by extension *60 Minutes* and CBS, potentially helped coerce Wigand into breaking the confidentiality agreement he signed when he was fired. At the time of the story, CBS was in the midst of a sale to the conglomerate Westinghouse, and a potential lawsuit could jeopardize that sale.

Hewitt decides to air an edited version of the story, one that sanitizes Wigand's remarks to the point that the bombshell story becomes a dud. Wallace confronts CBS News President Eric Kluster after watching a preview of the Wigand segment.

WALLACE: Where's the rest? Where the hell's the rest? (Hewitt and CBS lawyer Helen Caperelli enter the hallway and see Wallace yelling at Kluster.) You cut it. You cut the guts out of what I said.

KLUSTER: It was a time consideration, Mike.

WALLACE: (furious, yelling) Time? Bullshit. You corporate lackey. Who told you your incompetent little fingers had the requisite skills to edit me? I'm trying to Band-Aid a situation here, and you're too dim to . . .

CAPERELLI: (walking up to Wallace and Kluster, interrupting) Mike . . . Mike . . . Mike . . .

WALLACE: Mike? Mike? Try Mr. Wallace. We work in the same corporation doesn't mean we work in the same profession. What are you going to do now? You're going to finesse me, lawyer me some more? I've been in this profession (raising his voice even more) 50 fucking years. You, and the people you work for, are destroying the most-respected, the highest-rated, the most-profitable show on this network.

Wallace certainly is indignant, and possibly a bit pretentious, in this scene. However, his point is clear: corporate interests should never dictate news content. At this time, *60 Minutes* was respected, had strong ratings, and was highly profitable. With that kind of clout, corporate executives and lawyers—especially those with a conflict of interest because they stood to gain financially from a sale to Westinghouse—should have left the news decisions to trained and experienced news professionals such as Wallace, the screenwriters suggest.

Bergman eventually leaks the story about CBS not airing the full interview to the *New York Times* in an attempt to get it aired. The *Times* runs a front-page exposé, as well as a scathing editorial denouncing CBS for its actions in not running the story. (You can read these for yourself online.) The *Wall Street Journal* also runs a story on a dossier on Wigand, accusing those who created it of character assassination. They also run a transcript of Wigand's deposition in a big tobacco case in Mississippi. Those *Times* and *Journal* stories lead to a heated exchange between Bergman, Wallace, and Hewitt, who believes Bergman has betrayed CBS.

BERGMAN: This news division has been vilified by the *New York Times*. In print. On television. For caving to corporate interests.

HEWITT: *New York Times* ran a blow-by-blow of what we talked about behind closed doors. You fucked us.

BERGMAN: No, you fucked you. Don't invert stuff. Big tobacco tried to smear Wigand; you bought it. The *Wall Street Journal*, here, not exactly a bastion of anti-capitalist sentiment, refutes big tobacco's smear campaign as the lowest form of character assassination. And now, even now, when every word of what Wigand has said on our show is printed, the entire deposition of his testimony

in a court of law in the state of Mississippi, the cat *totally* out of the bag, you're still standing here debating. Don, what the hell else do you need?
HEWITT: Mike, you tell Lowell.
WALLACE: You fucked up, Don.

Wallace, here, shows that he agrees with Bergman that Hewitt made a mistake when he bowed to corporate pressure. *60 Minutes* finally runs the original segment with Wigand's full interview. After it airs, Bergman tells Wallace that he has resigned from CBS, saying, "What got broken here doesn't go back together." Bergman believes that he cannot give his word to sources to trust him because his and *60 Minutes'* credibility and integrity has been permanently stained by putting corporate interests above the public interest in this story.

The Insider suggests that the balance of the tension between financial support and public service should favor public service. There are other points of view. Beginning in the 1980s, news organizations such as CBS began moving toward making news "explicitly a commodity" (McManus, 1994, p. 1), selecting stories for the "issues and events that have the greatest ratio of expected appeal for demographically desirable audiences" (p. 114). Journalists' first goal in a market-driven newsroom would be providing news that could entice more readers or viewers, which, in turn, would lead to increased profitability. This shift toward news aimed at increasing profitability is in stark contrast to the traditional newsroom aim to inform the public in an attempt to strengthen democracy. The goal of a market-driven newsroom, then, is to entertain while possibly informing.

The journalists on Aaron Sorkin's *The Newsroom* (2012–2014) practice market-driven journalism, even when they clearly do not favor it. Ferrucci and Painter (2016) argue that the news organization in *The Newsroom* is in crisis; it previously adopted a market-based approach but is now challenged by the addition of Executive Producer MacKenzie McHale, who wants to separate economics from journalism. McHale and Executive Editor Charlie Skinner form a powerful alliance in an attempt to treat the news as a service rather than a product, but they initially are stymied by anchor Will McAvoy, who has grown accustomed to good ratings and the perks that go with them. The struggle is depicted in a newsroom argument between McHale and McAvoy during the series' first episode:

McHALE: You're terrified you're going to lose your audience, and you'd do anything to get them back. You're one pitch meeting away from doing the news in 3D.
McAVOY: This isn't nonprofit theater. It's advertiser-supported television. You know that, right?

McHALE: I'd rather do a good show for 100 people than a bad one for one million, if that's what you're saying.

McAVOY: What is it that you're talking to me about right now?

McHALE: I've come here to produce a news broadcast that more closely resembles the one we did before you got popular by not bothering anyone, Leno.

McAVOY: I think Jay and I would rather be employed if it's all the same to you.

McHALE: It's not all the same to me, you punk. I've come here to take your IQ and your talent and put it to some patriotic fucking use. And where does it say that a good news show can't be popular?

McAVOY: Nielsen ratings.

McHALE: We're going to do a good news show and make it popular at the same time.

McAVOY: That is impossible.

Commercial news organizations, including the fictional Atlantis World Media, the parent company of show-within-a-show *News Night*, concurrently trade in four markets: the market for audience, competing for readers and viewers; the stock market because most firms trade stock and desire higher valuations; the advertising market, competing for advertising revenue; and a market for sources, competing for information to disseminate (McManus, 1994). Market theory holds that these four markets should operate efficiently and consistently to produce the type of high-quality news that would both inform and attract the public; however, serving the public often conflicts with a focus on profitability and serving the market (Barnouw, 1997; McManus, 1994). As Robert McChesney (1999) argued, a corporate media system set up to serve the needs of Wall Street and Madison Avenue cannot and does not serve the needs of the majority of the population.

Discussion Question

Executives at Atlantis World Media adhere to the notion of stockholder theory. How might the newsroom within the show look if they instead adhered to Patricia H. Werhane's ideas of stakeholder theory?

Atlantis World Media is corporate owned and publicly traded, although Leona Lansing and her family own a controlling interest. Still, there are instances on *The Newsroom* where news coverage by Skinner, McHale, McAvoy, and their team directly or indirectly affects the larger organization. McAvoy converts to McHale's ideas about hard-hitting news in the public service, and he anchors a show meant to investigate, explore, and explain the Tea Party movement. This switch to serious news does not sit well with

Lansing, who holds a meeting with Skinner where she orders him to call off the dogs regarding the Tea Party.

> SKINNER: (in boardroom, just him and Lansing) Leona, you can't possibly expect us to tailor our news coverage to what best suits our corporate . . .
> LANSING: (putting up hand to silence Charlie) Let's start over, and, this time, disabuse yourself of the idea that this is a conversation between equals where I make an argument, you make a counterargument, and we agree to disagree. Our cable news division accounts for less than 3 percent of AWM's annual revenue. (Pointing finger at Charlie) You don't make money for stockholders, which I have a fiduciary responsibility to do. Well, last night, the voters ousted 21 percent of Congress, including seven members of the House Subcommittee on Communications and Technology. Three of those seven are AWM's most reliable friends on the Hill. Now, the Congressmen that will be replacing them are the same people that Will has been making look like fucking morons for the last six months.
> SKINNER: They've done a pretty good job making themselves look like morons.
> LANSING: I have business before this Congress, Charlie, and whatever you may think of these people, which is the same thing I think of them, they hold the keys to the future of AWM. Anything more than a pack of gum, and I have to go to Congress for permission. I don't make the rules, but I do abide by them.

In talking about her "fiduciary responsibility," Lansing is arguing for stockholder theory, which places an emphasis on corporate responsibility to stockholders for publicly traded corporations. In stockholder theory, increasing the share price is the single, overriding, and legally binding promise made by corporations and their leaders to those who purchase stock. Whatever legal means enacted to secure the ends of an increasing share price is ethically right, according to Milton Friedman, who first articulated stockholder theory. Stockholders, then, are placed above other stakeholders such as employees, advertisers, and the general public.

Some businesses, however, have a public responsibility that extends beyond individual stockholders, according to business ethicist Patricia H. Werhane (2006). Such companies should operate from an "enriched stakeholder" model, which puts an entity other than the corporation at the center of the "stakeholder" map, as opposed to a profit-driven "stockholder" model. Changing the stakeholder map necessitates that other "promises" surface and that measures of success other than increasing a corporation's stock price take precedence. For a news organization, replacing a stockholder model with an enriched stakeholder model would mean that a media corporate manager would begin to use a different gauge of success, for example what benefits citizens living in communities most, as opposed to always placing profit first in every situation.

People or groups, such as the media, agree to provide needed services; the community, in turn, agrees to compensate them for the services and recognize their right to perform them (Gardner, Csikszentmihalyi, & Damon, 2001). Such a mutually beneficial relationship creates an authentic alignment. A professional realm is authentically aligned when the values of the culture are in line with those of the domain (knowledge, skills, practices, rules, and values), when the expectations of stakeholders (consumers, citizens, corporate shareholders and executives) match those of the field (the roles that individuals practice when working with symbols of the domain and institutions), and when the domain and the field are themselves in sync (Gardner et al., 2001). For Lansing and *News Night*, that might mean reporting hard-hitting, sometimes controversial stories that better inform their viewers about emerging political and social movements that might not be as "grassroots" as they seem. Such a shift in focus would align *News Night* more closely with two guiding principles outlined in the Society of Professional Journalists code of ethics: seek truth and report it as fully as possible, and act independently. Seeking the truth can be a personally and financially rewarding experience, something that stockholder theory avoids but enriched stakeholder theory demands.

LESS WITH LESS: ECONOMICS AND LEGACY MEDIA

The news organizations in *Network*, *The Insider*, and *The Newsroom* are all legacy publications—news organizations that existed prior to the Internet. Because of decreasing revenues, these news organizations have to do more with less or, as city editor Guy Haynes says in *The Wire* (2002–2008), "less with less." The semi-fictional *Baltimore Sun* depicted in the fifth season of *The Wire* faces fairly consistent staff buyouts and cutbacks, and the paper has been publishing without certain reporters, such as a transportation beat writer, so it does not report certain types of stories as often as it could or should (Ferrucci & Painter, 2018). Indeed, in one episode, court reporter Bill Zorzi confronts an assistant district attorney because the *Sun* was not alerted about an important press conference. The district attorney tells him that she called her contact at the paper; however, that reporter had taken a buyout and left the paper four months earlier. The ability of the *Sun* to cover Baltimore is further diminished when executive editor James Whiting III announces yet another round of layoffs despite the profitability of the paper:

> It's a bad time for newspapers, as you all know. The news hole is shrinking as advertising dollars continue to decline. Our circulation numbers are also down as we compete with a variety of media. Technology is driving distribution and

the Internet is a free source of news and opinions. Seeking a balance in this new world, we're now faced with hard choices. We opened our first foreign bureau in London in 1924. The *Sun*'s foreign coverage has been a source of pride ever since. So it is with tremendous regret that I tell you that Chicago has made it clear that bureaus in Beijing, Moscow, Jerusalem, Johannesburg, and London will all be shuttered. Elsewhere in the newsroom there will be a fresh round of buyouts. Chicago has given us some hard budgetary numbers that will force us into some hard decisions throughout the newsroom. We are quite simply going to have to find ways to do more with less.

The *Sun* depicted in *The Wire* is fictional, although the *Baltimore Sun* is, of course, a real newspaper, and several *Sun* reporters play themselves on the show. The depiction of a shrinking news staff, however, is all too real. Alden Global Capital, the hedge fund that owns the *Denver Post*, has reduced the paper's newsroom staff from more than 300 to less than 100 reporters. Similar layoffs have occurred at the *Dallas Morning News*, *Cleveland Plain Dealer*, and in many newsrooms across the United States. Newsroom employment fell by 23 percent and newspaper employment fell by about half from 2008 to 2019 (Grieco, 2020). The current era of cutbacks and consolidations has been noted by media researcher Robert McChesney (1997), who makes this analogy:

Imagine if the federal government demanded that newspaper and broadcast journalism staffs be cut in half, that foreign bureaus be closed, and that news be tailored to suit the government's self-interest. There would be an outcry that would make the Alien and Sedition Acts, the Red Scares and Watergate seem like child's play. Yet when corporate America aggressively pursues the exact same policies, scarcely a murmur of dissent can be detected in the political culture.

In addition to making the jobs of journalists more difficult—reporters only can do less with less—buyouts and cutbacks also have led to a decrease in newsroom morale, as illustrated in another scene from *The Wire*:

ROBERT RUBIN (a foreign correspondent returning to Baltimore after the London bureau was shuttered): They even sold the building in Kensington. I mean, we bought that sucker for nothing 50 years ago, and now Chicago sells it off for a couple million pounds.
HAYNES: Capitalization they call it.
RUBIN: These newspaper chain guys just don't give a fuck, do they?

Good journalism is expensive. As Whiting states, few newsrooms enjoy large, or even sufficient, budgets in an era of shrinking news holes and circulation numbers, decreased advertising dollars, and competition from "free" sources of news and information online. Legacy organizations such as the *Sun* first started publishing in an era of low to moderate economic competition. For example, while there were at times up to six daily newspapers in Baltimore in the early 19th century, the *Sun* and the *Baltimore News-American* soon dominated the market. The *Sun* enjoyed a nearly total monopoly in Baltimore when the *News-American* folded in 1986. Media scholar Steve Lacy (1989) predicted these low to moderate competitive environments would produce a quality news product based on individual organizations' financial commitment to news, which in turn was perceived as useful by audience members and sustained by a journalistic culture that valued excellence and public service.

In contrast, the contemporary media marketplace is one of hyper-competition driven by Internet access where supply substantially exceeds demand. News consumers have access to the product of nearly any news organization throughout the world—usually in the palm of their hand. Consequently, a large percentage of news producers in a hyper-competitive environment operate at a financial loss. Classical economic theory posits that hyper-competition cannot exist permanently. News is a product, but it's not like other products. News is an "experience and credence" commodity, meaning that news consumers cannot judge whether the product meets their needs until they have invested in and spent time with the news. News also is linked to social welfare, a category of products with significant external values not readily captured by price point or profit margin.

While these films focus on the business of journalism, there are similar fictional treatments of some of these same issues in advertising, for example *What Women Want* (2000) and its contemporary reboot *What Men Want* (2019). Rock biopics, for example the recent Oscar-winning *Bohemian Rhapsody* (2018), also deal with conflicts over "selling" art versus staying true to an artistic vision. And documentary films have long taken on the "undercovered" story—the story that was either too complex or too edgy to make any sort of newscast. The fictional film *The Big Short* (2015), based on a nonfiction book, is an entertainment-based example of the critique that documentaries such as *Inside Job* (2010) provide.

WHAT IS THE LANGUAGE FOR ALIGNMENT?

Philosopher Michael Sandel (2012) argues that economic language—where literally everything has to be marketed and incentivized—has crowded out moral thinking, changing our idea of Aristotle's concept of a good life with authentic flourishing. However, there are areas of life, Sandel argues, where the market does not belong: paying schoolchildren to get good grades, selling naming rights to sports stadiums and national parks, creating a medical market for blood and kidneys. To these, we would add the public service role of a socially responsible media system. Sandel outlines two sets of basic objections to the kind of thinking that everything should be marketed and incentivized. The first is the notion of fairness and coercion. The second is the capacity to fuel corruption and degradation. Traditional economists tend to think of qualities including altruism, generosity, solidarity, and civic duty as scarce resources; Sandel, however, thinks of them as a muscle that strengthens with repeated use. Each of these qualities speaks to notions of the good life, so when the language of morals is replaced by the language of markets, then the good life itself is degraded.

Discussion Question

Michael Sandel argues that there are places and areas of life where the market simply doesn't belong. Is the news one of these places/areas? Is entertainment programming?

How an institution promotes a good, moral life remains a vibrant question for this century, one that certainly includes the media. The good life, as philosophers define it, doesn't appear to have a ready corporate sponsor. The question thus remains: if Americans get only what we are willing to pay for, how can we more closely align our economic choices with the impact we would expect, or at least hope, those choices to have?

Social Justice

A Moving, Aspirational Target

Central Concepts

- Ethical and philosophical roots of the concepts of justice and fairness
- The history and role of social justice in documentary film
- Fault lines in fictional films, with a particular examination of gender
- Social justice through the lens of individuals and institutions

---

"**G**od didn't mean for people to own people," says Cynthia Erivo as Harriet Tubman in the 2019 fictional film *Harriet*.

In that one line, the screenwriters provide audiences with the concept that infuses not merely the film but the historical character's life on which it was based. Justice—social justice in the United States in the 1860s—was defined at this baseline. Slavery—the ownership of one person by another—was unjust.

However, the film *Harriet* didn't exist in 1860. If you saw the movie, you did so more than 160 years after the events depicted in it. As a nation, we have had almost 250 years of experience in what it means to try to knit a more just society: a society that is trying to overcome its history of profound social injustice. America is hardly the first nation to embark on such an effort. The ancient Greeks invented the word *barbarian* to mean everyone who was not Greek. If you were Greek (and male), you could speak and vote in Athens. If you were a barbarian, you were something less than human. In 1789, the French slaughtered most of their nobility as part of a revolution with the political goal of providing more equality of opportunity and income. The same could be—and was said—of the Russian Revolution of 1917 and the Chinese revolution of 1949 when Mao Zedong became the longtime political leader of a country and a group of people who had literally marched more than 6,000 miles to change a balkanized and profoundly unjust political and social system.

What are some of the messages about social justice tucked in *Harriet*? First, Harriet Tubman herself said she was motivated because her family, and particularly her sisters, had been sold "down south" as part of the larger economic institution of slavery. Family separation—the contemporary term—has more than 400 years of history that the film only begins to explore. But that particular working out of injustice in contemporary American society must include the mass incarceration of people of color, a subject tackled by (and compared to slavery in) the 2016 documentary *13th*. When families were separated in the pre–Civil War South, people were transported in cages. In 2019, at the U.S. border with Mexico and in some places in Europe, people—refugees—were housed in facilities that provided for only the most minimal of basic human needs, and documented instances show where even those needs were not met. Children were separated from their parents; sometimes they wound up in cages.

Discussion Question

What are some of the messages about social justice tucked into other contemporary films about race such as *12 Years a Slave* (2013), *Selma* (2014), *Black Panther* (2018), *When They See Us* (2019), and *Just Mercy* (2019)? How are these messages similar or dissimilar to those found in the *New York Times*'s 1619 Project?

These cinematic choices of plot and visuals are deliberate. They also illustrate some important philosophical elements of justice. Here, social justice refers to a branch of philosophy and social philosophy that connects individual acts to their societal consequences and the societal understanding to a range of possible individual actions.

Justice is comparative. It is not possible to explain the term without reference to other people and to the social and political systems in which they live.

What is *just* may initially depend on your point of view. After all, the Greeks believed that they had developed a just society. Today we would criticize it as a society that lacked political equality for the majority of people involved.

Points of view emerge from specific times in history; they also are informed by history. What was *just* in 1860—ridding the country of slavery—is considered only a starting point for what would be considered just in 1960 . . . or 2021.

This chapter is divided into two parts. The first takes a long look at the history of documentaries. These films often explore issues of social justice, typically from the point of view of the "other" or the "underdog." They also have impacted fictional films—many of which are based on real people or events. The second half of the chapter focuses on the concept of fault lines. By taking a deep dive into the representation of gender in popular culture, we examine how fault lines can be a useful lens to explore social justice issues. Political and social philosophy form the basis for looking at social justice on the individual and institutional levels.

Whether it's in film or philosophy, how we evaluate whether something is just involves not just looking at individuals but at the social and political systems that they "invent" and in which they currently live. The concept of justice allows us to make critical evaluations of both ourselves as individuals and our communities. Justice informs our moral imaginations. We aspire to be more just while recognizing that too often we fall short.

PHILOSOPHICAL THINKING ABOUT SOCIAL JUSTICE

Having just read that the concept of justice has evolved with history and can vary by point of view, it is tempting to argue that the concept is relative and hinges on who and what groups can make the loudest arguments. However, philosophical thinking has developed some important principles that are far from relative. Among the best established is the work of philosophers John Rawls and Amartya Sen. Both base their thinking on human reason, and both connect individual actions with the social and political institutions of the day.

Rawls defines justice as fairness. His work attempts to compensate for some of the major shortcomings of utilitarian theory, specifically to account for long-term consequences. Long-term consequences are the purview of institutions. "Justice is the first virtue of social institutions, just as truth is of systems of thought. . . . Laws and institutions no matter how efficient and well-arranged must be reformed or abolished if they are unjust. . . . An injustice is tolerable only when it is necessary to avoid a greater injustice. Being first virtues of human activities, truth and justice are uncompromising" (Rawls, 1971, p. 3–4). Because Rawls was writing in the 20th century, his work acknowledges that current social institutions promote outcomes that are unjust. It is the job of philosophers, politicians, and citizens to take this admittedly imperfect and unlevel playing field and make it less imperfect and more level. Rawls's work accepts that such changes will be incremental, that they will be imperfect, but that, over the long haul, a more just society will emerge. Taken in the framework of *Harriet*, the initial social institution—slavery—was profoundly unjust. Outlaw slavery—what Thomas Jefferson referred to as America's "peculiar institution"—and the long-term problem is not solved because outlawing the institution of slavery does not repair the generational damage to families ripped apart because people were viewed as chattel (the social institution of family) or provided unequal access to economic opportunity (slaves were seldom educated or allowed to be educated and hence to begin to amass some wealth and economic security). With the Civil War and subsequent passage of the 13th Amendment to the U.S. Constitution, American society became a more just society, but it still has not become a perfectly just society. The country needed—on the individual and institutional level—to imagine the next, necessary changes.

Rawls places that need to imagine the "next step" in the form of a thought experiment he called the "veil of ignorance." When individuals move behind the imaginary veil of ignorance, they lose everything but their essential humanity—their gender, their social class, their education, their access to various social and political goods, their ethnicity . . . anything that would allow them to divide themselves into subgroups. Having jettisoned these distinctive but superficial qualities behind the veil, there is no guarantee that, when people emerge from the veil, they will retain those attributes that distinguished their social and economic status before they began the thought experiment. Behind the veil of ignorance, people are asked to develop rules of living that would be just when they emerge from behind the veil—when they might emerge as "something other" is a variety of ways. Rawls said that a rational response to the thought experiment would be these two rules of "living": (1) provide the freedom to access social and political goods to the widest possible number of people, and (2) protect whomever emerges as the weaker party. With equal emphasis on individual freedom and institutions crafted to reduce inequality, Rawls theorizes a more just society will emerge. That more just society, in turn, would provide the baseline understanding that can be criticized and ultimately changed, but only in ways that will promote more fairness. Rawls asserts that people will not want to develop institutions that are less fair than those that currently exist, hence the long-term progress toward justice at the individual and institutional level. He accepts that human beings may not perfectly understand the long-term consequences of institutional arrangements, hence the goal of justice is continual. In this, it is very like the goal of truth telling; it's something we must make continuing decisions about.

Rawls's theory of justice as fairness argues for iterative changes in existing social institutions. Sen (2009), on the other hand, criticizes Western philosophy for being preoccupied with finding the *most* just solution. Instead, Sen demands a public discussion of various just alternatives. He emphatically argues that there can be plural just solutions because there is an inescapable plurality of competing principles. Like Rawls, Sen asserts the necessity of re-examining existing social institutions; unlike Rawls, Sen is willing to accept partial solutions. Theoretically, Sen employs what political scientists call the rational choice model of decision-making. Practically, Sen is seeking to change human behavior at the individual level and acknowledges that institutions can promote or retard such change. Again, think of the example in *Harriet*. Slavery as an economic institution made certain choices much more likely—regardless of individual desires. Harriet Tubman had to travel alone for more than 100 miles before she could cross the border from a slave state to a free state. She could not save all her family members. Slavery circumscribed her choices; she believed that the choices for her sisters were even more restrictive.

SOCIAL INSTITUTIONS UNDER THE CINEMATIC LENS: THE ROLE OF DOCUMENTARY FILM

About 50 years before you are reading this book, documentary film was only a niche genre. Practitioners were rare, documentaries did not make money, and about the only places you could see one was in an "art house" theater.

Times have changed. Beginning with Michael Moore's *Roger and Me* (1989), which told the story of General Motors leaving Flint, Michigan, audiences discovered documentary film as an enjoyable, thought-provoking form of narrative. Money followed audiences; if "docs" could get butts in seats, then studios and directors would be willing to fund them, particularly because even the most expensive documentary takes millions of dollars less to produce then the latest entry in the Marvel universe. Technology helped; film cameras became more portable. Editing could be done on laptops. Filmmakers could shoot some—or all—of their films on the phone. Documentary film festivals sprang up—not just at places such as Sundance and Tribeca, but also in more out-of-the way locations such as Columbia, Missouri, where the True/False Film Festival attracts more than 40,000 people annually and where filmmakers come not to sell a product but to see how audiences react to it. With the explosion of content providers in this century, Netflix, Amazon, and Hulu have financed some documentaries and purchased others. The genre itself invaded narrative films, some of which, like *Harriet*, were based on real people and real events. *Erin Brockovich* (2000), for which Julia Roberts won the Best Actress Oscar, was a narrative film based on a real court case. More and more fiction films—*Deepwater Horizon* (2016), *Dark Waters* (2019),

Figure 7.1.   Michael Moore (right) from *Roger and Me*. Copyright 1989, Warner Bros.

Bombshell (2019)—are based on real events. So, as documentaries became both more profitable and more popular, audiences and filmmakers rediscovered that truth was sometimes better in the retelling than any fictional account might have been.

Historically, documentaries have been preoccupied with issues of social justice. And, more often than not, they have explored the concept of social justice from the vantage point of "the other." They have taken the relational elements of justice seriously and embodied them in remarkable ways. The effective documentary takes our aspirations for justice; holds our current social, political, and individual arrangements up to it; and asks audiences if they are satisfied with what they see. Two of the most historically influential (on other filmmakers) were Edward R. Murrow's *Harvest of Shame* (1960), about hunger in America, and Barbara Koppel's *Harlan County USA* (1976), about the months-long coal miners' strike in Harlan, Kentucky. Murrow's made-for-television documentary had the avowed goal of changing policy in the United States, particularly on issues involving migrant workers. It was unsuccessful, but the cinema verité techniques he used and the fact that he gave women and people of color equal time and screen space with those who were more privileged (white, male politicians) influenced broadcast journalists and documentary filmmakers for generations. The PBS series *Frontline* has a 30-year history in the tradition of Murrow. Koppel's work—the first documentary to employ a musical soundtrack—introduced many to the life of coal miners in Appalachia and remains one of the few films to examine the impact of coal mining and the ownership of mining companies on generations of poor people who had little political power. Elements of her soundtrack can be found in fictional films such as *O Brother, Where Art Thou?* (2000). Contemporary documentary producers acknowledge that a soundtrack is now an important and sometimes essential element in documentary film.

Discussion Question

What might John Rawls say about the documentary *Harvest of Shame* or *Harlan County USA*? What would Amartya Sen say?

Documentaries have been politically influential as well. John Fox's *Gasland* (2010 for part one, 2013 for part two) examined the environmental impact of fracking, particularly on individuals who had relatively little power and were, at best, middle class. Not only did his film elevate the issue, it actually led to changes in the law in states such as Texas. *Inside Job* (2010), which won the Oscar in 2010, explained the elements of the 2008 banking and financial crisis in accessible terms. *The Big Hack*, the 2018 film examining the work of Cambridge Analytica (and that firm's attempt to influence elections in more than 20 countries, including the United States), raised questions about social media that journalists working for powerful and sophisticated organizations were struggling to make accessible for readers and viewers. Work such as *One Child Nation* (2019) has exposed international audiences to the inner workings of China's one-child policy (which was rescinded in 2017), including forced late-term abortions. Even the *New York Times* has gotten into the documentary business with its weekly television show that examines the paper's reporting on a specific story. Finally, there have been documentaries focusing on journalism itself. Perhaps the most viewed is *The Reporter* (2009), which focuses on *New York Times* columnist Nicholas Kristof, particularly as he covers African warlords at considerable personal risk.

Finally, there is the sort of documentary with which the generation of students reading this book are probably the most familiar: street tapes. While this approach to documentary film began in the 1960s, its real impact awaited the lightweight video camera and later the cell phone. A cross between news

stories and documentary "shorts," most street tapes traded some level of production sophistication for powerful content. Whether it was the video of Minneapolis police officers killing George Floyd, the subsequent videos of brutal
police responses to nationwide protests, tapes of various responses to natural
disasters, or smuggled content of meetings by government or corporate actors
that were meant to remain secret, street tapes often focused on specific incidents and particular political causes. The fact that they exist owes a great deal
to the combination of technological innovation, the development of a 24-hour
news cycle for media outlets that include both broadcast and print, and the
realization by professional journalists that audience engagement provides an
important point of view. That realization can make street tapes problematic:
the focus on specific incidents sometimes ignores the context that actually
can provide a deeper meaning.

These documentaries surface injustice. Philosophers and politicians,
among them Mahatma Gandhi, have argued that in order to remedy injustice, you have to make it visible. Contemporary life is complex; documentaries, even for a brief time, can submerge audience members in a different
point of view. They do not take the place of the veil of ignorance, but they
provide audiences with some insight into what it might be like to emerge
from the veil as someone who has a different set of circumstances and a
different history than that which has informed their lives to date. While
documentaries are often done from a particular point of view, some incorporate multiple points of view by allowing those with different perspectives
to speak. This balancing of point of view with the need to hear "all sides
of the issue" continues to provoke internal debate in the documentary film
community. Many, but not all, documentarians argue that their films provide audiences with a point of view that has been overwhelmed by more
traditional news media, by cultural and social institutions that dismiss certain kinds of people or certain sorts of concerns, or by journalism that is
both episodic and shallow.

While many documentaries point out the places where injustice resides,
some provide audiences with insight on what a different sort of society might
look like. Philosopher Martha Nussbaum discusses justice through what she
calls the capabilities approach. This affirmative vision argues that justice and
inclusiveness are intrinsic values, made real by cooperation and altruism,
as well as economic cooperation. She argues that "language and imagery"
(Nussbaum, 2016, p. 413) allow individuals to reconceptualize their relationship to "the other." Her approach suggests things that people "might" do (not
just what they should avoid doing) and ways in which people might be encouraged to act. Nussbaum's thinking about justice provides a vision of what
a more just society might be like.

Born into Brothels, which won the Oscar for best documentary film in 2004, provided insights into the potential and possible futures for the children of sex workers in India. *Twenty Feet from Stardom* (2013) reminds every viewer that it's the backup singers who make the hits and that the women in this role have, through struggle, claimed both agency and choice for their artistic contributions. The 2018 documentary *Won't You Be My Neighbor* about Fred Rogers provided in-depth insights into why *Mr. Rogers' Neighborhood* positively influenced generations of viewers and their parents. All speak to capabilities and community through language and imagery—a way of operationalizing justice that documentary filmmakers and journalists can—and sometimes do—share with their readers, viewers, and listeners.

FAULT LINES AND SOCIAL JUSTICE

One useful tool for ensuring social justice is using Robert C. Maynard's concept of fault lines. Maynard originally conceived of five fault lines: race and ethnicity, class, gender and sexual orientation, geography, and generation (Maynard Institute, 2014). Viewers can see each of these fault lines play out in a variety of popular media. Race, for example, is prominent in movies both contemporary (*Get Out*, 2017; *Crazy Rich Asians*, 2018; *Parasite*, 2019) and classic (*In the Heat of the Night*, 1967), as well as television shows from *All in the Family* (1971–1979) to *The Wire* (2002–2008). Much of the critical acclaim of the original *Roseanne* television show (1988–1997) came from its unflinching portrayal of the struggles of a working-class family, while shows such as *Friends* (1994–2004) have been criticized for inaccurately depicting the well-to-do lifestyles of twentysomethings in often low-paying jobs who, in reality, would be hard-pressed to live comfortably in New York City. Class also has a long history in music. During the Vietnam War, bands such as the Rolling Stones ("Street Fighting Man") and Creedence Clearwater Revival ("Fortunate Son") sang about the poor fighting a rich man's war. The sentiment was expressed most clearly, however, in Black Sabbath's epic "War Pigs": "Politicians hide themselves away / They only started the war / Why should they go out to fight? / They leave that role to the poor." Class also has a long history in rap and hip-hop—think Jay-Z's "Hard Knock Life," Tupac Shakur's "Keep Ya Head Up," or Ice Cube's "It Was a Good Day" in which a "good day" is one where he did not have to shoot someone with an AK-47 assault rifle.

Subsequent scholars have expanded Maynard's fault lines list to include religion, disability, and political affiliation as potential fault lines, though this list is not meant to be exhaustive. Like the original fault lines, these additions are seen regularly in popular culture. For example, *Gentleman's Agreement* (1947)—one of only three films about journalism to win a Best Picture Oscar—centers on a magazine journalist who goes undercover to experience and document anti-Semitism and bigotry in New York and its ritzy Connecticut suburbs. More recently, films such as *Spotlight* (2015) and *Philomena* (2013) focus on abuses by the Catholic Church. In the latter, former BBC correspondent Martin Sixsmith begins reporting a human-interest story about an older woman, Philomena Lee, attempting to find the son she was forced to give up for adoption in the 1950s. Philomena had become pregnant out of wedlock and was sent to the local Irish convent. The story, however, turns into an investigative piece when Sixsmith discovers that nuns in the convent ran a years-long scheme to sell children to wealthy Americans.

Maynard argued that we, both as journalists and as society, cannot and should not pretend that differences do not exist. These fault lines should, and often do, extend to popular culture. The key is providing context and history through understanding and utilizing fault lines. For journalists, fault lines can better help them reflect the interests, decisions, and actions of sources in a different social group. They also can provide a way to identify missing cultural voices, as well as story angles and perspectives that could offer a way to reframe a story or add complexity.

GENDER AS A FAULT LINE

In popular culture, female journalists typically are not depicted as fully developed human beings. Instead, as Loren Ghiglione (1990) argues, "The contemporary newswoman, while regularly cast as a tough, talented pro, often bears the burden of being depicted as an emotionally empty Super Bitch or Super Whore" (p. 126). This concept of female journalists in popular culture falling on either end of a "Super Whore" and "Super Bitch" spectrum will be explored further here by focusing on two characters: Zoe Barnes in the first two seasons of *House of Cards* (2013–2014) and Miranda Priestly in *The Devil Wears Prada* (2006).

ZOE BARNES IS A "SUPER WHORE"

When first introduced to viewers in *House of Cards*, Zoe Barnes is a cub reporter for the *Washington Herald*. She is seen as a second-tier reporter, covering Fairfax County Council and angling for a meatier beat or an online column. That changes after she attends a gala at the National Center for the Performing Arts; there, while wearing a very short, very tight white dress, she's noticed—not for her reporting chops but instead for her curvaceous backside—by House Minority Whip Frank Underwood (Painter & Ferrucci, 2017). Later that night, she shows up unannounced at his house. He doesn't recognize her—again, she is a second-tier reporter, and he's a powerful member of Congress—but invites her in for a drink.

> UNDERWOOD: OK, so why are you here, Ms. Barnes? (Takes a drink.)
> BARNES: I need somebody I can talk to.
> UNDERWOOD: We're talking. Tell me what we're talking about.
> BARNES: I protect your identity. I print whatever you tell me, and I'll never ask any questions.

Underwood becomes Barnes's primary source after this encounter, and the level of flirting increases to the point that, by episode four, she invites Underwood to her apartment. Thus begins a sexual and professionally shady relationship that continues throughout most of the series' first season. As Underwood feeds Barnes information—sometimes truthful, sometimes fabricated, but always from a high-ranking source—her star rises at the *Herald*, and later at the *Politico*-like *Slugline*, because she is able to break a lot of terrific, although sometimes woefully inaccurate or fabricated, stories based on the information Underwood provides her (Painter & Ferrucci, 2017).

Throughout season one—really, until Underwood murders her in season two—Barnes is shown to be a stenographer, not a reporter. She publishes any information Underwood gives her, even if she questions its veracity or knows outright that the information is wrong. The professional relationship is symbiotic: Barnes gets her byline on big and important stories, and Underwood gets to set the political agenda through an uncritical press. These stories are important, with wide-ranging implications for the direction of the nation. Barnes effectively kills a liberal version of an education bill by writing about an early draft, ruins the nomination of potential secretary of state Michael Kern, and leaks the names of two potential vice presidential candidates. She also trumps up the nomination of a second secretary of state nominee, Katherine Durant, as well as Congressman Peter Russo's run for Pennsylvania governor, sparking the political careers of two of Underwood's allies. Barnes is rewarded for this lack of professionalism by *Herald* editor Tom Hammerschmidt, who offers her the White House correspondent job, as well as *Slugline* editor Carly Heath, who essentially tells Barnes that she will publish anything she writes without editing it first (Painter & Ferrucci, 2017).

Discussion Question

Social Justice is a branch of philosophy and political philosophy that connects individual acts to their societal consequences and the societal understanding to a range of possible individual actions. How do Zoe Barnes's individual acts intersect with other ethical concepts discussed in this book (choose one: truth telling, loyalty, public service, accountability, media economics)? What are the actual or potential societal consequences of her acts?

In season one, episode nine, Barnes directly compares herself to a prostitute. She attempts to end her sexual relationship with Underwood, although she wants to maintain her favored professional status. Underwood retaliates by cutting Barnes out of the insider loop, and after a couple of days of being frozen out of stories, she capitulates and restarts their sexual relationship.

> BARNES: So you need a whore? Which makes you a pimp.
> UNDERWOOD: I'm not a pimp. Just a very generous john.
> BARNES: Fine. As long as we're clear about what this is, I can play the whore. Now pay me.

Barnes shows here, and really throughout her time on the show, that she is willing to trade sexual favors for stories.

The creators of *House of Cards*, however, do not stop with one journalistic "whore." Janine Skorsky initially is depicted as a hard-line reporter, serving as a model hard-news journalist for much of season one. She often is shown reporting, taking bits of information and questioning those in power. She also is shown to be a positive mentor for Barnes, coaching her to become a better, more fearless reporter. Skorsky does have a positive influence on Barnes, who begins to do real journalistic work, tracking down sources and serving as a watchdog instead of Underwood's stenographer (Painter & Ferrucci, 2017). However, Skorsky eventually tells Barnes about her own unethical past when the two are in the *Slugline* office in episode nine:

> SKORSKY: We've all done it. I used to suck, jerk, and screw anything that moved just to get a story.
> BARNES: Really? Like who?
> SKORSKY: You want dish?
> BARNES: No, it's just . . .
> SKORSKY: The comm. director on Ben Schroeder's Senate race. A staffer in the Defense Department. My very own White House intern. He was a real blabbermouth when he wasn't eating me out.

BARNES: Wow.

SKORSKY: And I even had a fling with a Congressman.

BARNES: Which one?

SKORSKY: You tell me yours, and I'll tell you mine.

BARNES: I've never been with any.

SKORSKY: Oh, come on. You're hot. You're telling me that none of them have come on to you.

BARNES: I haven't really been in those circles.

SKORSKY: You are now.

BARNES: I guess I don't really give off that vibe.

SKORSKY: Oh, you mean the slut vibe? (Both laugh.) Look, I don't do that shit anymore because once word got out, it was like I hit a wall, and nobody took me seriously. So a piece of advice as far as career strategies go: it's not worth fucking your way to the middle.

Barnes, Underwood, and Power

Rawls's "veil of ignorance" is a way to ensure fairness by reducing or eliminating power imbalances. There certainly are major differences in relative power between Barnes and Underwood in *House of Cards.*

The most obvious is actual political power. When we first meet Underwood, he is the House majority whip, serving as the No. 2 ranking member of the congressional leadership. He later becomes vice president and finally president. Barnes, in contrast, is a cub reporter fighting for stories and space, though her star quickly rises after she begins her sexual and professional relationship with Underwood.

Underwood also is much older and more established. This difference becomes clear during a scene at Barnes's apartment in season one:

UNDERWOOD: Do your parents know you live like this?

BARNES: No. They haven't visited.

UNDERWOOD: Are you cared for?

ZOE: How do you mean?

UNDERWOOD: Do you have a man who cares for you? An older man?

ZOE: No.

UNDERWOOD: But you've been with older men before.

ZOE: Yes.

UNDERWOOD: Then you know they hurt you. (Zoe swallows hard.) And after they hurt you, they discard you.

This particular imbalance is even more pronounced in the British version of the series, where Mattie Storin (the Barnes character) literally and continually refers to Francis Urquhart (the Underwood character) as "Daddy."

Underwood also is physically more powerful than Barnes, which becomes evident during Barnes's final scene in season two, episode 14. Barnes meets Underwood at a subway station and confronts him about his possible involvement in the murder of U.S. Representative Peter Russo.

> BARNES: I'm trying to protect us both. These are questions anyone could ask.
> UNDERWOOD: But no one is except you. I can't imagine what you're after.
> BARNES: I took a chance. Showed up at your house and placed myself at your feet. Crossed ethical lines—professionally, physically—and I hold myself accountable for that. Those were my choices, and I can live with them. I'd like to move forward, but I need to know exactly what I was a part of. That I wasn't a part of someone's (pause) . . .
> UNDERWOOD: Finish your thought.
> BARNES: Part of someone's murder. (Subway train begins to enter the station.)
> UNDERWOOD: Jesus. (Starts to walk away.)
> BARNES: (chasing Frank) I want to believe you, Francis . . .

Underwood responds by grabbing Barnes and pushing her in front of an oncoming subway train. He then quickly walks away.

For Rawls (1971), justice as fairness would result in a fair agreement or bargain benefitting everyone, in particular the least advantaged members of society. Here, Underwood's inherent advantages of position, status, and strength would be negated. The fault lines are perpetuated. Barnes's star might not rise at the *Washington Herald* and *Slugline*; however, she also most likely would not be manipulated into helping Underwood wreck democracy, and she almost assuredly would not be murdered by Underwood once her tough questions meant that she was a threat instead of an asset to him.

Female Journalists Often Depicted as "Whores"

Barnes and Skorsky are far from the only female journalist "whores." Indeed, it's a stock character in film and television, and a female reporter seducing a source for a story, or having sex with her source or subject, is a tired narrative trope. Most audience members first encounter the reporter as love interest when they are children. In the *Superman* comic series (Action Comics No. 484, published in June 1978), *Daily Planet* reporter Lois Lane first marries Clark Kent. Then, after discovering that Kent is really Superman in disguise, she goes with the superhero to his Fortress of Solitude to renew their wedding vows in a Kryptonian ceremony.

Female journalists in movies as far-flung as *Trainwreck* (2015), *Top Five* (2014), *Crazy Heart* (2009), *Iron Man* (2008), *Three Kings* (1999), *Thank You for Smoking* (2005), *Scoop* (2006), *Absence of Malice* (1981), *Mr. Deeds*

(2002), *How to Lose a Guy in 10 Days* (2003), *Never Been Kissed* (1999), *The Hudsucker Proxy* (1994), and *Adaptation* (2002) have sex with or seduce their sources. Same with characters in television shows such as *Scandal* (2012–2018), *Parks and Recreation* (2009–2015), *Sharp Objects* (2018), and *Gilmore Girls* (2000–2007, 2016). Carrie Bradshaw has a series of flings in *Sex and the City* (1998–2004), though, to be fair, she is a sex and relationships columnist. When female journalists aren't sleeping with sources, they're having sex—or at least trying to have sex—with co-workers in movies such as *Anchorman* (2004), *Broadcast News* (1987), *Whiskey Tango Foxtrot* (2016), and *Nightcrawler* (2014).

The most egregious recent example is *Richard Jewell* (2019), the Clint Eastwood–directed film about the media frenzy surrounding a man wrongly accused of bombing the 1996 Atlanta Olympics. In the film, *Atlanta Journal-Constitution* reporter Kathy Scruggs exchanges sex with an FBI agent for a news tip that Jewell is under suspicion for the bombing. Scruggs, unlike Zoe Barnes and most of the other journalists above, was a real person. She did break the story that Jewell was the FBI's prime suspect; however, there is no evidence that she traded sex for information. Further, she cannot defend herself; Scruggs died in 2001. Kelly McBride, an ethicist at the Poynter Institute, said the *Richard Jewell* depiction is "condescending and insulting to my profession—and grossly inaccurate both in the specific instance of Kathy Scruggs, and in the broader instance of how women reporters do their jobs" (Humphries, 2019).

Miranda Priestly Is a "Super Bitch"

Miranda Priestly is the proverbial devil in *The Devil Wears Prada* (2006). Priestly is the editor-in-chief of the fictional *Runway* magazine, the premier women's fashion and lifestyle periodical. She's loosely based on Anna Wintour, the editor of *Vogue*, herself the subject of the 2009 documentary *The September Issue*. *The Devil Wears Prada* centers around Priestly's professional relationship with Andy Sachs, an aspiring "real" journalist who just graduated from Northwestern but is slumming as Priestly's co-assistant until she can find a job at a hard-news publication.

Priestly is condescending and at times cruel to Sachs. Take this exchange early in the film:

PRIESTLY: You have no sense of fashion.
SACHS: I think that depends on . . .
PRIESTLY: No, no. That wasn't a question.

Figure 7.2. Miranda Priestly from *The Devil Wears Prada*. Copyright 2006, 20th Century Fox

Sachs is reminded repeatedly that she has no sense of fashion. Priestly scolds Sachs when she laughs at a conversation between Priestly and some art assistants trying to choose between two similar belts that look nearly indistinguishable from each other.

PRIESTLY: Something funny?

SACHS: No, no, no. Nothing's . . . You know, it's just that both of those belts look exactly the same to me. You know, I'm still learning about all this stuff, and . . .

PRIESTLY: This . . . stuff? Oh, OK, I see. You think this has nothing to do with you. You go to your closet and you select . . . I don't know . . . that lumpy blue sweater, for instance, because you're trying to tell the world that you take yourself too seriously to care about what you put on your back. But what you don't know is that that sweater is not just blue. It's not turquoise. It's not lapis. It's actually cerulean. And you're also blithely unaware of the fact that in 2002, Oscar de la Renta did a collection of cerulean gowns. And then I think it was Yves Saint Laurent, wasn't it, who showed cerulean military jackets? I think we need a jacket here. And then cerulean quickly showed up in the collections of eight different designers. And then it, uh, filtered down through the department stores, and then trickled on down into some tragic Casual Corner where you, no doubt, fished it out of some clearance bin. However, that blue represents millions of dollars and countless jobs, and it's sort of comical how you think that you've made a choice that exempts you from the fashion industry when, in fact, you're wearing the sweater that was selected for you by the people in this room from a pile of stuff.

Having no sense of fashion is a no-no in the world of fashion journalism. So is being unattractive. Sachs, played by Anne Hathaway, repeatedly is ridiculed for being "fat" (she's a size 8) by Priestly and her underlings—Nigel

Kipling, the magazine's art director, and Emily Charlton, Priestly's other co-assistant. She also is told that she is not taking her job seriously enough, that she isn't trying hard enough, that she's unappreciative for the chance to work with Priestly, a job that "a million girls would kill for."

While a million girls would kill for Sachs's job, Priestly's unreasonable demands are killing her. For example, Priestly tasks Sachs with getting a copy of the upcoming but still unpublished *Harry Potter* manuscript for her children and later tells Sachs to find a plane to fly her home from Florida after all flights have been grounded because of a possible hurricane. When Sachs asks reasonable questions about her job—really the kind of questions that a competent assistant should ask—she is met by Priestly with more condescension:

PRIESTLY: I need 10 or 15 skirts from Calvin Klein.
SACHS: What kind of skirts?
PRIESTLY: Please bore someone else with your . . . questions.

Sachs transforms throughout the movie. With Kipling's help, she starts dressing more fashionably. She also slowly becomes a mini-version of Priestly. Her transformation distances her from her longtime boyfriend, and she edges out Charlton for a coveted spot on a trip to Paris Fashion Week. She also becomes almost unconditionally devoted to Priestly, which becomes evident during the Paris trip when Sachs learns that Jacqueline Follet has been tapped to replace Priestly at *Runway*. Sachs unsuccessfully tries to tell Priestly of the coup; however, Priestly announces during a speech at a luncheon that Follet is set to be the new creative director for James Holt (a position that Kipling told Sachs he had been offered and accepted). Later, Priestly tells Sachs that she knew about the plot to replace her, so she had to sacrifice Kipling's career aspirations in order to keep her job.

Sachs is repulsed, but Priestly reminds her that she did the same thing—pushing Charlton aside to further her own career ambitions. That's when Sachs realizes her choice: she can stay at *Runway* and continue to turn into a "devil" like Priestly, or she can leave. When we last see Sachs, she's working at a New York newspaper, where she originally wanted to work before being led astray to the "dark side" of fashion journalism.

Priestly is far from the only "Super Bitch" in popular culture. Really, any hard-changing female reporter, editor, or broadcaster has at least some elements of the "Super Bitch" in her. Veronica Corningstone tampers with the teleprompter to ridicule Ron Burgundy in *Anchorman* (2004), Amy Archer deceives the lovable but gullible Norville Barnes in order to get a scoop in *The Hudsucker Proxy* (1994), and Louise "Babe" Bennett does likewise with the "Cinderella Man" Longfellow Deeds in *Mr. Deeds Goes to Town* (1936). Hildy Johnson forgoes marriage and a "normal" life to hide a possible murderer and get an exclusive in *His Girl Friday* (1940). Diane Christiansen in *Network* (1976) and Alicia Clark in *The Paper* (1994) cynically put profits over public service journalism, ridiculing and arguing with those journalists—all men—who still believe in the power of good work. In Gus Van Sant's *To Die For* (1995), Suzanne Stone-Maretto seduces high school students in order to manipulate them into killing her husband, who she believes is standing in the way of her desire to become a world-famous broadcast journalist.

Impact of the "Super Whore" and "Super Bitch"

These depictions could be harmful to the broader field of journalism. As McBride says, "We know from broader cultural studies that entertainment has the ability to influence public opinion" (Humphries, 2019). One way that these depictions could hurt is by influencing young, aspiring female journalists and journalism students to enter a different field instead.

This, in turn, could lead to an underrepresentation of women in media, which could result in certain constituent groups being uncovered or miscovered. Further, female journalists are not monolithic; individual-level differences such as life experiences and values might influence news coverage and viewpoints (Len-Ríos, Hinnant, & Jeong, 2012; Meeks, 2013). Greater numbers of women in the newsroom, therefore, ensure greater diversity by allowing various women's perspectives to be represented while also better reflecting culturally diverse communities (Harp, Bachmann, & Loke, 2014).

Additionally, gender might influence editorial content, framing, and sources (Armstrong, 2004; Correa & Harp, 2011; Desmond & Danilewica, 2010; Grandy, 2014; Hardin & Shain, 2005; Liebler & Smith, 1997), as well as format and tone (Meeks, 2013). Women in leadership positions also might influence newsroom culture and structure (Everbach, 2006; Geertsema, 2009). Culturally defined sex roles cultivate distinct areas of gender ownership for certain issues (Elmore, 2009; Meeks, 2013; Van Zoonen, 1998). Journalism historically and presently is male-dominated (Beam & DeCicco, 2010), so "masculine" issues such as economics, security, and politics (Meeks, 2013) are favored over "feminine" issues such as children, women's health, workplace equality, education, poverty, family life, and social protest (Craft & Wanta, 2004; Everbach, 2006; Len-Ríos, Hinnant, & Jeong, 2012; Mills, 1997; Smith, 2015). Consequently, masculine news topics generally are worthy of front-page placement while feminine topics are published in less visible places (Chambers, Steiner, & Fleming, 2004; Van Zoonen, 1998).

8

Sell Me Ethics

Advocacy, Objectivity, and Strategic Communication

Central Concepts

- Advocacy as an ethical principle
- Advocacy vs. objectivity
- Depictions of strategic communicators almost always negative
- Evaluating ethical choices based on motivation

Strategic communicators rate highly on ethical tests when compared to other professionals. Public relations professionals—118 of them—outscored orthopedic surgeons, Navy enlisted men, and business professionals on a test of moral development called the Defining Issues Test (Coleman & Wilkins, 2009). They also ranked only 0.1 percent below nurses, who ranked sixth overall. According to this study, these public relations professionals are good ethical thinkers; the single biggest predictor of a good score on the DIT is education, and public relations professionals as a group have less formal education than most of the professions with scores "above" them, meaning that these findings are significant. They also performed significantly better when the ethical dilemmas were about public relations issues than when they were not, indicating domain expertise on ethical issues.

These findings are fairly consistently and have been replicated for advertising executives (Castleberry, French, & Carlin, 1993; Schauster, Ferrucci, Tandoc, & Walker, 2020) and public relations executives (Lieber, 2008; Plaisance, 2015). Cunningham (2005) did find that advertising professionals demonstrated considerably lower ethical reasoning scores than most other tested professions, and adults in general. Advertisers' scores, though, mostly aligned with those of other business professionals. The group did score lower on ethical reasoning when presented with advertising-specific dilemmas, suspending moral judgment to instead focus on the financial implications of a decision for themselves and their clients.

The results are mixed, but mostly positive. They are not consistent, however, with the depiction of strategic communicators in popular culture. These portrayals—from protagonists such as *Mad Men*'s Don Draper, *Thank You for Smoking*'s Nick Naylor, and *Our Brand Is Crisis*'s "Calamity" Jane Bodine, to lesser roles in *The Wire* and *Parks and Recreation*—are almost uniformly negative. So, if strategic communicators score higher than many other fields in ethical measures such as the Defining Issues Test, then why are they often seen as scoundrels in popular culture? There are two primary reasons. First, there is a general lack of strategic communicators depicted in popular culture overall, so, unlike their journalist counterparts, negative portrayals of strategic communicators are not counterbalanced by heroic depictions. Second, advocacy as an ethical principal connotes negatively, at least when compared to other ethical principles such as truth telling or loyalty. Both of these ideas will be explored in more depth toward the end of this chapter. But first, let's meet the strategic communicators featured in popular culture.

THE DEVILISH AD MAN

Don Draper is a bad man.

Draper, the central character in *Mad Men* (2007–2015), is a criminal. He actually started life as Dick Whitman but changed his name during the Korean War. Whitman enlisted in the Army in order to escape a pretty bad life in Illinois only to discover that he is stationed to help build a field hospital under the command of Lieutenant Don Draper. Whitman and Draper are alone; everyone else reporting to Draper has been killed, captured, or has deserted. During an artillery attack, Whitman accidently causes an explosion that kills his commanding officer, Don Draper. Scared and wanting to get out of the war without having to go back to his old life, a wounded Whitman switches dog tags with the deceased Draper. In one act, Whitman has committed two crimes. First, he committed identity theft; Whitman symbolically dies while Draper is awarded a Purple Heart. Second, Whitman deserted the Army during wartime. Both crimes—and Whitman-turned-Draper's attempts to keep them hidden—become a major part of his life and actions. Viewers do not know this information when they first meet Draper; instead, it is slowly revealed throughout the duration of the series.

Figure 8.1. Don Draper (standing) from *Mad Men*. Copyright 2007, Lionsgate Television

Draper is unfaithful to his family. First, Draper, or Whitman, faked his death, which, of course, led his immediate family to believe Whitman was dead. His half-brother, Adam, eventually tracks down Draper in New York. Draper, however, coldly rejects Adam, telling him that he needs to leave his past life in the past. Adam is despondent and ultimately commits suicide. Draper's rejection of Adam at least is quick. His rejection of his wife, Betty, is constant but prolonged. Throughout the first two seasons of *Mad Men*, Draper has a string of adulterous flings and affairs with a bohemian artist, the heiress of an upscale department store, the wife and manager of a comedian who pitches a product for one of Draper's clients, and his elementary-age daughter's schoolteacher.

Draper has mental health issues. He is depicted as a raging alcoholic who routinely blacks out and drives drunk. He even makes pitches to prospective clients while drunk at least twice. Following the second incident, a disastrous pitch to Hershey Chocolate, Draper is fired—or, in the parlance of advertising agencies, forced to take a "leave of absence"—by the firm that he helped create. Part of the alcoholism stems from Draper's apparent post-traumatic stress disorder. He certainly was affected by his experiences in the Korean War, especially being badly injured and watching his commanding officer—and, really, the only other soldier he regularly had contact with in the war zone—die because of a mistake that Draper (then Whitman) made. Whitman also had a traumatic childhood. He is the son of Archie Whitman, an abusive alcoholic, and an unnamed prostitute who died in childbirth. A 10-year-old Dick Whitman watched while his drunk father was accidentally kicked to death by a spooked horse. From there, he initially is raised by Archie's wife, Abigail, and then by his Uncle Mac, who ran a brothel where Dick is raised after leaving the family's Illinois farm. At the brothel, he is placed under the care of a prostitute named Aimée, who molests the young Dick. In summary, Dick Whitman lived a traumatic life before assuming the identity of Don Draper, and his alcohol abuse is one way he attempts to cope with his past.

Don Draper is a bad man. He is an unfaithful, alcoholic criminal.

However, he is a great ad man. This contradiction focuses on one of the key ethical questions that haunts strategic communication: when—if ever—does acting for personal gain include promoting a larger, less personal good?

Discussion Question

We state, "Advocacy here, though, does not mean simply serving the needs of a particular client and that client's desires; instead, the advocate also has moral duties to self and others connected to the functions they perform, as well as particular communities and the greater society." What moral duties does Don Draper have to himself, to others in his advertising firm, to the larger advertising profession, and to the greater society?

The character Don Draper is partially inspired by Draper Daniels, a 1950s advertising executive who worked on the "Marlboro Man" campaign while serving as the creative director at the Leo Burnett advertising agency. Burnett was one of the real "Mad Men" credited with spearheading the 1960s creative revolution in advertising. Burnett and his team often focused on sentimental ads appealing to Midwestern values. Burnett created many iconic advertising characters such as Ronald McDonald, Tony the Tiger for Frosted Flakes, Mr. Clean, the Keebler Elves, the Pillsbury Doughboy, and, as mentioned, the Marlboro Man. The other major real-life "Mad Men" were Bill Bernbach, who focused on developing "image" for products by emphasizing creativity over formulaic advertising, and David Ogilvy, who coined the phrase "If it doesn't sell, it isn't creative." Ogilvy, who also served as inspiration for Draper, used market research to drive advertising, stressed the benefits of the products, and valued sales results.

Throughout the series' seven-season run, Draper repeatedly is shown to be one of the best, most creative advertising men in the business. Probably the most iconic pitch occurred in the first season episode "The Wheel" when he relies heavily on nostalgia and the bittersweet longing to remember and recapture family memories for an advertising campaign for Kodak's latest product, the "Carousel." Draper begins, "This device isn't a spaceship; it's a time machine. It takes us to a place where we ache to go again . . . to a place where we know we are loved." All the while, he switches to pictures from his personal family album. First, there is a picture of his daughter, Sally, sitting on Don's shoulders. Next is a picture of his wife, Betty, holding Sally as a newborn baby. Finally, there is a picture of Don carrying his then new bride over the threshold. One of Don's colleagues, Harry, rushes out of the room crying. It's difficult for the intended audience, the Kodak executives, not to follow his lead. The pitch is moving, and the resulting ad is literally award-winning; Draper wins a Clio Award for the campaign. Traditional ethical theory does not include creativity as the virtuous equivalent of wisdom or courage, but English philosopher G. E. Moore argued that we intuitively link creativity in the arts to a kind of excellence that includes a concept of "the good."

One of Draper's greatest advertising triumphs, however, is not an ad itself—it's changing the narrative after a disaster. Lucky Strike cigarettes is, by far, his firm's biggest client. When the tobacco company fires the firm in season four, the partners know that they need new business in order to not be seen as dead or decaying. Draper makes a pitch to Philip Morris, another big tobacco manufacturer, for a brand of women's cigarettes. However, they later learn that Philip Morris was simply using them in order to get a better price from their current advertising agency. In response, Draper writes a letter that runs as a fictional full-page ad in the *New York Times*:

> Recently, my advertising agency ended a long relationship with Lucky Strike cigarettes, and I'm relieved.
>
> For over 25 years, we devoted ourselves to peddling a product for which good work is irrelevant, because people can't stop themselves from buying it. A product that never improves, that causes illness, and makes people unhappy. But there was money in it. A lot of money. In fact, our entire business depended on it. We knew it wasn't good for us, but we couldn't stop.
>
> And then, when Lucky Strike moved their business elsewhere, I realized, here was my chance to be someone who could sleep at night, because I know what I'm selling doesn't kill my customers.
>
> So as of today, Sterling Cooper Draper Pryce will no longer take tobacco accounts. We know it's going to be hard. If you're interested in cigarette work, here's a list of agencies that do it well: BBDO, Leo Burnett, McCann Erickson, Cutler Gleason & Chaough, and Benton & Bowles.
>
> As for us, we welcome all other business because we're certain that our best work is still ahead of us.

Draper didn't really give up cigarettes. He remains an avid smoker, and his wife, Betty, later dies of lung cancer as a result of her longtime cigarette habit. Draper, however, needed the story to be about something other than Lucky Strike ending its relationship with his advertising firm. His explanation: "If you don't like what's being said, change the conversation."

And if you cannot change the conversation, then run away. Draper runs multiple times, the final time culminating in his greatest triumph. The series finale ends with Draper in a hippie colony in November 1970. His life is crashing. He's traveling West after being fired, and he then learns from his daughter that his ex-wife, Betty, the mother of his children, is dying of lung cancer and is planning for the children to live with her brother and sister-in-law instead of Don. He eventually reaches California and reunites with Stephanie Draper, the niece of the widow of the real Don Draper (who is also, technically, Whitman-turned-Draper's first wife), whose identity Don stole, and she convinces him to join her at a spiritual retreat. While there, he calls Peggy Olsen, his associate and longtime friend and confidant, and confesses stealing another man's identity, as well as breaking his familial and professional vows. The show ends with Draper, on the verge of a mental breakdown, still at the retreat: the camera stops on a frontal shot of Draper meditating, and then a smile comes to his face. The show then cuts to its final scene, the iconic Coca-Cola "Hilltop" commercial, implying that Draper envisioned and created it. In the ad, a multicultural and multiethnic group of young men and women sing about how they would like to "teach the world to sing in perfect harmony" and, most importantly for the brand, "buy the world a Coke."

The real-life commercial was conceived by Bill Backer, an ad man for McCann-Erickson, in January 1971 after heavy London fog forced his plane to land in Shannon, Ireland. The next morning, Backer saw many of his fellow passengers at the airport café laughing, talking, and drinking bottles of Coke. That's when he envisioned the idea for the ad campaign:

> In that moment [I] a saw a bottle of Coke in a whole new light. . . . [I] began to see a bottle of Coca-Cola as more than a drink that refreshed a hundred million people a day in almost every corner of the globe. So [I] began to see the familiar words, "Let's have a Coke," as more than an invitation to pause for refreshment. They were actually a subtle way of saying "Let's keep each other company for a while." And [I] knew they were being said all over the world as [I] sat there in Ireland. So that was the basic idea: to see Coke not as it was originally designed to be—a liquid refresher—but as a tiny bit of commonality between all peoples, a universally liked formula that would help to keep them company for a few minutes. (Hartmann, 2015)

The ad became such a tremendous hit that the song "I'd Like to Teach the World to Sing (In Perfect Harmony)" eventually topped the Top-40 charts in both the United States and United Kingdom. Backer had reached the advertiser's mountaintop—or, more precisely, hilltop: the song led to millions of dollars of free advertising because every time it was played on the radio in essence became a free ad for Coke.

While the ad is full of sweetness and light, there also is an undercurrent of cynicism. The ultimate message is centered on peace, community, and harmony—but that is all in the name of selling a product, specifically Coke. Of course, tapping into the cultural zeitgeist is a key component of advertising, so co-opting the peace and love vibes of the last days of the 1960s hippie movement is, if not natural, then par for the course for advertisers. As Joe Strummer sang in the Clash song "(White Man) In Hammersmith Palais": "You think it's funny, turning rebellion into money."

Pepsi, in a divisive 2017 commercial featuring Kendall Jenner, attempted to emulate Coke's "Hilltop" ad for a new generation. The commercial "depicted Jenner drinking a Pepsi and walking through a group of diverse, protesting marchers. Eventually, Jenner notices a large group of protesters being watched intently by some police officers. She then pulls off a wig and struts toward one of the officers, hands him a Pepsi, and the protestors cheer wildly" (Ferrucci & Schauster, 2020, p. 1). After controversy surrounding the commercial ensued, actors within and outside the advertising industry argued that the ad violated ethical strategic communication boundaries by co-opting a social issue, acting as a form of cultural appropriation, and serving as an example of brand activism gone awry (Ferrucci & Schauster, 2020). Several brands, both commercial (Aunt Jemima, Land O' Lakes) and artistic (Dixie Chicks—now the Chicks, Lady Antebellum—now Lady A), faced similar reckonings in 2020 from consumer backlash over racist or racially charged words or images, especially after renewed Black Lives Matter protests prompted by the police killings of George Floyd and Breonna Taylor.

CIGARETTES AND ELECTIONEERING

While Draper is the protagonist in *Mad Men*, he often is portrayed negatively. He is not alone. Most popular culture depictions of advertising and public relations practitioners are negative.

Nick Naylor, the chief protagonist in *Thank You for Smoking* (2005), describes himself as having "moral flexibility." Others describe him in harsher terms. During an interview with Heather Holloway, a reporter for *The Washington Probe* writing a profile on Naylor, she says that her other sources have "pinned you as a mass murderer, bloodsucker, pimp, profiteer, child killer, and my personal favorite, yuppie Mephistopheles."

Naylor is the spokesman for the Academy of Tobacco Studies, a pseudo-research firm funded by Big Tobacco to deny and obfuscate a link between smoking and lung cancer and heart disease. Of course, Naylor, like everyone else at Big Tobacco, knows that such a link exists. As Naylor says while introducing himself to viewers at the beginning of the movie: "I make a living fronting an organization that kills 1,200 human beings a day." He knows that he is on the wrong side of history, so why does he do it? There are times when Naylor tries to fool himself: "Why do I do what I do? Defending the defenseless. Protecting the disenfranchised corporations that have been abandoned by their very own consumers. The logger. The sweatshop foreman. The oil driller. The landmine developer. The baby seal poacher." Other times, however, he is more honest with himself, albeit with a hint of sarcasm. Why does Naylor defend the deplorables? "To pay the mortgage," he jokes throughout the film.

Figure 8.2. Polly Bailey, Bobby Jay Bliss, and Nick Naylor (left to right) from *Thank You for Smoking*. Copyright 2005, Room 9 Entertainment

Naylor is part of the self-labeled M.O.D. Squad, or "Merchants of Death" Squad, with the chief lobbyists for the alcohol (Polly Bailey) and firearm (Bobby Jay Bliss) industries. The lunchtime group later is joined by spokespeople for the oil, fast food, and pharmaceutical industries. The Merchants of Death are much like the Merchants of Doubt in the Naomi Oreskes and Erik M. Conway book (2010) of the same name. In that book, they argue that a group of politically conservative scientists have "played a disproportionate role in debates about controversial questions" surrounding global warming, tobacco use, acid rain, DDT, and the hole in the ozone layer. These scientists—like the fictional Naylor, Bailey, and Bliss—influenced public opinion and policy-making by spreading doubt and confusion after a scientific consensus had been reached. Here, Naylor is not trying to argue that cigarettes do not cause cancer. That is a losing argument. Instead, he argues—often based on shady science funded by Big Tobacco—that scientists cannot agree about whether cigarettes cause cancer.

Throughout the film, Naylor is shown to be exceptionally good at his job. With his help, the bad guys win again and again. Early in the film, Big Tobacco is facing a crisis. Sales are down. His boss, B. R., yells at a roomful of tobacco advertising and public relations executives that they are not effectively doing their jobs: "We sell cigarettes. And they're cool, and available, and addictive. The job is almost done for us." The job, however, has gotten tougher. Cigarette smokers are not instantly seen as being cool. Naylor, however, has a solution: work with Hollywood executives to get cigarette placement in upcoming movies. Naylor is successful. For a fee, producer Jeff Megall will write a post-coital cigarette scene into a space movie within the movie starring Brad Pitt and Catherine Zeta-Jones.

Naylor, however, has a second job to do in Los Angeles. He's tasked to deliver bribe money to Lorne Lutch, the original "Marlboro Man," who is now dying of cancer and speaking out about the dangers of cigarettes. While Lutch and the movie meeting are pure fiction, five "Marlboro Men" died of lung cancer or other cigarette-related causes. Two "Marlboro Men" later became anti-smoking advocates. Wayne McLaren spoke out for anti-smoking legislation, and Eric Lawson appeared in an American Cancer Society public service announcement that parodied the "Marlboro Man" ad. In the film, Lutch initially is loath to see Naylor; in fact, he threatens to shoot Naylor as soon as he steps out of his car on Lutch's ranch. However, Naylor talks his way into the man's living room—and then talks him into taking the bribe.

Throughout the movie, Naylor battles Senator Ortolan Finistirre, who is promoting a bill to add a skull-and-crossbones poison warning to cigarette packaging, which already happens in places such as Australia and the European Union. During a Senate hearing, Naylor admits to the dangers of smoking. Naylor, though, holds true to one of his guiding principles: "If you argue correctly, you're never wrong." He argues against the packaging on three counts. First, he says that additional packaging is unnecessary because public awareness of the dangers of cigarettes already is high. Second, he emphasizes consumer choice and responsibility. Finally, he says that if tobacco companies are guilty of tobacco-related deaths, then states such as Finistirre's home state of Vermont should be responsible for high rates of obesity and heart disease caused by the high cholesterol in cheese. Naylor's argument is an example of a "red herring," a logical fallacy meant to confuse and distract by pointing to a piece of information that initially seems relevant but is actually off topic.

While Naylor is great at his job, he does screw up in his personal life—sometimes to the detriment of his job. He begins a sexual relationship with reporter Heather Holloway after their interview, and he spills secrets about tobacco, alcohol, and firearms lobbying. B. R. fires him, saying that his job "relied on your ability to keep secrets and spin the truth." B. R. later congratulates Naylor for his Senate speech attacking Finistirre and offers him his old job, but Naylor decides to start his own firm instead. His first client: cell phone manufacturers. In the final scene, Naylor is shown coaching his new clients on how to sow doubt: "Gentlemen, practice these words in front of a mirror. Although we are constantly exploring the subject, currently, there is no direct evidence that links cell phone usage to brain cancer."

In *Our Brand Is Crisis* (2015), "Calamity" Jane Bodine is a political strategist with "no kids, no family, no life" who comes out of self-imposed retirement to run a Bolivian presidential campaign. She's pitted against a longtime rival, Pat Candy; both are among the best in the business, though neither speaks Spanish or seemingly cares about the election. For both, it's initially about money and later about winning by destroying the other one.

Like Draper in *Mad Men*, Calamity Jane is all about the narrative. Early in the film, there is an incident where her candidate, Pedro Castillo, punches a man who jumped a security barricade and broke an egg on his face. The incident was a setup by Pat Candy to provoke a negative response from Castillo, whose team wants to craft an apology before Jane tells them that it's the wrong move. Echoing Draper, she says, "You don't change the man to fit the narrative. You change the narrative to fit the man." The new narrative is that Castillo is a tough guy who won't back down from Bolivia's problems. People are motivated by fear, Jane says, so Castillo's campaign strategy should be to convince people that Bolivia is in the midst of a social and economic crisis, at a crossroads, and that the only man who can lead them is a fighter such as Castillo. "This is no longer an election," Jane says. "This is a crisis. And our brand, what we are selling, is crisis."

Thereafter, Calamity Jane repeatedly refers to the campaign as a war, quoting Sun Tzu and calling the opponent the enemy. She has a ready-made stash of dirty tricks, including circulating a picture of Castillo's political opponent standing next to a man in a Nazi uniform. She also has a ready-made rationalization to explain away all of her bad deeds, which she expresses in a shouting match with Castillo during debate prep: "I am a good person, but the ends justify the means, and the nasty, terrible things that I have done, I've done for people like you. So now you owe me. I am this close to winning this thing, and I'm not going to stand here and watch you ruin it." The "ends justify the means" quote is typically—and inaccurately—attributed to Machiavelli. In *Discourses*, Machiavelli tried to articulate the implications of overthrowing a tyrant: "For although the act condemns the doer, the end may justify him" (I, 9). More so than many political theorists, Machiavelli was concerned with how citizens or political leaders might displace or even depose tyrants. This question is complex and layered, one many political theorists writing within 300 years of Machiavelli's work either sought to avoid or left to the actions of a deity (Augustine) or the inchoate exercise of the general will (Rousseau). The sentiment certainly fits the experience-informed understanding that morally bad actions sometimes are needed to ensure morally good outcomes. Just war theory emerges from this thorny question. Calamity Jane might believe that her actions are for the greater good, that Castillo would make a better president for Bolivia. However, it's just as likely that she only wants to win—she does say, "*I* am this close to winning"—and is searching for a way to justify her bad actions.

Ultimately, Calamity Jane knows that her actions are unethical. She has a moment of clarity while giving a television interview after the election: "Is it soul stealing? Yeah, it's soul stealing. It's advertising. You convince people of something they don't need, and then you give it to them, and then you profit from it. You know, we want the money and the power. We want to grab that brass ring." Ultimately, the film leaves Jane where it began—in self-imposed exile. She becomes a repentant sinner, leaving political campaigns to become the outreach coordinator for the Latin American Solidarity Network, a place where she believes she can actually make a difference in the lives of young Bolivians.

Other campaign managers are just as self-serving, willing to do almost anything to get the desired win. In *The Wire*, City Councilman Tommy Carcetti hires his friend and former lover Theresa D'Agostino when he decides to run as the "Great White Hope" mayor in predominantly Black Baltimore. D'Agostino and Carcetti devise a plan to encourage another councilman, Anthony Gray, to also run in an attempt to split the Black vote between Gray and incumbent Clarence Royce. Drafting Gray is underhanded—Carcetti doesn't initial tell Gray that he also is planning to run for mayor, and the tactic basically destroys both their friendship and working relationship. For Carcetti and D'Agnostino, however, the ends justify the means; the most important thing for both is to win, and any tactic that ensures that outcome is OK. *The Wire* is a drama, but campaign managers also are played for laughs in shows such as *Parks and Recreation*. When Leslie Knope runs for Pawnee City Council, her opponent, Bobby Newport, the unqualified and just plain stupid son of a local candy tycoon, hires Jennifer Barkley, a political whiz from Washington, to run his campaign. Barkley embarks on a series of surprises—having Newport announce that his father will move his factory to Mexico if Knope is elected, sabotaging Knope's campaign by paying companies not to rent needed campaign supplies to her, and capitalizing on the death of Newport's father to make Knope look cold and heartless. Like D'Agnostino, Barkley doesn't really care about the election or who is best qualified to lead the city. Instead, she only cares about winning.

ADVOCACY AS AN ETHICAL PRINCIPLE

Advocacy is a core ethical value in strategic communication. Indeed, the first tenet in the Public Relations Society of America Code of Ethics states that its members "serve the public interest by acting as responsible advocates for those we represent. We provide a voice in the marketplace of ideas, facts, and viewpoints to aid informed public debate." As such, public relations practitioners are just one of several fields and professions—including marketing, advertising, sales, law, and politics—that engage in advocacy and persuasion and share core ethical issues and considerations (Baker, 2009). Advocacy here, though, does not mean simply serving the needs of a particular client and that client's desires. Instead, the advocate also has moral duties to self and others connected to the functions they perform, as well as particular communities and the greater society (Baker, 2009). Those communities, or constituent groups, include the public, the advertisers, the media, and the agencies themselves, according to the American Association of Advertising Agencies code of ethics.

Sherry Baker (1999) lays out a "five baselines" framework that "allows conceptual clarity both about differing motivations that underlie action in professional persuasive communication and differing rounds or baselines which action is justified." Each successive baseline represents higher moral ground than the one before it:

1. Raw Self-Interest: assumes legitimacy in pure self-interested egoism, even to the detriment of others; advocates may use society for their own benefit even if it damages the social order.
2. Entitlement Model: Position that (a) all clients, legal products, and causes are entitled to professional assistance and representation, (b) professional persuaders have a right to advocate for legal products and causes even if they are harmful, (c) that "let the buyer beware" is a morally acceptable position.

3. Enlightened Self-Interest: Businesses do well financially by doing good ethically, so it is in their bottom-line interest to behave ethically.
4. Social Responsibility: Assumes people in society are interdependent, so the focus of one's actions and moral reasoning should be on responsibilities to others within one's community.
5. Kingdom of Ends follows Kant's principle of humanity to treat others "never merely as an end, but always at the same time as an end."

Advocacy, therefore, does not run counter to ethical principles and values, especially in Baker's fourth and fifth baselines. However, advocacy—and by extension advocates such as strategic communicators—are still often seen as less ethical than those pursuing "high" ideals such as the truth or performing the role of providing news and information in order for citizens to make informed decisions. One reason is that advocacy runs counter to the ideal—or at least the popular conception of the ideal—of the concept of objectivity.

A second, and equally important, issue is that the number of strategic communicators seen on the big and small screen is relatively small. Indeed, strategic communicators vastly outnumber their journalistic counterparts in the real world, but those numbers are reversed in the fictional realm of popular culture.

LACK OF PORTRAYALS

The rise of public relations as a field in the 20th century mirrors the rise of film and television as popular mediums. As discussed previously, public relations and advertising practitioners have been the subject of a number of movies and television shows; however, there is a popular fascination with journalism that is absent from strategic communication even though practitioners of the latter are more numerous, better paid, and live lifestyles that are probably just as glamorous, if not more so (McNair, 2010). In this sense, popular culture reflects another of the embedded problems with strategic communication—equality of access. If the only voices who can afford to have their messages in the marketplace promote a single point of view, then advocacy itself paints an unrealistic picture of reality and of the range of options open to individuals.

As can be seen with the depictions of Don Draper in *Mad Men*, Nick Naylor in *Thank You for Smoking*, and "Calamity" Jane Bodine and Pat Candy in *Our Brand Is Crisis*, strategic communicators are rarely portrayed as heroes. There also are plenty of negative portrayals of journalists in popular culture. However, these villains are countered by an equal or, probably, greater number of heroes.

Discussion Question

What positive portrayals of strategic communicators (advertising, public relations, marketing) have you seen in popular culture? What made those portrayals positive?

Negative depictions of strategic communicators, however, are not readily countered by the strategic communicator hero. A similar dearth of depth spawned Hari Kondabolu's 2017 documentary *The Problem with Apu*. In that film, Kondabolu explores *The Simpsons* character Apu Nahasapeemapetilon, a thickly accented Indian immigrant who owns and runs the Kwik-E-Mart convenience store in the Simpsons' fictional Springfield hometown. When the character first appeared in 1990, he was the only South Asian character to regularly appear on mainstream U.S. television (Itzkoff, 2020). Apu also was voiced by Hank Azaria, leading Kondabolu in his documentary to call the character "a white guy doing an impression of a white guy making fun of my father." *The Problem with Apu* explores negative and sometimes racist stereotypes, racial microaggressions, and racist slurs and bullying against people of Indian and South Asian heritage as a result of the *Simpsons* character. In January 2020, Azaria announced that he would no longer voice Apu, although it was unclear if the character would remain on the show.

The problem with strategic communicator depictions such as Draper, Naylor, and Calamity Jane, much like the problem with Apu, is not that these depictions are negative. Instead, the problem is that negative or problematic depictions are the *only* depictions of strategic communicators that audiences see. Again, there are a lot of newspaper and broadcast scoundrels on the big and little screen. Those, however, are counterbalanced by the vast number of heroes who engage in witnessing injustice, holding powerful people and institutions accountable, and defending freedom (McNair, 2010). In some ways, popular culture portrayals of journalists are more realistic and multidimensional—more objective—than the popular culture portrayals of strategic communication professionals. That lack of objectivity has both fictional and real-world consequences.

OBJECTIVITY AS AN ETHICAL CONSTRUCT

The concept of objectivity is ingrained, both by professionals and by the public at large. As David Mindich writes: "If American journalism were a religion, as it has been called from time to time, its supreme deity would be 'objectivity.' The high priests of journalism worship 'objectivity'; one leading editor called it the 'highest original moral concept ever developed in America and given to the world'" (2000, p. 1). But just what is objectivity? How is it defined? How is it used? The first problem with any study focusing on objectivity is how to define the concept. That has proven to be a bit tricky.

In *News Reporting and Writing*, one of the more highly used handbooks in journalism education, objectivity is defined as "the rules that mainstream journalists follow in attempting to arrive at the best obtainable version of the truth" (Brooks, Kennedy, Moen, & Ranly, 2005, p. 14). In this sense, objectivity can mean that "a person's statements about the world can be trusted if they are submitted to established rules deemed legitimate by a professional community. Facts here are not aspects of the world, but consensually validated statements about it" (Schudson, 1978, p. 7).

To that end, objectivity could be considered the journalistic equivalent of the scientific method (Brooks et al., 2005). "Objective" methods include relying on observable facts and using transparent techniques to pursue the truth. However, observable facts and transparent techniques are an incomplete version of the scientific method: "In science, transparency means that the researcher explains his objectives, his methods, his findings and his limitations. In journalism, only part of that methodology is usually followed" (Brooks et al., 2005, p. 15).

Stephen J. A. Ward calls the concept of objectivity "based on absolute standards or facts, as ascertained by neutral, perspective-less agents" outdated and unrealistic (2004, p. 261). Instead, he argues for pragmatic objectivity, which places the emphasis on process because while "objective truth is a worthy goal, there are many occasions when we are not sure of having reached it" (Ward, 2004, p. 264). For Ward, journalistic objectivity must "talk about imperfect procedures and about standards that *point* in the direction of truth" (2004, p. 264). Ward's concept is related to but distinct from realism, or the idea that the path to truth would come from reporters digging out facts and ordering them together. The ideal of realism coincided with news organizations emphasizing accuracy, the invention of the inverted pyramid, and the death of the partisan press era; it was at that time that the public began to believe in the necessity of a press that was "fair, accurate, balanced, dispassionate, uninvolved, unbiased, and unprejudiced" (Dicken-Garcia, 2005, p. 94).

A third conceptualization of objectivity is the "belief that one can and should separate facts from values" and opinions (Schudson, 1978, p. 5). This concept of objectivity has its roots in the Enlightenment. In ethical traditions, "an objective thinker was an impartial judge who adopted a 'common view' when considering the rightness or wrongness of an action" (Ward, 2004, p. 70). Enlightenment thinkers discussed objectivity through "epistemological quarrels over how the mind could know nature" or how ideas could represent objects (Ward, 2004, p. 74). This idea of objectivity later was expressed through the ideas of Karl Popper, who wrote about two types of knowledge or thought. The first is *"knowledge or thought in an objective sense,* consisting of problems, theories, and arguments as such. Knowledge in this objective sense is totally independent of anybody's claim to know; it is also independent of anybody's belief, or disposition to assent; or to assert, or to act. Knowledge in the objective sense is *knowledge without a knower*: it is *knowledge without a knowing subject"* (1979, p. 108–109). For example, a book is more than just ink on paper regardless of whether it is ever read or understood. Instead, a book contains objective knowledge regardless of any other factor. This is different than knowledge in a subjective sense, or knowledge "consisting of a state of mind or consciousness or a disposition to behave or react" (Popper, 1979, p. 108). This type of knowledge would include the ideas in a book once that book is opened, read, thought about, and possibly discussed.

The Enlightenment view of truth also was compatible with democracy and its emphasis on rational government. People who could reason together could arrive at some shared "truth" of how they could govern themselves. Information was essential to government, for it allowed citizens to scrutinize government. As long as truth was ascertainable, government could function. Citizens and government needed information in order to continue their rational function. Information, and the notion that it corresponded in some essential way with the truth, carried enormous promise.

This version of objectivity became the professional standard in the early 1900s. Media organizations shifting from a partisan to a commercial press needed large audiences and the subsequent advertising dollars they could command; consequently, alienating a large swath of the public for partisan political ends was not a financially viable journalistic strategy. Journalists view objectivity as refusing to allow individual bias to influence what they report or how they cover it. It is in journalism that all facts and people are regarded as equal and equally worthy of coverage. Culture, an individual sense of mission, and individual and organizational feelings and views do not belong in objective news accounts. An Enlightenment view of truth allowed objectivity to be considered an attainable ideal, and objectivity often was linked to the end result of reporting and editing: the individual news story or media outlet.

All of these conceptualizations of objectivity are different from the popular misconception that an "objective" journalist is one who is fair, balanced, and free of bias. There are major drawbacks to this definition of objectivity. Glasser (1992) offers three ways that a strict adherence to objectivity could bias news coverage. The first is that "objective reporting is biased against what the press typically defines as its role in a democracy—that of a Fourth

Estate, the watchdog role, an adversary press" (Glasser, 1992, p. 176). Objectivity makes the press biased against its watchdog role because it forces reporters and editors to rely on official sources, which propagates the status quo by leading journalists to rely on established power holders as primary sources of news and comment. The second is that "objective reporting is biased against independent thinking; it emasculates the intellect by treating it as a disinterested spectator" (Glasser, 1992, p. 176). In strict adherence to objectivity, journalists are forced to remain impartial and neutral, which means that they should just report the "facts" as they are told instead of interpreting events through a critical lens. The third is that "objective reporting is biased against the very idea of responsibility; the day's news is viewed as something journalists are compelled to report, not something they are responsible for creating" (Glasser, 1992, p. 176). In this ideology, news exists as something for a journalist to gather "out there." A journalist has completed the job if he or she reports that a fact claim has been made; he or she can report such a claim "without moral impunity—even if he or she knows the content of the claim to be false" (Glasser, 1992, p. 176).

The problem with ideology—Glasser and other scholars use this word deliberately—is that it seldom neatly fits multiple, daily experiences. Most definitions of objectivity suggest that elements of human society such as culture should not determine what is reported as news or how that news is reported. Yet, there are multiple studies of news coverage that have found that culture is an essential component of how journalists report the news, whether it is the "domestication of foreign news" or the racialization of poverty. As Walter Lippmann (1922) noted a century ago in his book *Public Opinion*, "we define first, and then we see." In both the foregoing examples, culture—in the first American political culture and in the second systemic racism—has influenced not just what is reported but how it is covered. Without ever meaning to, both of these examples provide evidence of persuasion—what is normally considered the realm of strategic communication. Thinking about "news" and "strategic communication" as exercises in symbol formation provides a way to reintroduce ethics into a shared professional conversation. As Baker notes, authentic, ethical persuasive messages place the good of the community, or, in Nussbaum's framing, the capabilities of individuals within community, ahead of sales, profit, and individual glory. The process of using data (quantitative and qualitative) to develop creative pitches that communicate objective reasons—reasons that would persuade you as well as us—to buy a product, give to a particular charity, or follow the instructions of public servants attempting to promote the public welfare can inform strategic communication every bit as much as news reporting. Objectivity as a process as opposed to an end is applicable to the creative efforts of strategic communication professionals.

Does Motivation Matter?

More than many other elements of ethics and popular culture, visions of strategic communication professionals on the large and small screen ask audiences to consider an important question: does the motivation for a particular choice matter in how it is evaluated ethically? Classical ethical theory has provided multiple answers. Immanuel Kant, for example, would respond with a categorical "no." Moral choice, for Kant, should be informed exclusively by duty. For Aristotle, the answer is less clear. He wrote that ethical acts sprang from virtue, but writing as he did about 3,000 years before Sigmund Freud and modern psychology, he was silent on how the virtues were to be cultivated except through practice and general education. Utilitarianism, at least the work of Jeremy Bentham and John Stuart Mill, as well as the modern and significant additions to it by John Rawls, tie ethical actions to what is the domain of the common good. There is little to no discussion of whether public perception of the common good can be wrongheaded. Pragmatism ties ethical thinking to life experience to a certain extent but not necessarily to motivation. Only feminist ethics, with its emphasis on care, brings motivation—and hence emotion—to the forefront.

Discussion Question

The chapter concludes with this question: Does the motivation for a particular choice matter in how it is evaluated ethically? Should motivation matter? Why or why not? Is the answer different for a hard-news journalist than for a strategic communicator? Why or why not?

However, none of these theories suggest that motivation should be the driving force in ethical decision making. We understand Draper's troubled motivations for many decisions in his life, but those psychologically informed understandings do not excuse his ethical lapses. As your mother or father may have told you, "The road to hell is paved with good intentions," a pithy summary of the impact of relying exclusively on motivation without resort to reason. All of us have had the experience of thinking we were doing the "right" thing because we were motivated to do so by a particular emotion or set of circumstances only be confronted seconds to years later with the realization that our actions—despite our motivation for them—had harmed others. Calamity Jane is a fictional rendition of our own, individual real-life experiences. One of the real challenges of ethical theory in the 21st century is to incorporate the impact of emotions and hence motivation on ethical choice without dismissing them entirely. In this effort, popular culture is leading the way—at least when it comes to asking a smart and persistent question.

9

When Mock Watchdogs Bark

Media Accountability in Satirical News

Central Concepts

- Methods of media accountability
- Differences between responsibility and accountability
- Constituent groups owed accountability
- The history and purpose of political satire and mock news

Accountability machinery, inside and outside of government, largely is taken for granted but is a major part of life in contemporary society. Hugh Helco, in his book *On Thinking Institutionally*, argues that we have an increasingly layered system of guardians monitoring guardians. Congress investigates the president. The major news outlets cover the daily actions of Congress, and relatedly the federal courts, during its investigation. Readers, viewers, and listeners—and increasingly people who do none of the above—take to social media to comment on news coverage, as well as the actions by members of each branch of government. There are few moments of thoroughgoing accountability and thousands of tiny instances of giving procedural accounts of this or that action. However, adding up micro-accountabilities is not likely to produce macro-accountability; indeed, it is more likely than not to obscure it (Helco, 2008).

Journalists rhetorically have placed themselves as one of the chief accountability mechanisms for the republic. They're the Fourth Estate. They're the watchdog that barks when government or big business engages in corruption. They comfort the afflicted and afflict the comfortable. Accountability to the public is one of the central norms of journalists. However, who really is watching the watchdog? And what can we, as a society, do when that watchdog doesn't bark?

There are a multitude of mechanisms used to assure press accountability. This chapter focuses on one of those: media critics and reporters regularly covering journalism. Specifically, we focus on mock news—those political satirists who use humor to point toward falsehoods, exaggerations, and absurdities often found on "real" newscasts. These mock newscasters are funny, but they also function as a "Fifth Estate" when individual journalists and the larger media system in which they operate fail in their public service role. The argument in this chapter is rooted in the ethical traditions of accountability and duty.

Discussion Question

Democratic nations have devised a number of means to assure press accountability, including: (a) journalism reviews, (b) codes of ethics, (c) ombudsmen, (d) journals put out by professional organizations, (e) trade and academic publications, (f) press councils, (g) op-ed pages, (h) regular critical reviews by schools of journalism and mass communication, (i) public and civic journalism initiatives, (j) media critics and reporters regularly covering journalism. Which of these accountability means do you see as being most effective? Which is least effective? Why?

In the United States, journalistic accountability legally cannot and ethically should not be subject to the power of government alone. Methods of regulating professional conduct, such as licensing, are forbidden in the United States because of the First Amendment, which states, in part, that "Congress shall pass no law . . . abridging the freedom . . . of the press." Because of the First Amendment, legal and social structures in the United States are derived from the sense that government can hold journalists accountable for their behaviors only after the fact through libel, privacy, obscenity, and copyright law. Indeed, enforcing accountability could have a chilling effect on the press and the First Amendment (Lambeth, 1992). So, in the absence of government regulation, democratic nations have devised a number of means to assure press accountability, including journalism reviews, codes of ethics, ombudsmen, journals put out by professional organizations, trade and academic publications, press councils, op-ed pages, regular critical reviews by schools of journalism and mass communication, public and civic journalism initiatives, and media critics and reporters regularly covering journalism.

The final mechanism, media critics, is the focus on this chapter. The Hutchins Commission (The Commission on Freedom of the Press, 1947) wrote, "If the press is to be accountable—and it must if it is to remain free—its members must discipline one another by the only means they have available, namely, public criticism" (p. 94). We are not arguing here that late-night comedians are journalists, even when they play the role of "journalist" so convincingly as to be almost indistinguishable from the real thing. However, we are arguing that late-night comedians often are doing journalism. Indeed, the argument here is that a wide range of comedic material—from *The Daily Show* and its various spinoffs and competitors to print publications such as *The Onion*—serve as an accountability mechanism by holding traditional news outlets' feet to the fire while simultaneously teaching audiences the basic concepts of media literacy. Before diving into the likes of Trevor Noah and John Oliver, however, we need to step back and look at just what ethicists mean when they say "accountability."

MEDIA ACCOUNTABILITY

Media accountability is the process by which media could or should be expected or obliged to report a truthful and complex account of the news (Pritchard, 2000), as well as the media's willingness to answer for their acts and how to secure accountability where there is unwillingness (Christians, Glasser, McQuail, Nordenstreng, & White, 2009). Accountability refers to "the willingness of the media to answer for what they do by their acts of publication, including what they do to society at large, and refers as well to the feasibility of securing accountability where there is unwillingness. Being accountable is normally linked to accepting, or being given, certain responsibilities, tasks, or goals" (Christians et al., 2009). Answerability involves explaining actions or conduct to groups or individuals (Blatz, 1972), so to say that media organizations "are accountable for their behavior means that they can be called to judgment in respect of their obligations" (Christians, 1985/1986, p. 16).

News media in the United States have on the whole accepted some form of accountability, though those methods have varied widely from advanced forms (e.g., National News Council from 1973 to 1984) to elementary obligations (e.g., corrected errors and responding to criticisms) (Lambeth, 1992). Media accountability typically is demonstrated by certain indictors such as corrections, feedback such as letters to the editor or comments sections after online posts, and ombudsmen (McIntyre, 1987). Still, the only watching that most of the watchdogs get comes from their audiences, codes of ethics, ombudsmen, news councils (whether those are local, regional, or national), in-house critics, journalism reviews, accuracy and fairness citizen groups, readers' and viewers' panels, and research institutes. While that list might seem extensive, each of those accountability mechanisms is incomplete and unable to do a thorough job of holding media organizations accountable.

If a media organization deviates from public accountability norms, it typically faces one of two possible consequences. The first is more coercive: adversarial liability for the consequences of publication (Blatz, 1972; Christians, 1989), which may take the form of legal sanctions and institutional authority (Murthy, 2007; Christians et al., 2009). The second is less coercive: nonconfrontational answerability (Blatz, 1972; Christians, 1989), which may take the form of market pressure such as a loss of viewers, public pressure such as a call for explanations, or professional self-regulation such as rebukes and criticisms (Murthy, 2007; Christians et al., 2009). Journalists typically hold that others in their field can and should be called to judgment by the public and by other journalists (Black, Steele, & Barney, 1999). Media criticism, however, only is meaningful as self-regulation if it encourages "reflection about journalistic norms" in such a way that it has a "clear influence on the practices and standards journalists consider acceptable" (Bunton, 2000, p. 73). Another type of nonconfrontational accountability is ridicule from a mock news program (Borden & Tew, 2007; Painter & Hodges, 2010).

The term *media accountability* is applied simultaneously to individual journalists and to the larger media ecology of which they are a part, raising the issue of whether organizations or institutions are morally blameworthy for acts that can truly be collective in nature. Individual responsibility is not obliterated by collective decision making in organizations and agencies. By selective recruiting, socializing organizational habits and norms, and exerting pressure to conform, organizations influence individual members to identify strongly with the organization and absorb its standards as their own (Helco, 2008).

It's important here to distinguish between the terms *responsibility* and *accountability*; though both are used somewhat interchangeably, there are important distinctions between them. Responsibility refers to obligations that are attributed to the media (McQuail, 1997) and asks the question, "To what social needs should we expect journalists to respond ably?" (Hodges, 1986, p. 14). Accountability refers to the process through which media are evaluated for meeting, or not meeting, their obligations (McQuail, 1997) and asks the question, "How might society call on journalists to account for their performance of the responsibility given to them?" (Hodges, 1986, p. 14).

In other words, responsibility is about defining proper conduct while accountability is concerned with compelling proper conduct. Therefore, it is possible to have a press that is both free and responsible; however, it is not possible to have a press that is both totally free and accountable (Hodges, 1986). This distinction is at the heart of John C. Merrill's (1990) argument that if the press is regulated, controlled, or directed from any power attempting to make the press "responsible" or "accountable," then that press no longer is free and autonomous. However, others argue that while accountability implies some constraint on freedom, and enforced accountability is a denial of freedom, some forms of accountability—for example, certain laws and regulations, market and public pressure (either by the general public or by organized pressure groups), and professional self-regulation—are quite compatible with media freedom as it is generally understood (Christians et al., 2009).

ACCOUNTABILITY TO WHOM?

German philosopher Immanuel Kant argued that rationality and autonomy support the dignity of every human being, that everyone is entitled to some level of respect because of these traits. Our practices of holding one another accountable for deeds and misdeeds is a direct consequence of our autonomy. Because we are free and rational human beings, Kant wrote, we are morally responsible for our choices and actions. As such, we also are fit for praise and blame because of those choices and actions.

Media organizations are linked to society by ties of attachment, obligation, and subordination; these influences work as internal lines of control and also as a way of interaction with external agents (Christians et al., 2009). Media constituents include external agents such as individuals in the intended audience and the wider public; other social institutions, groups, and organizations that depend on the media; government and regulatory agencies; and clients, sponsors, and news sources and subjects; as well as internal agents such as editors, publishers, owners, clients, sponsors, and peers and colleagues (Christians et al., 2009; Murthy, 2007; Pritchard, 2000). A journalist or other mass communicator owes accountability to all of those whose lives and well-being are significantly affected by his or her conduct. Journalists owe moral accountability to anyone they can harm through their work (e.g., the audience, the sources and subjects of news stories, and the journalism field at large), and they owe that moral accountability whether or not those people have the power to demand it (Foreman, 2016).

Discussion Question

To whom do mock newscasters such as John Oliver owe accountability? Does that answer change if Oliver and his ilk are considered journalists as opposed to comedians?

Media organizations and individual journalists typically say that their main constituents are the public and political society (see numerous codes of ethics, such as those from the Associated Press, the Society of Professional Journalists, and the Radio-Television Digital News Association, as well as most basic reporting textbooks). At its heart, "a news organization's social responsibility is to provide honest, impartial, and reliable information about current events that their fellow citizens need to make democratic institutions work" (Foreman, 2016). It is impossible for the media to be accountable to every competing interest all the time (Hirst & Patching, 2005), so when interests compete, for example, between an advertiser and the public, the ethical obligation is to serve the interests of the public. The ethical argument for why journalists must be accountable to the public is threefold.

First, journalists are morally accountable to anyone they can harm through their work, and this entitlement should be demanded and given regardless if those people have the power to demand accountability (Foreman, 2016). Journalists are powerful because they hold and disseminate vast amounts of often very personal information. A profession is defined largely by its specialized knowledge, which is a source of substantial power in today's information society (Helco, 2008). With that power comes the obligation to use it in a way "that is in the interest of the people they affect" (Elliott, 1986, p. 36). It's a similar sentiment to the principle expressed by Spider-Man's Uncle Ben (though tracing its roots at least as far back as the Bible and the 1793 French National Convention) that "with great power comes great responsibility." Consequently, the news media should need to fulfill the Hutchins Commission's mandate to give "a truthful, comprehensive, and intelligent account of the day's events in a context which gives them meaning" (The Commission on Freedom of the Press, 1947, p. 20–21) because the media have "the power to affect the lives of individuals and groups within society" (Elliott, 1986, p. 35).

Second, individual journalists should aspire to the highest professional standards (Keeble, 2001). Bill Kovach and Tom Rosenstiel (2007) argue that "the purpose of journalism is to provide people with the information they need to be free and self-governing" (p. 12). To that end, they offer five base norms relevant to the current discussion: (1) journalism's first obligation is to the truth, (2) its first loyalty is to citizens, (3) it must serve as an independent monitor of power, (4) it must keep the news comprehensive and proportional, and (5) its practitioners must be allowed to exercise their personal conscience. Accountability here moves beyond the realm of duty to the realm of duty within a professional role.

Third, accountability leads to trust, and the public needs to be able to trust the media to report truthful and accurate information in order for the media to fulfill their watchdog role. Adherence to values of truth telling and avoiding harm by individual journalists allows for the creation of social trust, which John Dewey (1954) and others link to the creation and maintenance of a political community. The normative standard, then, starts with individuals but also applies to organizational and institutional acts. The ubiquity of the Internet has made accountability more important than ever because citizens form an army of factcheckers calling attention to journalists' mistakes, and the web's interactivity fosters a conversation between journalists and the audience (Foreman, 2016, p. 34).

THE EVER-GROWING REALM OF MOCK NEWS

Jon Stewart didn't create the mock news format, but his version of *The Daily Show*, which ran from 1999 to 2015, can be seen as the lynchpin for the current proliferation of such comedic programming. Many former *Daily Show* correspondents now host (or have hosted) their own programs, including Stephen Colbert on *The Colbert Report*, John Oliver on *Last Week Tonight*, Samantha Bee on *Full Frontal*, Larry Wilmore on *The Nightly Show*, Jordan Klepper on *The Opposition*, Michelle Wolf on *The Break*, and Hasan Minhaj on *Patriot Act*. There also are similar shows, often inspired by *The Daily Show*, in countries worldwide, such as *The Real News* in Pakistan, *Wonderful Country* in Israel, *Heute-Show* in Germany, *If I Were Prime Minister* in Japan, and *Static* (filmed in the United States but with an Iranian target audience).

Stewart's *Daily Show*, and most of the programs that followed, are a structural parody of news reporting that appropriate the common structure of broadcast news and rely on viewer's familiarity with its iconography, style, and narrative structure (Fox, 2011; Morreale, 2009; Spicer, 2011). The common tropes of broadcast news—prominent anchor's desk, slick background, television monitor with iconic images and logos, special reports, breaking news, headlines, etc.—all can be seen in most mock news programs (Day, 2009; Fox, 2011). These shows, however, focus on three specific aspects of television news that are ripe for parody because of viewer familiarity.

First, these shows deconstruct the practice of sending reporters to read statements "on location," which creates the illusion of immediacy and

Figure 9.1.   Jon Stewart (left) and the *Daily Show* correspondents. Copyright Comedy Central

transparency (Barbur & Goodnow, 2011; Fox, 2011). Of course, the mock correspondents seldom actually leave the television studio; instead, they read their segment in front of a green screen depicting a scene of wherever they are supposed to be. The ruse is intended to be obvious to viewers because the live-audience laughter can be heard during the "on-location" report, and the correspondent often ends the segment by appearing in the studio to answer questions from the mock news anchor. There is no real immediacy or transparency, but the greater point is that the continual use of on-location reports, often from correspondents who have only been in the news location for a couple of days, often is not transparent nor offers relevant hard news. Local television news, which was the target of *The Daily Show* when Craig Kilborn hosted (1996–1998), use live on-location spots that offer little more than a backdrop—for example, a closed public courthouse for the 11 p.m. broadcast.

Second, these shows use absurdly inflated, incredibly story-specific, and constantly varying titles and areas of expertise for correspondents' pieces (Barbur & Goodnow, 2011; Day, 2009; McGeough, 2011; Spicer, 2011). For example, *The Daily Show*'s Roy Wood Jr. is listed as the Senior Mars Correspondent, Senior Wall Street Correspondent, Senior Campaign Correspondent, Senior Immigration Correspondent, and the Senior Hollywood Correspondent. The joke, of course, is that Wood could not be an expert in all of these fields. Similarly, the joke for other "senior correspondent" fields is that they would not be specialized beats in a typical broadcast but are needed for specific stories being covered by *The Daily Show*. Finally, the joke behind Jaboukie Young-White's title of "Senior Youth Correspondent" is twofold: first, that the title itself is an oxymoron, and second that Young-White's only specialized knowledge is that he's only 25 years old. The use of such titles undermines traditional newscasters' claims of authority by claiming unfound expertise, suggesting broadcast journalists likewise lack such expertise.

Third, the shows themselves are presented as a news parody, complete with reporters in the field, interviews with faux experts, as well as graphics, charts, and other trappings of a modern cable news program (Young & Esralew, 2011). One long-running gag on *The Daily Show* is the use of clever puns to title various long-running segments. Some examples include "Moscow in the Meddle" (Russian interference during the 2016 presidential campaign), "Commander in Beef" (focusing on Donald Trump's various Twitter feuds), "Guantanamo Baywatch" (detailing the U.S. prison camp in Cuba), "Mess O'Potamia" (about the Iraq War), and "Baracknophobia" (focusing on Fox News's irrational fears of candidate-then-president Barack Obama). The longest-running *Daily Show* segment is the show-closing "Your Moment of Zen," which typically features a humorous clip that relates to a topic discussed earlier in the show. The "Moment of Zen" parodies local television news' penchant for ending each broadcast with a quick, light-hearted story to balance the typically bad news that preceded it.

Comedy laughs at a fool to offer redemption, not to seek the destruction of the unsalvageable, as long as the target of ridicule demonstrates worthiness of redemption (Buerkle, 2011). The key point is to dramatically enact the underlying critique of the media by showing that the mainstream news is altogether artificial, constructed according to formulas and processes easily decoded by comedy writers and attentive viewers (Tally, 2011). Mock news programs accomplish this task in four ways. First, the joke is just how incompetent mainstream news is, as it inevitably gets the story wrong. Second, they look into the active masking or concealing of reality by purportedly objective news organizations. Third, they reveal that mainstream media's coverage is of something nonexistent entirely, or perhaps the coverage is of a news item of such little consequence that any coverage is a clear misuse of resources. Finally, there is the inevitable notion of news as a self-perpetuating image-generation machine where the very news to be reported is only that of other news reports (Tally, 2011). By making fun of traditional television news while pulling back the curtain on the fake Wizards of Television Oz, mock newscasters endear themselves to an audience already skeptical of traditional news sources (Mullen, 2011).

BITING THE HAND THAT FEEDS

As stated in the previous section, mock news programming offers a broad satire of the larger ills of the news genre and the hypocrisies within the day's news stories. However, mock newscasters also depend on mainstream news media because the genre is based on borrowing and re-contextualizing content from other media, congressional hearings, and press conferences. Because the jokes are based on political and news content reported by mainstream outlets, viewers must have the requisite knowledge of civics, current events, and the political landscape (i.e., must be embedded in the political system) in order to fully appreciate the jokes (Fox, 2011; Self, 2011). The comedians require audiences to have some working knowledge of the issues at hand and of the misinformation, biases, and inadequacies portrayed on serious news broadcasts in order to join the fun of mocking the media and political actors on those broadcasts (Wisniewski, 2011).

Watching mock news programs, therefore, could lead to increasing consumption of regular news outlets. They also promote media literacy and, in many instances, critical thinking. By piggy-backing political content onto entertainment material, mock news programs provide a gateway to increased audience attention to news and public affairs (Feldman, Leiserowitz, & Maibach, 2011). This gateway potential is largest among audience members with the least amount of formal education, those that are initially less politically engaged, and those who are only "marginally attentive" to politics and other forms of news (Feldman et al., 2011; Xenos, Moy, & Becker, 2011).

The end result is that most mock news viewers consume *more* news, not less. Indeed, few Americans rely exclusively on one media source for their information. They tend to get their news from various types of media (e.g., network and cable television, newspapers, social media, radio, etc.), as well as various news outlets within a particular medium (e.g., ABC, NBC, CBS, Fox News, MSNBC, and CNN for television). Adding a news-via-entertainment source such as *The Daily Show* then becomes just one more source of news and information in a well-balanced news diet. Further, political information does not primarily emanate from news broadcasts or newspapers, and sources of information typically are not clearly and consistently labeled as "news" or "entertainment," blurring the line between news and other forms for politically relevant programming (Williams & Delli Carpini, 2011).

Discussion Question

If news is worthy of criticism or parody, can the same be said for advertising? What would a mock "sponsorship" show look like? Can you envision some continuing segments? Would it serve the same normative function as mock news? Why might such a show be more problematic for media organizations?

Few people, if anyone, would call comedy routines the ideal way to communicate substantive and nuanced information about our democratic system

(Lichter, Baumgartner, & Morris, 2015). However, mock newscasters are a positive accountability mechanism for those times that traditional broadcasters fail to adequately inform the public. The argument made by many mock newscasters is that the news media is not performing its responsibility to the public with informed deliberation about real social issues because mainstream journalists are bound by professional norms and routines to remain factual, neutral, objective, and serious in their coverage (Fox, 2011; Hess, 2011b). For example, Jon Stewart positioned himself as an outsider speaking for the ordinary citizen's displeasure with those in power, including a press that, in his view, was not adequately doing its job (Gray, Jones, & Thompson, 2009; McGeough, 2011). At their best, mock newscasters can be seen as a positive alternative form of journalism that challenges the norms of objectivity, holds politicians accountable, and deconstructs the symbiotic relationship between journalists and politicians (Young & Esralew, 2011). At their worst, however, these shows are parasitic upon the work of journalists, depending upon them for both a basic understanding of the day's significant events and the specific stories upon which their satire is based while failing to acknowledge this dependence, to praise the high-quality reporting, or to recognize the current crisis of journalism or offer any solutions (Williams & Delli Carpini, 2011).

THE DEEP DIVE

John Oliver, the host of *Last Week Tonight* and a former *Daily Show* correspondent, does give credit to good journalistic work in both print and broadcast outlets. For example, in the August 7, 2016, segment titled "Journalism," Oliver said, "Stupid shows like ours lean heavily on local papers. In fact, whenever this show is mistakenly called journalism, it is a slap in the face to the actual journalists whose work we rely on." He then gives the example of a segment on state lotteries that relied heavily on the work of Harry Esteve at *The Oregonian*. Similarly, in the July 2, 2017, segment "Local News" (explored further later in this section), Oliver said that his show relies on the work of local broadcast outlets "all of the time," citing pieces on civil forfeiture and problems with the 911 emergency telephone system.

One major component of most mock news programs is the deep dive into a given topic. The hosts dedicate significant time on their shows to doing extended deconstructions of current events, spending several minutes actively reporting on an ongoing story, replaying footage seen on other news programs but with a decidedly comedic angle (e.g., highlighting particular statements within a longer speech or making faces of mock incredulity), and employing physical comedy (e.g., facial expressions and slapstick antics

Figure 9.2.   John Oliver from *Last Week Tonight*. Copyright HBO

such as a spit take) (Fox, 2011; Mullen, 2011). The result is that mock news programs tend to develop stories in greater depth, devoting more time, more background, more historical context, and more long-running series of stories (Barbur & Goodnow, 2011).

These long, in-depth segments stand in marked contrast to the types of stories typically found on network or cable news programming. The networks' flagship nightly newscasts seldom spend more than a couple of minutes on any given topic. While there are a few long-form journalism series, for every *60 Minutes*, there are 10 shows such as *Dateline* and *48 Hours* that focus more on true crime and less on the intricacies on political information. Similarly, when Ted Turner co-founded CNN, he said that the promise of a 24-hour news channel was the ability to devote time and resources to important stories that didn't fit neatly into a two-minute segment. However, CNN, along with Fox News and MSNBC, tends to cover the same five or so stories ad nauseam and then devote primetime programming to opinion talking heads such as Sean Hannity, Laura Ingraham, Rachel Maddow, and Anderson Cooper.

Gerald Baldasty (1992) argued that news values have been commercially redefined to include a concern for the bottom line, and news itself has been defined as a commodity to be shaped and marketed with an eye for profit. The tension is how to balance doing the best possible news with how to get the biggest audience while simultaneously keeping a clear separation between news and advertising content. In *The Newsroom*, fictional news anchor Will McAvoy apologizes to his audience. During the apology, he gets to the heart of the tension between news, audiences, and advertising:

The reason we failed isn't a mystery. We took a dive for the ratings. In the infancy of mass communication, the Columbus and Magellan of broadcast journalism, William Paley and David Sarnoff, went down to Washington to cut a deal with Congress. Congress would allow the fledgling networks free use of taxpayer-owned airwaves in exchange for one public service. That public service would be one hour of airtime set aside every night for informational broadcasting, or what we now call the evening news. Congress, unable to anticipate the enormous capacity television would have to deliver consumers to advertisers, failed to include in its deal the one requirement that would have changed our national discourse immeasurably for the better. Congress forgot to add that under no circumstances could there be paid advertising during informational broadcasting. They forgot to say the taxpayers will give you the airwaves for free, and for 23 hours a day you should make a profit, but for one hour a night, you work for us.

None of this is to say that network and cable news programs do not, at times, do good, hard-hitting journalism. Nor is it to say that mock news programs also are not driven, in part, by a quest for bigger audiences and the ratings and ad dollars that come with them. It is to hit the central premise of most mock news programs: that driven by ratings and a 24-hour time slot, modern news programs report and present the world in an excessively stylistic manner that lacks real substance (Hess, 2011a). Comedic news hosts make media coverage of events their topic, illustrating the complicity in coverage of orchestrated political events, the lack of substance behind much political discourse, the way that news focuses on the sensational and spectacular, and the proliferation of spin by politicians and corporations with little interrogation by the news media (Day, 2009; Morreale, 2009).

Last Week Tonight host John Oliver is known for his 20- to 30-minute segments exploring the intricacies of a variety of topics, from gerrymandering to deaths in professional wrestling to the proliferation of SLAPP (strategic lawsuit against public participation) lawsuits. Oliver himself was the defendant in a SLAPP lawsuit by coal baron Bob Murray—a longtime Republican donor who is best known for his climate change denial and mine-safety concerns following the death of six workers in his Crandall Canyon Mine in Utah—after another long-form segment about Murray's business practices.

In July 2017, Oliver devoted a segment to exploring the Sinclair Broadcast Group after a viral video showed dozens of the company's local TV anchors reading the exact same script about "fake news." Sinclair owns or operates 193 stations in more than 100 markets, reaching more than 40 percent of American households, especially ABC and Fox affiliates in the South and Midwest. Oliver began the segment by stating his thesis: that local broadcast news fills an important role in finding stories that the national networks miss or don't care about, but that there are potentially problems related to the corporate consolidation of local news. Specifically, he targets Sinclair, which, he says, "may be the most influential media company that you've never heard of."

Oliver's major argument is that Sinclair skews "hard right" politically in news, opinion, and even the advertising it allows on its stations. One big concern is the use of "must-run" segments that are produced at Sinclair's headquarters in Maryland and then sent to its affiliates nationwide with the edict that they must be aired. Sinclair also writes "must-read" scripts for local anchors, dictating local news content and injecting what Oliver describes as "Fox-worthy" content into trusted local news anchors.

Oliver highlights two recurring news segments produced by Sinclair. The first is a series of poll questions that "can range from benign to pretty leading." He then showed a clip of several polls, including this question: "Why are cable news channels airing so much coverage of the Trump/Russia story? (1) Bias against the President, (2) Higher Ratings, (3) *Anchor reads with a questioning voice*, It's a really important story." Oliver joked about this "inevitable" poll: "How would you describe how Trump looks in athletic wear? (A) Adonis-like, (B) Herculean, (C) Striking for a man his age, (D) Not my thing, but I'd still hit it." Even the poll questions, though, are not as ubiquitous, and misleading, as the daily "Terrorism Alert Desk," which runs no matter if there is real terrorism-related news or not. One story was about an ISIS flag hanging in a yard in New Hampshire. "Alert Desk" reports also include debunked "news" items. The worst, however, are stories that are not about terrorism; Oliver highlighted an item about "burkinis" that, as he said, had nothing to do with terrorists, just Muslims. "By that definition, terrorism is anything a Muslim does," Oliver said, exasperated. "Tonight, Mahershala Ali on the cover of *GQ*, Kareem Abdul Jabbar sneezed in an airport, and happy birthday to Fareed Zakaria. This has been your Terrorism Alert Desk."

Even the advertising on Sinclair stations "sometimes put[s] a thumb on the scale," according to Oliver. In 2010, a Pittsburgh affiliate pulled a 30-second ad by the Democratic Congressional Campaign Committee because some claims were unsubstantiated. However, the same station, and others, later aired a 25-minute attack ad that inferred that Barack Obama took campaign money from the terrorist group Hamas. "If you're going to make up scary donors to the Obama campaign, why stop with Hamas?" Oliver said. "Just keep going. 'He won't say where the money came from. One reason may be that it originated with this gang of coyotes that has made billions selling human babies to other, hungrier coyotes.'" Oliver's speech was accompanied by a visual featuring coyotes wearing sunglasses, smoking cigarettes, riding motorcycles, and wearing leather jackets while surrounding four babies and a briefcase full of money.

The overriding point of the "Local News" deep dive is that there are negative effects to a community when its local, trusted broadcast news source is bought by a corporate conglomerate that produces "must-run" segments, especially if those segments have a deeply partisan bent. Oliver doesn't have the demands of a daily newscast, and his show airs on HBO, not a network that potentially includes Sinclair-owned affiliates. The combination of those two factors allows Oliver to dive deeply into an issue and serve as an accountability mechanism for traditional broadcast news stations.

MOCK NEWS: PRINT EDITION

Mock news, of course, did not start with *The Daily Show* or other television programming. Indeed, print versions of mock news predate the birth of the republic, going back in the United States at least as far as Benjamin Franklin's *Poor Richard's Almanac*. Probably the most well-known and most popular current mock newspaper is *The Onion*, which bills itself sardonically as "America's Finest News Source." In reality, *The Onion* is a satirical and often laugh-out-loud mix of political, cultural, and just plain weird stories.

The layout of the newspaper, including the digital version, mimics traditional news. There is a featured story with a dominant graphic and several smaller articles on a variety of "general-interest" topics. For example, the featured story at the time of this writing is "One-Eyed Man Who Kamala Harris Locked Up 25 Years Ago Quietly Removes Tulsi Gabbard Mask." Secondary stories ranged from the political ("British Royal Family Condemns Media's Ugly Attacks on Their Traditional Practice of Sexual Abuse") to the cultural ("Washboard Player in Jug Band Tired of Spoons Guy Getting All the Chicks"). *The Onion* also includes secondary features common in traditional media such as horoscopes, man-on-the-street opinion polls, infographics, videos, and political cartoons. However, each of these also has a satirical twist.

At least twice, *The Onion* writers touched on a social nerve with reporting that hit audiences in the head and the gut.

The first was the 9/11 issue, published September 27, 2001. The old cliché is that tragedy plus time equals comedy. *Saturday Night Live* received a lot of media attention for its first broadcast following the terrorist attacks—when producer Lorne Michaels asked then New York mayor Rudy Giuliani if they were allowed to be funny and Giuliani deadpanned, "Why start now?"—but both *The Daily Show* (on September 20) and *The Onion* (on September 27) had already decided that enough time had passed to turn the tragic into laughs.

The Onion writers perfectly captured the combination of vengeance, fear, and bewilderment following the terrorist attacks with stories including "U.S.

Vows to Defeat Whoever It Is We're at War With," "American Life Turns Into Bad Jerry Bruckheimer Movie," and "Not Knowing What Else to Do, Woman Bakes American-Flag Cake." They also continued to skewer traditional news coverage, dubbing the continuing coverage "Holy Fucking Shit: Attack on America" with a graphic of a U.S. map seen through crosshairs. A front-page teaser, "Massive Attack on Pentagon Page 14 News," was based on the joke that an airplane crashing into the heart of the American military ordinarily would be reported as the lead story but here was not even worthy of a place on Page One.

The second is the long-running series "'No Way to Prevent This,' Says Only Nation Where This Regularly Happens." The full text of the original May 27, 2014, story is less than 200 words:

> ISLA VISTA, CA—In the days following a violent rampage in southern California in which a lone attacker killed seven individuals, including himself, and seriously injured over a dozen others, citizens living in the only country where this kind of mass killing routinely occurs reportedly concluded Tuesday that there was no way to prevent the massacre from taking place. "This was a terrible tragedy, but sometimes these things just happen and there's nothing anyone can do to stop them," said North Carolina resident Samuel Wipper, echoing sentiments expressed by tens of millions of individuals who reside in a nation where over half of the world's deadliest mass shootings have occurred in the past 50 years and whose citizens are 20 times more likely to die of gun violence than those of other developed nations. "It's a shame, but what can we do? There really wasn't anything that was going to keep this guy from snapping and killing a lot of people if that's what he really wanted." At press time, residents of the only economically advanced nation in the world where roughly two mass shootings have occurred every month for the past five years were referring to themselves and their situation as "helpless."

The story subsequently has appeared 13 more times following mass shootings, with only the date, location of violence, and number of people killed changing. The repetition is intended to highlight that mass shootings are a regular occurrence in the United States (and no other country), tapping into a shared sense of frustration, futility, and hopelessness.

10

Conclusions

The Play's the Thing

Central Concepts

- Why thinking about evil is crucial in ethics
- How human beings develop as moral beings
- How might you—and your teachers—contribute to our understanding of the link between popular culture and understanding ethical theory

---

It's rare that people know the era in which they are living is one of historic, fundamental change *while that change is happening*. However, that's the position that most Americans find themselves in today. Popular culture—and for that matter elite art—is just as likely to detect those changes and some of their implications than the more traditional academic fields or even average people going about their changing daily lives. Popular culture helps us begin to understand the impact of those changes by asking us to imagine things differently. It's a relatively low-cost thought experiment because you can imagine change without having to go through the effort of making the change itself.

But, with a history that extends for more than 3,000 years, ethical decisions continue to focus around the central issues of duty, virtue, and consequence while allowing us to examine the philosophical principles that undergird truth, privacy, and accountability, among others. This is not because philosophy is somehow "behind." It is that over millennia, these issues remain current. History asks us to consider them in a different light, and as we know more in a scientific and social scientific sense, we can deepen our understanding of the morally relevant facts and the implications of specific choices. And that, by the way, is one of the central themes of this book. Regardless of theory, and regardless of the book, film, television show, meme, or song, ethical actions require choice. And so does evil.

A DIFFERENT SORT OF QUESTION

As a philosophical concept, evil is not written about as much as what is right or what is good. Too often, because ethics is about doing the right thing for the better reason, it sometimes seems that making the wrong choice is simply a mistake in thinking. Unethical, yes, but understandable, too. After all, you were trying to do the right thing; you did not intend to screw up. Sometimes that's exactly the case. But we suggest that, at least as often, acting unethically is a conscious decision. We mean to do it. We even take pleasure in it. Evil and intentional malevolence are part of our ethical universe; we have all experienced it. However, thinking through the ethics of responding to evil is something that popular culture has had multiple responses to. In this sense, popular culture, more than philosophy, has taken on the concept of evil.

So, this chapter begins with a discussion of evil, what philosophers have said, and how once upon a time in a galaxy far, far away, evil is realized and perhaps defeated. How people can choose to act ethically one day and behave in a different way the next day is the focus of the second portion of this chapter: moral development. The patterns in moral thinking, and how we become more sophisticated in reasoning through moral problems, is the focus of this field of academic research. Finally, we articulate a potential research agenda for those who think that popular culture has something to say about ethics. These research questions are meant to apply to students and faculty alike. Just as important, we hope you take them with you as you watch films and the news, listen to music, and game—socially distanced or not.

But, for now, we turn to the dark side.

EVIL IS A CHOICE

For the purposes of this book, we are using a non-religious definition of evil. Like many elements of ethics, religion has historically informed thinking about the term. The poet William Blake framed the question gently: "Tyger, tyger burning bright . . . what immortal hand or eye could frame thy fearful symmetry?" Did a god who created good also create evil? It is beyond the scope of this book to address this question in a religious sense, but we acknowledge that many of you will have addressed it in other settings.

Philosophers have focused not so much on how evil comes to be but how to define and recognize it. Most begin with the concept of pain and harm. Some philosophers, for example Kant, view causing pain and harm as an individual act, what he termed "radical evil." Other philosophers, most prominent among them Hannah Arendt, who in the 20th century wrote some of the most thoughtful work about evil as she tried to explain Fascism and the rise of Nazi Germany, have said political and social community is essential for evil to emerge. In *Origins of Totalitarianism*, Arendt (1951/1973) analyzes evils that result from systems put in place by totalitarian regimes. In this work, her analysis does not consider individual culpability. *Unmasking Administrative Evil* by Guy Adams and Danny Balfour (1994) extends this line of thought. In their evaluation of why Nazi scientists were allowed to immigrate into the United States after World War II, Adams and Balfour conclude that political goals and immigration procedures were as much at fault as any single individual act. The United States needed expertise in rocket building—for both the space program and long-range nuclear missiles—and Nazi physicists had it. Samantha Powers (2002), in *The Problem from Hell*, the Pulitzer Prize–winning book about the genocides of the 20th century, comes to much the same conclusion. Genocide for most is unimaginable; it is easy for multiple institutions, including the media, to ignore or dismiss the beginning of a genocidal political policy as "impossible or unlikely" until it is too late.

Discussion Question

Revisit—or watch for the first time—any of the three *Godfather* films. Do these films provide audiences with a vision of evil? In what way? How do the films respond to the "reality" of surviving a corrupt system?

This notion of a system—a set of plans and objectives including economic arrangements and political structures—that promotes and sustains evil is the focus of popular culture as well. *Rogue One* (2016), the *Star Wars* spin-off that takes as its inspiration the development of the atomic bomb as part of the Manhattan Project in the United States, focuses on the role of the individual scientist within a larger system of science and intellectual advancement that becomes the core from which evil emerges. "Galen Urso is the scientist essential to the development of their weapons," the rebel commander tells Cassian Andor. "There will be no extraction. You find him, you kill him." Robert Moses, an urban planner who worked in New York City for four decades during the 20th century, set in place such a system. By controlling the height at which bridges and overpasses were built, Moses made it impossible for public buses to travel from the urban core to more suburban environments. Robert Caro (1974), Moses's biographer, concludes in *The Power Broker* that this planning choice enforcing racial segregation in New York City lasted for decades after Moses left public service. The system outlived the individual who built it.

Arendt (1963) coined the phrase "the banality of evil" in her study of the role of Nazi functionary Adolf Eichmann. She argues that the average Nazi, like Eichmann, was "thoughtless" but not stupid when he followed orders to exterminate prisoners in concentration camps. She described Eichmann as a "terrifyingly normal" human being who did not think deeply about the nature of the orders he was being given. This focus on the individual—why it is that people will make evil choices—has been the impetus for much psychological research in the United States. The notion that people who are terrifyingly normal will make abhorrent choices is affirmed by the work of Stanley Milgram and Philip Zimbardo; put Stanford undergraduates in a prison-like environment, and they will behave like the worst sort of prison guards imaginable. So community, just as Arendt describes, has something to do with sustaining evil choices. Rebecca Skloot's book *The Immortal Life of Henrietta Lacks* (2010) describes similar treatment by the medical establishment of an African-American woman, Henrietta Lacks, whose cells were used without her consent for a variety of medical procedures. Lacks died from her cancer, but her "immortal" cells became the basis of the pap smear, a test for cervical cancer. In her case, "the system" cost Lacks her life, but her humanity—her cells—has saved millions of women. Finally, because community is implicated in the emergence and the sustaining of evil, media content itself has been the focus of research. More than 6,000 studies have been conducted into whether violent media content—from television and films to gaming and the Internet—promotes violent behavior. The underwhelming answer: we still don't know definitively. However, we do know that media content can encourage pro-social behavior (Greitemeyer, 2011). We began this book with references to Mr. Rogers for multiple reasons, this among them.

Media ethicist Clifford Christians has tackled the problem of evil, as most ethicists do, by positing the "inverse" of evil. For Christians (2019), a sound philosophy of media ethics in the 21st century is based on what he calls "proto-norms," the assertion that as human beings we have inescapable claims on one other. Abandon the claim, and we abandon our common humanity. The three proto-norms that Christians argues are essential to a robust discussion of media ethics in the 21st century are the sacredness of human life, truth, and nonviolence. Invert these proto-norms through conscious choice and evil emerges. Treat life as transactional or as a means to another end (the story of Henrietta Lacks), obscure truth (one instrument of propaganda essential to totalitarian regimes), and wage war or encourage poverty, racism, and sexism (the abandonment of nonviolence), and evil is a predictable consequence.

Discussion Question

Gandhi said that poverty is the worst form of violence. What films, television shows, or music reflect this view? Does this view make poverty the equivalent of evil?

So, while most scholars have subdivided the question somewhat erratically into "the systemic reasons for evil" and "individual motivations to act evilly," creators of culture seem to have intuitively understood that it takes the right person at the right time—what Erik Erikson (1967) called "the historical moment"—for evil to emerge and have profound consequences.

Especially a long time ago in a galaxy far, far away.

THE CASE OF KYLO REN

The nine-film *Star Wars* series has had an indelible impact on popular culture because it deals with a myth structure that resonates globally. *Star Wars* is about people as they face themselves and the challenges that life provides. While the focus is on the Jedi and the force that connects all living things, the subplot of the films has always demanded villainy and, in the person of Kylo Ren, a human being who choses evil despite many opportunities to do otherwise.

Audiences don't meet Ren until the final three films in the series, but when they do, the screenwriters have stripped away the excuses that many of us, in our post-Freudian age, might provide him. Ren, who starts life as Ben Solo, comes from a good, in fact high-achieving family. Deprivation and want are not part of his childhood; indeed, in his mother, Leia, he is exposed to Jedi-trained goodness and strength from the earliest age. His mentor is Luke Skywalker, the Jedi who has grappled with the dark side and knows its power. Luke blames himself for Ben Solo's attraction to the dark side, but it is clear that the dark side is a path that Ben chose to walk of his own volition despite multiple examples of choosing other things and a childhood that was obviously filled with love. Modern psychology does not explain these choices very well.

Kylo Ren chooses evil. He chooses to kill his father—an example of the death he inflicts wherever he goes. He chooses to challenge Luke and is defeated only at great cost. Having killed his father, he also chooses to kill his mentor in the dark side: Snoke. This was not spur-of-the-moment opportunity; it is clear that Ren seeks the power to rule and to control and is willing to use others as instruments in his struggle. Finally, Ren pursues Rey, literally across the galaxy, deceiving her about her parentage, taunting her with his seemingly omniscient knowledge about her life, all the while ensnaring her in a plot to murder her biological grandfather and hence gain supreme power in the *Star Wars* universe.

Audiences in this galaxy are not asked why evil exists or even how it comes to be; instead, they are asked how to defeat it. The answers: "They win by making you think you are alone," a steadfastness of purpose that chooses life at every opportunity, even in the face of evil, and of the creation and maintenance of community that values commitment more than pre-existing stature. And that includes the droids, who should not be underestimated. In the final moments of the plot, compromise and cooperation between the Jedi (Rey) and the Sith (Ren) are rejected. Defeating Ren costs many lives. It also results in the creation of a "new" system, at least for the *Star Wars* universe, summarized by a single act: Rey, whose birth name is Palpatine, chooses to take for her last name Skywalker, to honor Luke and Leia, their beliefs in the force, and the community they brought into being. Defeating the evil that Ren represents requires the fusing of self-reflection about the consequences of specific actions and the steadfast willingness to adhere to duty in community.

The *Star Wars* plot encourages audiences to acknowledge that evil does exist—that the psychological explanations we are willing to provide are incomplete. At one point in the film, Ren tells Rey that the "dark side is in all of us," something that poets have understood but contemporary social science and philosophy have had some trouble accepting. The *Star Wars* plot also encourages us to think about evil systemically and to understand that almost any system can be used for evil purposes, or at least as a way to subvert the purposes for which it was originally intended. In a cultural sense, it leaves us with questions. If the ideals of journalism, primary among them a focus on truth, have been subverted, what new system must be "invented" to replace it? How might we articulate duties in this new professional universe? How might professional community buttress individual choice? If we reinvented journalism, public relations, and strategic communication in the 21st century, what would we change—like Rey's adoption of a new last name—and what might be retained—the ethics of duty and capability that permeate creation of something new?

ETHICAL BUILDING BLOCKS

The good news is that there is evidence that morality is grounded in biology. Ethicists have argued that we evolved a moral instinct, a capacity that naturally grows within each child and is designed to generate rapid judgments about what is morally right or wrong based on an unconscious grammar of action (de Waal, 2013, 2006; Hauser, 2006). In other words, we're born with ethical building blocks—among them justice, fairness, kindness, and reasonableness—that enable us, from an early age, to begin making ethical decisions. Is it fair that my older brother gets to watch the latest *Star Wars* movie while I'm stuck watching *Finding Nemo* for the tenth time because *Star Wars* is too violent for a kid my age? What if big brother gives me a hug when I begin to cry at the perceived injustice? Both, on some level, are ethical decisions. This biology of choice does not determine which specific ethical decision will be made, only that human beings have the capacity to recognize that an ethical question is involved.

These building blocks are not learned (though, of course, some learning and refining takes place, but we'll get to that); they're hard wired. Take the example of Frans de Waal's experiments with capuchin monkeys. On day one, both monkeys are given the same task. When completed, they both get a cucumber slice as a reward. All is good. On day two, both monkeys again are given the same task. When completed, they both get a grape, a far superior reward. All is even better. However, trouble arises on day three when the monkeys are once again given the same task. When completed, one monkey gets a cucumber slice while the other gets a grape. The monkey that got the short end of the stick—or cucumber if you will—freaks out and throws a tantrum. (Some even throw the cucumber at de Waal or his colleagues.) Why? It's not fair. It's not just. It's not reasonable. The same is true for capuchin monkeys' close cousins: humans.

In humans, we call the process of learning and internalizing ethics moral development. Scholars argue that people can develop morally just as they can learn to think critically (Clouse, 1985). They base that assertion on four premises. First, moral development occurs within the individual; people develop morally when they become aware of their reasons for acting in a certain way. Second, moral development parallels intellectual development; the two could proceed at a slightly different pace, but there can be little moral development without a certain intellectual capacity. Third, moral development occurs in a series of universal, unvarying, and hierarchal stages (more on this a bit later). Finally, moral development occurs through conflict; "a fundamental reason why an individual moves from one stage to the next is because the latter stages solve problems and inconsistencies unsolvable at the present developmental stage" (Kohlberg, 1973, p. 13).

LEARNING ABOUT MORAL
DEVELOPMENT BY WATCHING BOYS AND GIRLS

Swiss psychologist Jean Piaget developed his theories on moral development by watching boys between the ages of 3 and 12 play marbles, later testing his assumptions about their playground behavior in interviews. He theorized four stages of moral development in his book *The Moral Judgment of the Child* (1932/1965). Boys, he argued, began with no understanding of what a marble was, let alone how the game was played. Indeed, in the first stage, which largely occurred until age 2, the boys' interest in marbles was purely motor-oriented. For example, a young boy would put the marble in his mouth. Slowly, however, boys would learn and internalize the rules of the game. From 3 to 7, boys would play marbles with their friends but would make up their own rules—changing the rules by playmate and game. Starting at about age 7, they would start following a set of rules handed down from on high (typically from older children); though they did not understand the reasoning behind the rules, they obediently followed them because an authority figure (again, typically a slightly older boy) should not be challenged. Finally, the boys began to develop autonomy around age 11, characterized by internalizing rules, understanding that rules ensure fair play, and justifying rules violations such as allowing younger children to "cheat" or break the rules to level the playing field.

Piaget's work is foundational, but, of course, it is incomplete. He studied boys until 12, leaving out two major components of the population—women and girls, and everyone over the age of 12. Carol Gilligan and Lawrence Kohlberg, two subsequent psychologists influenced by Piaget, would help fill those gaps.

Harvard psychologist Lawrence Kohlberg (1973) mapped six stages (divided into three levels) of moral development by studying college students in the 1960s. Kohlberg's six stages are descriptive, not prescriptive. Doing right, fulfilling one's duties, and abiding by the social contract are the pillars upon which the stages of Kohlberg's work rest. Under Kohlberg's arrangement, justice—and therefore morality—is a function of perception; as you develop, more activities fall under the realm of duty than before. Kohlberg dubbed his first level "preconventional." People in this level display simple obedience (stage 1) or follow rules only when they are deemed to be in one's self-interest (stage 2). As people advance to the "conventional" stage, they mostly are motivated by societal expectations to conform to one's role (stage 3)—as, for example, a daughter or neighbor—and to fulfill agreed-upon societal duties (stage 4) such as respecting authority and upholding laws. The third, "postconventional" level begins with stage 5, which is based on the social contract and individual rights. Here, a person becomes aware that the social contract demands that we uphold laws agreed to by due process even if they are contrary to our best interests because they provide the greatest good for the greatest number. The only exceptions—the only times when those laws are allowed, and even obligated, to be broken—are when they conflict with values such as life and liberty that supersede majority opinion. Kohlberg argued that most people live their lives in the two conventional stages motivated by society's expectations. Few rise to the fifth stage, and only a select handful—Socrates, Gandhi, Martin Luther King Jr., Mother Teresa—ever achieved the sixth stage of moral development, where one is guided by universal ethical principles self-selected by each individual. The principles that guide this person include equality of human rights and respect for the dignity of all humans.

Discussion Question

The concept of moral development makes us think that moral growth may be inevitable. Examine the character Oskar Schindler in either the book or the film *Schindler's List*. Evaluate Schindler's moral growth—or lack of it. What questions does the cinematic version of a real-life hero raise for you in terms of moral development? Apply the same analysis to the protagonists in *Crazy Rich Asians*.

Gilligan (1982) posited that the moral development literature was flawed. The traditional conceptualization of justice and the rights of others as the dominant basis for moral development, she argued, meant that women and girls almost always were found to be lacking—not because they were morally deficient but because they deemed another ethical principle to be more important. Gilligan found that women making moral choices define themselves in relation and connection to other people, that a woman comes to know herself through relationship with others. In other words, identity is related to intimacy. The moral imperative that emerged repeatedly during Gilligan's interviews with women was an injunction to care, a responsibility to discern and alleviate the "real and recognizable" trouble in this world (Gilligan, 1982). In this ethics of care, moral growth emerges not from conflict but from understanding the concept of community—either a community of two (i.e., mother and child) or the larger community. Moral development, according to the proponents of care, emerges from understanding the concept of "we" instead of the concept of "I" espoused by rights-based scholars such as Piaget and Kohlberg.

BOYS AND GIRLS DEVELOP
MORALLY THROUGH POPULAR CULTURE

Psychologists such as Piaget watched children to study moral development. Children watch TV and movies, play video games, read books, and listen to music. While the impetus for consuming popular culture is entertainment, the ethical lessons embedded in popular culture lead to a high degree of moral development.

Many young children are first exposed to popular culture through books read to them by their parents. As Confucius wrote, "You cannot open a book without learning something," and children learn ethical and moral lessons from these books. These lessons include gratitude in Dr. Seuss's *Did I Ever Tell You How Lucky You Are*, generosity in Shel Silverstein's *The Giving Tree*, truth telling in Berkeley Breathed's *Edwurd Fudwupper Fibbed Big*, perseverance in Watty Piper's *The Little Engine That Could*, and reciprocity and sacrifice in E. B. White's *Charlotte's Web*. When they begin to grow older, they're introduced to children's programming including *Mr. Rogers, Neighborhood* and *Daniel Tiger*—both discussed in chapter 1. *Sesame Street* both teaches lessons and very likely introduces children to their first journalist—Kermit the Frog, who reports from the scene of fairy tales from "Three Little Pigs" and the "Tortoise and Hare" to "Humpty Dumpty" and "Alice in Wonderland."

Slightly older children might begin exploring the fictional worlds of superheroes. The most interesting characters are neither purely good nor purely evil. Take, for example, Sandman, one of the supervillains in the movie *Spider-Man 3* (2007). The character begins as Flint Marko, a small-time thug and thief; his daughter is dying, and Marko steals money to help pay for her cancer treatment. Stealing obviously is wrong, yet even Christian teaching holds "people do not despise a thief if he steals to satisfy himself when he is starving" (Proverbs 6:30)—though tell that to Jean Valjean in *Les Misérables*. Magneto is sometimes a superhero and other times a supervillain in the *X-Men* series. Like the X-Men, Magneto is a powerful mutant. He's also a Holocaust survivor, whose methods and philosophy—his aim is for mutants, which he calls *Homo superior*, to replace humans as Earth's dominant species—are derived in part from his experiences and fears of a world that persecutes mutants.

These children also might begin to watch professional wrestling—a mythological fight between good and evil. Roland Barthes (2005) argued that wrestling is meant to portray a purely moral concept: justice. In the 1980s, justice was served when heroes such as Hulk Hogan vanquished evildoers such as Iranian wrestler the Iron Sheik and the Soviet—though really Croatian-American—Nikolai Volkoff (who would sing the Russian national anthem before matches). This good versus evil dynamic became more complicated in the 1990s "Attitude Era" when headliners "Stone Cold" Steve Austin, the Rock (who later became a movie star under his given name, Dwayne Johnson), the Undertaker, and others straddled the often thin line between hero and villain. The most consistent villain was wrestling promoter Vince McMahon, who played the part of an evil media baron attempting to destroy the careers of his disobedient employees.

The impact of gaming on individual behavior, especially during adolescence, mirrors the contentious decades of scholarly research on the impact of violent television programming and film: there are as many studies that say such content promotes and encourages violent behavior as there are studies that find no or weak relationships between media content and specific behavior. However, in a small study that examined the impact of imaginative gaming (Dungeons & Dragons) on moral growth, researchers found that "imaginative role-playing games can serve as an enjoyable medium for promoting (and protecting) moral growth. In particular, gaming that involves the encounter of morally relevant situations appears to facilitate a shift away from concern for one's own personal interests and toward the interests of others, both in one's reasoning about moral scenarios and in the expression of one's values" (Wright, Weissglass, & Casey, 2017, p. 20). A single study, of course, is not definitive, but it does suggest the need for additional research.

As children grow into teenagers, they begin to read and watch more mature content, including *The Hunger Games* trilogy (discussed in depth in the "Privacy" chapter). The *Harry Potter* and *Star Wars* series—both directed at young adults but beloved and revered by nearly every age group—are morality lessons in good versus evil (discussed earlier in this chapter). In both worlds, good and evil are not strictly black and white; most characters exist in a gray world. Think of "The Force," a metaphysical power that can be wielded by both good (the Jedi) and evil (the Sith) characters. Evil also can be redeemed—such was the case with Anakin Skywalker, who turned to the "dark side" and became Darth Vader before sacrificing himself to save his son in *Return of the Jedi*.

Finally, we become adults. Our moral development doesn't stop as we continue to progress toward ever more difficult fare. The works in previous chapters all contribute to our moral development and understanding. We'll add one more here: *The Good Place* (2016–2020), a sitcom inherently about moral development. The "Good Place" is a utopian, highly selective afterlife designed as a reward for a righteous life. Those who don't live a righteous life end up in the "Bad Place," where they will be tortured by demons with methods such as "bees with teeth," an endless stack of *New Yorker* magazines, and the "Bad Place" theme song (the Kars4Kids jingle). When Eleanor Shell-strop figures out early in season one that she was mistakenly assigned to the Good Place, she enlists the help of her assigned soulmate, the moral philosopher Chidi Anagonye, to help her become a better person to earn her spot in the Good Place. What follows is four seasons of moral growth and development, including the work of actual philosophers ranging from John Locke and David Hume to Peter Singer and Derek Parfit. There's also a brilliant rendition of the classic ethical thought experiment the "Trolley Problem" in season two.

The point here is that we learn moral development in many ways—through education; through parents, family, and peers; and also through popular culture. Psychologists Jean Piaget, Lawrence Kohlberg, and Carol Gilligan watched us to gain insight into moral development. Collectively, we've turned to popular culture to aid our moral development. What popular culture can do is engage our moral imaginations and help us think about the different ways to solve the problems that confront us in real life. However, we don't develop morally until we can actually make the choice and learn from the experience.

WHERE TO GO FROM HERE

Throughout this book, we've highlighted the ethical lessons in popular culture with a special emphasis on *media* ethics. We've discussed some of the core concepts in media ethics: truth telling, loyalty, privacy, public service, media economics, social justice, advocacy, and accountability. We've also discussed some of the classic portrayals of journalists in popular culture both fictional (Howard Beale in *Network*, Hildy Johnson in *His Girl Friday*, Henry Hackett in *The Paper*) and based on real life (Robby Robinson and his team in *Spotlight*, Bob Woodward and Carl Bernstein in *All the President's Men*, Lowell Bergman in *The Insider*).

On both fronts, however, we've only scratched the surface.

Future researchers could focus on how popular culture has addressed a multitude of ethical concepts: altruism, authenticity, autonomy, benevolence, dignity, fairness, independence, reciprocity, and transparency. This list is not meant to be exhaustive or definitive. Nor is there scientific or social science–based research to document whether and in what ways human beings, from childhood through adulthood, learn ethical concepts from popular culture. There is research documenting what people learn (and don't learn) from news and many sorts of persuasive messages, but learning from fiction is largely unexplored territory.

Similarly, there are a wealth of philosophers and philosophy that, due to focus or space restraints, are not included in this text. Finally, we have only begun to explore the wealth of media portrayals in popular culture. The Image of the Journalist in Popular Culture project includes a database with "more than 92,000 items on the images of journalists, public relations practitioners and media in films, television, radio, fiction, commercials, video games, comics, cartoons and other aspects of popular culture" (www.ijpc.org). Clearly, any book-length undertaking will be far from exhaustive considering the material available.

In addition to examining how popular culture portrays ethical concepts, we also need to ask whether it matters in terms of the decisions people actually make. This book is based on an assumption supported by some tantalizing evidence: children exposed to pro-social media content actually behave in more pro-social ways. And, seeing violent media content does not necessarily make you go out and beat up your neighbor. But there's so much more to learn. Are film audiences aware of the ethics lessons they are receiving on the big screen? If people watch *Star Trek* with its discussion of supererogatory and utilitarian behavior, do those lessons influence decisions about wearing a mask or declining to be socially distant under certain situations in both the short and long term? Does a play such as *Hamilton* promote learning about American history through a different lens, and what might be the long-term consequences of such learning? Does the link between music and emotion promote a different quality or kind of moral thinking than something like more traditional essays or even this book? Does popular culture actively provoke the moral imagination, or does it lull us into complacency, as some have argued? All of these questions could be the focus of empirical research. Equally important, they could add to the complexity of existing theory by providing context and constraints under which ethical choice is understood.

THE FINAL WORD

We began this book with a simple question: why popular culture? Our answer now remains the same as our answer then. At its most basic level, the answer is because you—just like the authors of this book—have spent thousands of hours with popular culture. Shakespeare and the ancient Greeks knew that if you want to tell a moral lesson and have it remembered, then embed it in a play—one that audiences are fond of seeing.

Few students—to be honest, few media ethicists—have read all or most of the major philosophical works by Aristotle, John Stuart Mill, Immanuel Kant, John Rawls, Thomas Hobbes, and John Locke. Even fewer have delved past what one media ethicist calls "the dead white guys" to explore non-Western philosophy or the works of major female ethicists such as Nel Noddings, Martha Nussbaum, and Sissela Bok.

While we are not arguing that popular culture is an equal substitute for delving into ethical works, we are saying that one can learn ethics from film, television shows, books, and other forms of entertainment. The fact that we can laugh along with John Oliver, get "as mad as hell" with Howard Beale, or imagine ourselves as crusaders such as Woodward and Bernstein or the *Spotlight* team who take on corrupt institutions is just an added bonus.

One last note: we hope that you've had as much fun reading this book as we've had writing it. Now it's time to pop some popcorn, dim the lights, and start the show . . .

Bibliography

Adams, G., & Balfour, D. (1994). *Unmasking administrative evil.* New York: M. E. Sharpe.

Akner, T. B. (2019, Nov. 13). This Tom Hanks story will help you feel less bad. *The New York Times.* Retrieved from https://www.nytimes.com/2019/11/13/movies/tom-hanks-mister-rogers.html.

Anderson, C. A., Berkowitz, L., Donnerstein, E., Huesmann, L. R., Johnson, J. D., Linz, D., Malamuth, N. M., & Wartella, E. (2003). The influence of media violence on youth. *Psychological Science in the Public Interest, 4*(3), 81–110.

Arendt, H. (1951/1973). *The origins of totalitarianism.* New York: Harcourt, Brace and Javonitch.

Arendt, H. (February–March 1963). Eichmann in Jerusalem. 5 parts. *The New Yorker.* Retrieved from https://www.newyorker.com/magazine/1963/02/16/eichmann-in-jerusalem-i.

Asimov, I. (1940–1950). *I, Robot.* Stories originally appeared in *Super Science Stories* and *Astounding Science Fiction*, compiled into a single book in 1950. New York: Gnome Press.

Aristotle. (1947). *Nicomachean ethics.* Translated by N. Rackham, edited by H. Jeffrey. Cambridge, MA: Harvard University Press.

Armstrong, C. L. (2004). The influence of reporter gender on source selection in newspaper stories. *Journalism and Mass Communication Quarterly, 81*(1), 139–154.

Baker, S. (2009). The ethics of advocacy: Moral reasoning in the practice of public relations. In C. G. Christians & L. Wilkins (Eds.), *The handbook of mass media ethics* (pp. 115–129). New York: Routledge.

Baker, S. (1999). Five baselines for justification in persuasion. *Journal of Mass Media Ethics, 14*(2), 69–81.

Baldasty, G. J. (1992). *The commercialization of news in the nineteenth century.* Madison: University of Wisconsin Press.

175

Barbur, J. E., & Goodnow, T. (2011). The arête of amusement. An Aristotelian perspective on the ethos of *The Daily Show*. In T. Goodnow (Ed.), *The Daily Show and rhetoric: Arguments, issues, and strategies* (pp. 3–18). Lanham, MD: Lexington Books.

Barnouw, E. (1997). *Conglomerates and the media*. New York: New Press.

Barthes, R. (2005). The world of wrestling. In N. Sammond (Ed.), *Steel chair to the head: The pleasure and pain of professional wrestling* (pp. 23–32). Durham, NC: Duke University Press.

Beam, R. A., & DeCicco, D. T. (2010). When women run the newsroom: Management change, gender, and the news. *Journalism & Mass Communication Quarterly, 87*(2), 393–411.

Bennett, W. (1993). *The book of virtues: A treasury of great moral stories*. New York: Simon and Schuster.

Bentham, J. (1789/1961). An introduction to the principles of morality and legislation. Garden City, NJ: Doubleday.

Black, J., Steele, B., & Barney, R. (1999). *Doing ethics in journalism: A handbook with case studies*. Needham Heights, MA: Allyn & Bacon.

Blatz, C. (1972). Accountability and answerability. *Journal of the Theory of Social Behavior, 6*(2), 253–259.

Bok, S. (1999). *Lying: Moral choice in public and private life*. New York: Random House.

Borden, S. L., & Tew, C. (2007). The role of journalist and the performance of journalism: Ethical lessons from "fake" news (seriously). *Journal of Mass Media Ethics, 22*(4), 300–314.

Bowman, P. (2012). *Culture and the media*. New York: Palgrave Macmillan.

Brooks, B. S., Kennedy, G., Moen, D. R., & Ranly, D. (2005). *News reporting and writing*. Boston: Bedford/St. Martin's.

Buerkle, C. W. (2011). Gaywatch: A Burkean frame analysis of *The Daily Show*'s treatment of queer topics. In T. Goodnow (Ed.), *The Daily Show and rhetoric: Arguments, issues, and strategies* (pp. 189–206). Lanham, MD: Lexington Books.

Bunton, K. (2000). Media criticism as professional self-regulation. In D. Pritchard (Ed.), *Holding the media accountable: Citizens, ethics, and the law* (pp. 68–89). Bloomington: Indiana University Press.

Caro, R. (1974). *The power broker: Robert Moses and the fall of New York*. New York: Knopf.

Castleberry, S. B., French, W., & Carlin, B. A. (1993). The ethical framework of advertising and marketing research practitioners: A moral development perspective. *Journal of Advertising, 22*(2), 39–46.

Chambers, D., Steiner, L., & Fleming, C. (2004). *Women and journalism*. New York: Routledge.

Christians, C. G. (1985/1986). Enforcing media codes. *Journal of Mass Media Ethics, 1*(1), 14–21.

Christians, C. G. (2010). The ethics of privacy. In C. Meyers (Ed.), *Journalism ethics: A philosophical approach* (pp. 203–213). Oxford: Oxford University Press.

Christians, C. G. (2019). *Media ethics and global justice in the digital age*. Cambridge: Cambridge University Press.

Christians, C. G. (1989). Self-regulation: A critical role for a code of ethics. In E. E. Dennis, D. M. Gillmore, & T. L. Glasser (Eds.), *Media freedom and accountability* (pp. 35–54). New York: Greenwood Press.

Christians, C. G., Glasser, T. L., McQuail, D., Nordenstreng, K., & White, R. A. (2009). *Normative theories of the media: Journalism in democratic societies*. Champaign: University of Illinois Press.

Clouse, B. (1985). *Moral development*. Grand Rapids, MI: Baker Book House.

Coleman, R., & Wilkins, L. (2009). The moral development of public relations practitioners: A comparison with other professions and influences on higher quality ethical reasoning. *Journal of Public Relations Research, 21*(3), 318–340.

Collins, S. (2009). *Catching Fire*. New York: Scholastic.

Collins, S. (2008). *The Hunger Games*. New York: Scholastic.

Collins, S. (2010). *Mockingjay*. New York: Scholastic.

The Commission on Freedom of the Press. (1947). *A free and responsible press*. Chicago: University of Chicago Press.

Correa, T., & Harp, D. (2011). Women matter in newsrooms: How power and critical mass relate to the coverage of the HPV vaccine. *Journalism and Mass Communication Quarterly, 88*(2), 301–319.

Craft, S. (2017). Distinguish features: Reconsidering the link between journalism's professional status and ethics. *Journalism Monographs, 19*(4), 260–301.

Craft, S., & Wanta, W. (2004). Women in the newsroom: Influences of female editors and reporters on the news agenda. *Journalism & Mass Communication Quarterly, 81*(1), 124–138.

Cunningham, A. (2005). Advertising practitioners respond: The news is not good. In L. Wilkins & R. Coleman (Eds.), *The moral media: How journalists reason about ethics* (pp. 114–124). Mahwah, NJ: Lawrence Erlbaum Associates.

Danesi, M. (2019). *Popular culture: Introductory perspectives* (4th ed.). Lanham, MD: Rowman & Littlefield.

Davies, J. C. (1963). *Human nature in politics*. New York: John Wiley & Sons.

Day, A. (2009). And now . . . the news? Mimesis and the real in *The Daily Show*. In J. Gray, J. P. Jones, & E. Thompson (Eds.), *Satire TV: Politics and comedy in the post-network era* (pp. 85–103). New York: New York University Press.

De Tocqueville, A. (1835/1985). *Democracy in America*. New York: George Dearborn.

De Waal, F. (2013). *The bonobo and the atheist: In search of humanism among the primates*. New York: W. W. Norton.

De Waal, F. (2006). *Primates and philosophers: How morality evolved*. Princeton, NJ: Princeton University Press.

Desmond, R., & Danilewica, A. (2010). Women are on, but not in, the news: Gender roles in local television news. *Sex Roles, 62*(11), 822–829.

Dewey, J. (1954). *The public and its problems*. Chicago: The Swallow Press.

Dicken-Garcia, H. (2005). *Fair & balanced: A history of journalistic objectivity*. Fairfield, CA: Vision Press.

Dominus, S. (2011, April 8). Suzanne Collins's war stories for kids. *New York Times Magazine.* Retrieved from http://www.nytimes.com/2011/04/10/magazine/mag-10collins-t.html?pagewanted=all&_r=1&.

Edelman, M. (1988). *Constructing the political spectacle.* Chicago: University of Chicago Press.

Ehrlich, M. C. (2004). *Journalism in the movies.* Urbana: University of Illinois Press.

Eichhorn, K. (2019). *The end of forgetting: Growing up with social media.* Cambridge, MA: Harvard University Press.

Elliott, D. (1986). Foundations for news media responsibility. In D. Elliott (Ed.), *Responsible journalism* (pp. 32–44). Beverly Hills, CA: Sage.

Elmore, C. (2009). Turning points and turnover among female journalists: Communicating resistance and repression. *Women's Studies in Communication, 32*(2), 232–254.

Ettema, J., & Glasser, T. L. (1998). *Custodians of conscience: Investigative journalists and public virtue.* New York: Columbia University Press.

Erikson, E. H. (1967). *Childhood and society.* New York: W. W. Norton.

Everbach, T. (2006). The culture of a woman-led newspaper: An ethnographic study of the *Sarasota Herald-Tribune. Journalism and Mass Communication Quarterly, 83*(3), 477–493.

Feldman, L., Leiserowitz, A., & Maibach, E. (2011). The science of satire: *The Daily Show* and *The Colbert Report* as sources of public attention to science and the environment. In A. Amarasignam (Ed.), *The Stewart/Colbert effect: Essays on the real impacts of fake news* (pp. 25–46). Jefferson, NC: McFarland & Company.

Ferrucci, P., & Painter, C. (2016). Market matters: How market-driven is *The Newsroom? Critical Studies in Television, 11*(1), 41–58.

Ferrucci, P., & Painter, C. (2018). On *The Wire*: A textual analysis of "the most realistic depiction of a newsroom ever." *Journal of Popular Television, 6*(1), 3–18.

Ferrucci, P., & Schauster, E. (2020). Keeping up with the ethical boundaries on advertising. Big soda, metadiscourse, and paradigm repair. Presented at the Association for Education in Journalism and Mass Communication, August 2020, San Francisco (virtually).

Fischer, C. T. (1980). Privacy and human development. In W. C. Beir (Ed.), *Privacy? A vanishing value* (pp. 37–46). New York: Fordham University Press.

Fletcher, G. (1993). *Loyalty: An essay on the morality of relationships.* Oxford: Oxford University Press.

Foote, P. (1977). *Virtues and vices: And other essays in moral philosophy.* Oxford: Oxford University Press.

Foreman, G. (2016). *The ethical journalist: Making responsible decisions in the digital age.* Malden, MA: Wiley-Blackwell.

Forsling, C. (2019, Aug. 2). The original "Top Gun" was a recruiter's dream—the sequel will be anything but. *Business Insider.* Retrieved from https://www.businessinsider.com/top-gun-sequel-unlikely-same-enlistment-increase-as-first-2019-8.

Fox, J. R. (2011). Wise fools: Jon Stewart and Stephen Colbert as modern-day jesters in the American court. In A. Amarasignam (Ed.), *The Stewart/Colbert effect:*

Essays on the real impacts of fake news (pp. 136–148). Jefferson, NC: McFarland & Company.

Gardner, H. E., Csikszentmihalyi, M., & Damon, W. (2001). *Good work: When excellence and ethics meet.* New York: Basic Books.

Geertsema, M. (2009). Gender mainstreaming in international news: A case study of the Inter Press Service. *Journalism and Mass Communication Quarterly, 86*(1), 65–84.

Ghiglione, L. (1990). *The American journalist: Paradox of the press.* Washington, DC: Library of Congress.

Gierzynski, A. (2018). *The political effects of entertainment media: How fictional worlds affect real world political perspectives.* Lanham, MD: Lexington Books.

Gilligan, C. (1982). *In a different voice: Psychological theory and women's development.* Cambridge, MA: Harvard University Press.

Glasser, T. L. (1992). Objectivity and news bias. In E. D. Cohen (Ed.), *Philosophical issues in journalism* (pp. 176–185). Oxford: Oxford University Press.

Good, H. (1986). *Acquainted with the night: The image of journalists in American fiction, 1890–1930.* Metuchen, NJ: Scarecrow Press.

Grandy, K. (2014). You've come a short way, baby: Gender of information sources in American and Canadian business magazines, 1991–92 and 2011–12. *Journalism & Mass Communication Quarterly, 91*(3), 578–589.

Gray, J., Jones, J. P., & Thompson, E. (2009). *Satire TV: Politics and comedy in the post-network era.* New York: New York University Press.

Greitemeyer, T. (2011). Effects of prosocial media on behavior: When and why does media exposure affect helping and aggression. *Current Directions in Psychological Science, 20*(4), 251–255.

Grieco, E. (2020, April 20). U.S. newspapers have shed half of their newsroom employees since 2008. Pew Research Center. Retrieved from https://www.pewresearch.org/fact-tank/2020/04/20/u-s-newsroom-employment-has-dropped-by-a-quarter-since-2008/.

Gündüz, U. (2017). The effect of social media on identity construction. *Mediterranean Journal of Social Sciences, 8*(5), 85–92.

Hardin, M., & Shain, S. (2005). Strength in numbers? The experiences and attitudes of women in sports media careers. *Journalism and Mass Communication Quarterly, 82*(4), 804–819.

Harp, D., Bachmann, I., & Loke, J. (2014). Where are the women? The presence of female columnists in U.S. opinion pages. *Journalism & Mass Communication Quarterly, 91*(2), 289–307.

Hartmann, M. (2015, May 18). The Coke ad in *Mad Men*: What you need to know to understand the finale. *Vulture.* Retrieved from https://www.vulture.com/2015/05/coke-ad-mad-men-finale-history.html.

Hauser, M. D. (2006). *Moral minds: The nature of right and wrong.* New York: Ecco.

Helco, H. (2008). *On thinking institutionally.* Boulder, CO: Paradigm Publishers.

Hendrickson, E., & Wilkins, L. (2009). The wages of synergy. *Journalism Practice, 3*(2), 3–21.

Herman, E. S., & Chomsky, N. (2002). *Manufacturing consent: The political economy of the mass media.* New York: Pantheon.

Hess, A. (2011a). Breaking news: A postmodern rhetorical analysis of *The Daily Show.* In T. Goodnow (Ed.), *The Daily Show and rhetoric: Arguments, issues, and strategies* (pp. 153–170). Lanham, MD: Lexington Books.

Hess, A. (2011b). Purifying laughter: Carnivalesque self-parody as argument scheme in *The Daily Show with Jon Stewart.* In T. Goodnow (Ed.), *The Daily Show and rhetoric: Arguments, issues, and strategies* (pp. 93–111). Lanham, MD: Lexington Books.

Hirst, M., & Patching, R. (2005). *Journalism ethics: Arguments and cases.* Oxford: Oxford University Press.

Hodges, L. W. (1986). Defining press responsibility: A functional approach. In D. Elliot (Ed.), *Responsible journalism* (pp. 13–31). Beverly Hills, CA: Sage.

Hoven, J. (2004). Privacy and the varieties of informational wrongdoing. In R. A. Sinello & H. T. Tavani (Eds.), *Readings in cyber ethics* (2nd ed.) (pp. 488–500). Boston: Jones and Bartlett Publishers.

Humphries, S. (2019, Dec. 16). Hollywood's woman journalist problem: Why does it endure. *Christian Science Monitor.* Retrieved from https://www.csmonitor.com/The-Culture/Movies/2019/1216/Hollywood-s-woman-journalist-problem-Why-does-it-endure.

Ibold, H., & Wilkins, L. (2008). Philosophy at work. In B. H. Winfield (Ed.), *Journalism 1908: Birth of a profession* (pp. 82–99). Columbia: University of Missouri Press.

The Image of the Journalist in Popular Culture. (2020). ijpc database. Retrieved from www.ijpc.org.

Itzkoff, D. (2020, Feb. 25). Why Hank Azaria won't play Apu on "The Simpsons" anymore. *New York Times.* Retrieved from https://www.nytimes.com/2020/02/25/arts/hank-azaria-simpsons-apu.html.

Jollimore, T. (2013). *On loyalty.* New York: Routledge.

Junod, T. (2019, December). My friend Mister Rogers. *The Atlantic.* Retrieved from https://www.theatlantic.com/magazine/archive/2019/12/what-would-mister-rogers-do/600772/.

Kant, I. (1970). On the common saying: "This may be true in theory, but it does not apply in practice." In H. Reiss (Ed.), *Kant's political writings.* Cambridge: Cambridge University Press.

Kantor, J., & Twohey, M. (2019). *She said: Breaking the sexual harassment story that helped ignite a movement.* New York: Penguin Press.

Keeble, R. (2001). *Ethics for journalists.* London: Routledge.

Keller, S. (2007). *The limits of loyalty.* Cambridge: Cambridge University Press.

Kohlberg, L. (1973). The contribution of developmental psychology to education. *Educational Psychologist, 10,* 2–14.

Koestler, A. (1967). *The ghost in the machine. The urge to self-destruction: A psychological and evolutionary study of modern man's predicament.* New York: The Macmillan Company.

Kovach, B., & Rosenstiel, T. (2007). *The elements of journalism: What news people should know and the public should expect.* New York: Three Rivers Press.

Lacy, S. (1989). A model of demand for news: Impact of competition on newspaper content. *Journalism Quarterly, 66*(1), 40–48.

Lambeth, E. B. (1992). *Committed journalism: An ethic for the profession* (2nd ed.). Bloomington: Indiana University Press.

Larson, R. (1995). Secrets in the bedroom: Adolescents' private use of media. *Journal of Youth and Adolescence, 24*(5), 535–550.

Len-Ríos, M., Hinnant, A., & Jeong, J. Y. (2012). Reporters' gender affects views on health reporting. *Newspaper Research Journal, 33*(3), 76–88

Liberman, N., Trope, Y., & Stephan, E. (2007). Psychological distance. In A. W. Kruglanski & E. T. Higgins (Eds.), *Social psychology: Handbook of basic principles* (pp. 353–381). New York: The Guilford Press.

Lichter, S. R., Baumgartner, J. C., & Morris, J. S. (2015). *Politics is a joke! How TV comedians are remaking political life.* Boulder, CO: Westview Press.

Lieber, P. S. (2008). Moral development in public relations: Measuring duty to society in strategic communication. *Public Relations Review, 34*(3), 244–251.

Liebler, C. M., & Smith, S. J. (1997). Tracking gender differences: A comparative analysis of network correspondents and their sources. *Journal of Broadcasting & Electronic Media, 41*(1), 58–69.

Lippmann, W. (1922). *Public opinion.* New York: Free Press.

Lowery, S. A., & DeFleur, M. (1995). *Milestones in mass communication research.* New York: Pearson.

Machiavelli, N. (1950). *The prince and the discourses.* Introduction by Max Lerner. New York: Modern Library.

MacIntyre, A. (1981). *After virtue: A study in moral theory* (3rd ed.). Notre Dame, IN: University of Notre Dame Press.

Maynard Institute. (2014). *Robert C. Maynard: Life and legacy.* Retrieved from http://mije.org/robertmaynard.

McChesney, R. W. (1997). *Corporate media and the threat to democracy.* New York: Seven Stories Press.

McChesney, R. W. (1999). *Rich media, poor democracy: Communication politics in dubious times.* Champaign: University of Illinois Press.

McGeough, R. (2011). The voice of the people: Jon Stewart, public argument, and political satire. In T. Goodnow (Ed.), *The Daily Show and rhetoric: Arguments, issues, and strategies* (pp. 113–127). Lanham, MD: Lexington Books.

McIntyre, J. (1987). Repositioning a landmark: The Hutchins Commission and freedom of the press. *Critical Studies in Mass Communication, 4*(2), 136–160.

McManus, J. (1994). *Market-driven journalism: Let the citizen beware?* Thousand Oaks, CA: Sage Publications.

McNair, B. (2010). *Journalists in film: Heroes and villains.* Edinburgh, UK: Edinburgh University Press.

McQuail, D. (1997). Accountability of media to society: Principles and means. *European Journal of Communication, 12*(4), 511–529.

Meeks, L. (2013). All the gender that's fit to print: How the *New York Times* covered Hillary Clinton and Sarah Palin in 2008. *Journalism & Mass Communication Quarterly, 90*(3), 520–539.

Merrill, J. C. (1990). *The imperative of freedom: A philosophy of journalistic autonomy.* New York: Freedom House.

Mill, J. S. (1861/1998). *Utilitarianism.* New York: Oxford University Press.

Mills, C. W. (1956). *The power elite.* New York: Oxford University Press.

Mills, K. (1997). What differences do women journalists make? In P. Norris (Ed.), *Women, media, and politics* (pp. 41–55). Oxford: Oxford University Press.

Mindich, D. T. Z. (2000). *Just the facts: How "objectivity" came to define American journalism.* New York: New York University Press.

Molina, A., & McKeown, C. (2012). The heart of the profession: Understanding public service values. *Journal of Public Affairs Education, 18*(2), 375–396.

Moore, M. (2010). What are the universal principles that guide journalism? Media-Shift. Retrieved from http://mediashift.org/2010/02/what-are-the-universal-principles-that- guide- journalism032/.

Morreale, J. (2009). Jon Stewart and *The Daily Show*: I thought you were going to be funny! In J. Gray, J. P. Jones, & E. Thompson (Eds.), *Satire TV: Politics and comedy in the post-network era* (pp. 104–123). New York: New York University Press.

Mullen, L. J. (2011). Visual aspects of *The Daily Show with Jon Stewart.* In T. Goodnow (Ed.), *The Daily Show and rhetoric: Arguments, issues, and strategies* (pp. 171–185). Lanham, MD: Lexington Books.

Murthy, D. V. R. (2007, December). Question of public accountability of the media: An analysis of journalists' perceptions. *Glossa, 3*(1), 142–184.

Neville, R. C. (1980). Various meanings of privacy: A philosophical analysis. In W. C. Bier (Ed.), *Privacy: A vanishing value?* (pp. 26–36). New York: Fordham University Press.

Nissenbaum, H. (2010). *Privacy in context: Technology, policy, and the integrity of social life.* Stanford, CA: Stanford Law Books.

Nussbaum, M. (2016). *Anger and forgiveness: Resentment, generosity and justice.* Oxford: Oxford University Press.

Oldenquist, A. (2002). Loyalties. In I. Primoratz (Ed.), *Patriotism* (pp. 25–42). Amherst, NY: Humanity Books.

Oreskes, N., & Conway, E. M. (2010). *Merchants of doubt: How a handful of scientists obscured the truth on issues from tobacco smoke to climate change.* New York: Bloomsbury Publishing.

Painter, C. (2020). Culture is normative. In C. Christians & L. Wilkins (Eds.), *The Routledge handbook of mass media ethics* (pp. 276–289). New York: Routledge.

Painter, C., & Ferrucci, P. (2017). Gender games: The portrayal of female journalists on *House of Cards. Journalism Practice, 11*(4), 493–508.

Painter, C., & Hodges, L. (2010). Mocking the news: How *The Daily Show with Jon Stewart* holds traditional broadcast news accountable. *Journal of Mass Media Ethics, 25*(4), 257–274.

Piaget, J. (1932/1965). *The moral judgment of the child.* Trans. by M. Gabain. New York: Free Press.

Plaisance, P. L. (2015). *Virtue in media: The moral psychology of excellence in news and public relations*. New York: Routledge.

Popper, K. R. (1979). *Objective knowledge: An evolutionary approach*. Oxford: Clarendon Press.

Postman, N. (1985). *Amusing ourselves to death: Public discourse in the age of show business*. New York: Penguin Books.

Powers, S. (2002). *The problem from Hell: America and the age of genocide*. New York: Basic Books.

Pritchard, D. (2000). The process of media accountability. In D. Pritchard (Ed.), *Holding the media accountable: Citizens, ethics and the law* (pp. 1–10). Bloomington: Indiana University Press.

Radin, M. J. (1982). Property and personhood. *Stanford Law Review, 34*(5), 957–1015.

Rawls, J. (1971). *A theory of justice*. Cambridge, MA: Harvard University Press.

Roberts, C. (2019). Codes of ethics. In T. Vos & F. Hanusch (Eds.), *The international encyclopedia of journalism studies*. Hoboken, NJ: John Wiley & Sons.

Rosen, J. (2000). *The unwanted gaze: The destruction of privacy in America*. New York: Random House.

Ross, W. D. (1930). *The right and the good*. Oxford: Clarendon Press.

Royce, J. (1908). *The philosophy of loyalty*. Nashville, TN: Vanderbilt University Press.

Sandel, M. J. (2012). *What money can't buy: The moral limits of markets*. New York: Farrar, Straus and Giroux.

Schauster, E., Ferrucci, P., Tandoc, E., & Walker, T. (2020). Advertising primed: How professional identity affects moral reasoning. *Journal of Business Ethics*. Advance online publication: https://doi.org/10.1007/s10551-020-04429-0.

Schudson, M. (1978). *Discovering the news*. New York: Basic Books.

Self, J. W. (2011). The (not-so) laughable political argument: A close-textual analysis of *The Daily Show with Jon Stewart*. In T. Goodnow (Ed.), *The Daily Show and rhetoric: Arguments, issues, and strategies* (pp. 59–76). Lanham, MD: Lexington Books.

Sellars, J. A. (2008, June 9). "The Hunger Games": A dark horse breaks out. *Publishers Weekly*. Retrieved from https://www.publishersweekly.com/pw/by-topic/childrens/childrens-book-news/article/9915-a-dark-horse-breaks-out.html.

Sen, A. (2009). *The idea of justice*. Cambridge, MA: The Belknap Press.

Shafer-Landau, R. (2012). *The fundamentals of ethics*. Oxford: Oxford University Press.

Shain, R. E. (1972). Effects of Pentagon influence on war movies, 1948–1970. *Journalism Quarterly, 49*(4), 641–647.

Shoemaker, P. J., & Vos, T. (2009). *Gatekeeping theory*. New York: Routledge.

Shoemaker, P. J., & Reese, S. J. (1996). *Mediating the message: Theories of influences on mass media content*. White Plains, NY: Longman.

Skloot, R. (2010). *The immortal life of Henrietta Lacks*. New York: Broadway Books.

Smith, V. (2015). *Outsiders still: Why women journalists love—and leave—their newspaper careers*. Toronto: University of Toronto Press.

Snow, E. (1937). *Red star over China*. New York: Grove Press.

Spicer, R. N. (2011). Before and after *The Daily Show*: Freedom and consequences in political satire. In T. Goodnow (Ed.), *The Daily Show and rhetoric: Arguments, issues, and strategies* (pp. 19–41). Lanham, MD: Lexington Books.

Stocking, S. H. (2008). What is good work? *Absence of Malice*. In H. Good (Ed.), *Journalism ethics goes to the movies* (pp. 49–57). Lanham, MD: Rowman & Littlefield.

Tally Jr., R. T. (2011). I am the mainstream media (and so can you!). In A. Amarasignam (Ed.), *The Stewart/Colbert effect: Essays on the real impacts of fake news* (pp. 149–163). Jefferson, NC: McFarland & Company.

Van Zoonen, L. (1998). One of the girls? The changing gender of journalism. In C. Carter, G. Branston, & S. Allan (Eds.), *News, gender, and power* (pp. 33–46). New York: Routledge.

Ward, S. J. A. (2004). *The invention of journalism ethics*. Montreal: McGill-Queens University Press.

Ward, S. J. A., & Wasserman, H. (2010). Toward an open ethics: Implications of new media platforms for global ethics discourse. *Journal of Mass Media Ethics, 25*(4), 275–292.

Warren, S., & Brandeis, L. (1890/1984). The right to privacy (the implicit made explicit). In F. D. Schoeman (Ed.), *Philosophical dimensions of privacy: An anthology* (pp. 193–220). Cambridge: Cambridge University Press.

Warzel, C. (2019, April 16). Privacy is too big to understand. *New York Times*. Retrieved from https://www.nytimes.com/2019/04/16/opinion/privacy-technology.html.

Werhane, P. (2006, February). Stockholder ethics in health care. Presented to the Association of Applied and Professional Ethics, San Antonio, Texas.

Westbrook, R. B. (1991). *John Dewey and American democracy*. Ithaca, NY: Cornell University Press.

Westin, A. (1967). *Privacy and freedom*. New York: Atheneum.

Wezner, K. (2012). Perhaps I am watching you now: Panem's panopticons. In M. F. Pharr & L. A. Clark (Eds.), *Of bread, blood and The Hunger Games: Critical essays on the Suzanne Collins trilogy*. Jefferson, NC: McFarland & Co.

Wilkins, L., & Patterson, P. (2020). Toward an institution-based theory of privacy. In C. Christians & L. Wilkins (Eds.), *The Routledge handbook of mass media ethics* (pp. 374–387). New York: Routledge.

Williams, B. A., & Delli Carpini, M. X. (2011). Real ethical concerns and fake news: *The Daily Show* and the challenge of the new media environment. In A. Amarasignam (Ed.), *The Stewart/Colbert effect: Essays on the real impacts of fake news* (pp. 181–192). Jefferson, NC: McFarland & Company.

Williams, R. (2000). Culture is ordinary. In I. Szeman & T. Koposy (Eds.), *Cultural theory: An anthology* (pp. 53–59). Malden, MA: Wiley-Blackwell.

Wisniewski, K. A. (2011). It's all about meme: The art of the interview and the insatiable ego of the Colbert bump. In A. Amarasignam (Ed.), *The Stewart/Colbert effect: Essays on the real impacts of fake news* (pp. 164–180). Jefferson, NC: McFarland & Company.

Wright, J., Weissglass, D., & Casey, V. (2017). Imaginative role-playing as a medium for moral development: Dungeons & Dragons provides moral training. *Journal of Humanistic Psychology*, *60*(1), 99–129.

Wright, S. A., Dinsmore, J. B., & Kellaris, J. J. (2013). How group loyalties shape ethical judgment and punishment preferences. *Psychology & Marketing, 30*(3), 203–210.

Xenos, M. A., Moy, P., & Becker, A. B. (2011). Making sense of *The Daily Show*: Understanding the role of partisan heuristics in political comedy effects. In A. Amarasignam (Ed.), *The Stewart/Colbert effect: Essays on the real impacts of fake news* (pp. 47–62). Jefferson, NC: McFarland & Company.

Young, D. G., & Esralew, S. E. (2011). Jon Stewart as heretic? Surely you jest: Political participation and discussion among viewers of late-night comedy programming. In A. Amarasignam (Ed.), *The Stewart/Colbert effect: Essays on the real impacts of fake news* (pp. 99–116). Jefferson, NC: McFarland & Company.

Zuboff, S. (2019). *The age of surveillance capitalism: A fight for a human future at the new frontier of power*. New York: PublicAffairs.

Subject Index

Cultural Artifact Index

About the Authors

Chad Painter is assistant professor of communication at the University of Dayton, where he teaches journalism and mass communication courses including Journalists in Film, Foundations of Mass Communication, and Multimedia Journalism. He studies media ethics with emphases on the depiction of journalists in popular culture, the alternative press, and diversity studies. He is the co-author of the book *Media Ethics: Issues and Cases*. His articles have appeared in the *Journal of Media Ethics, Journalism Studies, Journalism Practice*, and the *Newspaper Research Journal*; and he has authored book chapters in the *Routledge Handbook of Mass Media Ethics, Cross Cultural Journalism: Communicating Strategically About Diversity*, and *Alternative Media Meets Mainstream Politics: Activist Nation Rising*. Currently, he serves as the teaching chair for the Association for Education in Journalism and Mass Communication's Media Ethics Division.

Painter received his Ph.D. and M.A. in journalism from the University of Missouri and his B.A. in English from Capital University in Columbus, Ohio. Prior to academia, he worked for eight years as a reporter; music, film, and arts critic; and arts editor for the alternative newsweekly *The Other Paper* in Columbus and in corporate communications for JPMorgan Chase. He is a member of the Society of Professional Journalists.

Lee Wilkins is an award-winning teacher who is professor emerita at two different institutions, Wayne State University in Detroit and the University of Missouri School of Journalism. At Wayne State she chaired the Department of Communication in the College of Fine Performing and Communication Arts. Before then, she taught at the University of Missouri for 23 years, winning the campus's highest teaching award and then being named a Curator's

Distinguished Teaching Professor. She was a member of the school's broadcast news faculty. During her time at Missouri, she was a weekly panelist and later host of *Views of the News*, a program that examined the news media, which aired on public radio station KBIA. She earned her doctorate in political science at the University of Oregon, a master's degree from that same university in journalism, and a bachelor's of journalism and a bachelor's of arts with a major in political science from the University of Missouri. She has worked as both a reporter and editor at newspapers in the Midwest and West.

Wilkins's research focuses on how professionals make ethical choices. Her co-authored book, *The Moral Media* (with Renita Coleman, University of Texas–Austin), was among the first empirical studies to explore ethical decision making among journalists and public relations professionals. She is the co-editor, with Professor Clifford Christians, of both the first and second editions of the *Handbook of Mass Media Ethics*. She served for six years as the editor of the *Journal of Media Ethics* and remains on its editorial board. She has authored or co-authored more than 100 scholarly articles, book chapters, and books. Her other research interest centers on media coverage of the environment and risk communication. That work has been funded by the National Science Foundation, the Environmental Protection Agency, and, while at Wayne State, the World Health Organization.